Analyzing Telework, Trustworthiness, and Performance Using Leader-Member Exchange:

COVID-19 Perspective

Michael A. Brown Sr.
Right Fit Communications LLC, USA

A volume in the Advances in Human Resources Management and Organizational Development (AHRMOD) Book Series

IGI Global
PUBLISHER of TIMELY KNOWLEDGE

Published in the United States of America by
IGI Global
Business Science Reference (an imprint of IGI Global)
701 E. Chocolate Avenue
Hershey PA, USA 17033
Tel: 717-533-8845
Fax: 717-533-8661
E-mail: cust@igi-global.com
Web site: http://www.igi-global.com

Library of Congress Cataloging-in-Publication Data

Names: Brown, Michael A., Sr., 1956- author.
Title: Analyzing telework, trustworthiness, and performance using leader-member exchange : COVID-19 perspective / by Michael Anthony Brown, Sr.
Description: Hershey, PA : Business Science Reference, [2022] | Includes bibliographical references and index. | Summary: "Useful for people and organizations seeking answers to COVID-related issues of teleworking, this book a new look at teleworking, an examination of important factors, and a plan for improvement in the short and long term"-- Provided by publisher.
Identifiers: LCCN 2021041332 (print) | LCCN 2021041333 (ebook) | ISBN 9781799889502 (hardcover) | ISBN 9781799889519 (paperback) | ISBN 9781799889526 (ebook)
Subjects: LCSH: Telecommuting. | COVID-19 Pandemic, 2020-
Classification: LCC HD2336.3 .B76 2022 (print) | LCC HD2336.3 (ebook) | DDC 331.25/68--dc20
LC record available at https://lccn.loc.gov/2021041332
LC ebook record available at https://lccn.loc.gov/2021041333

This book is published in the IGI Global book series Advances in Human Resources Management and Organizational Development (AHRMOD) (ISSN: 2327-3372; eISSN: 2327-3380)

British Cataloguing in Publication Data
A Cataloguing in Publication record for this book is available from the British Library.

Advances in Human Resources Management and Organizational Development (AHRMOD) Book Series

ISSN:2327-3372
EISSN:2327-3380

Editor-in-Chief: Patricia Ordóñez de Pablos, Universidad de Oviedo, Spain

MISSION

A solid foundation is essential to the development and success of any organization and can be accomplished through the effective and careful management of an organization's human capital. Research in human resources management and organizational development is necessary in providing business leaders with the tools and methodologies which will assist in the development and maintenance of their organizational structure.

The **Advances in Human Resources Management and Organizational Development (AHRMOD) Book Series** aims to publish the latest research on all aspects of human resources as well as the latest methodologies, tools, and theories regarding organizational development and sustainability. The **AHRMOD Book Series** intends to provide business professionals, managers, researchers, and students with the necessary resources to effectively develop and implement organizational strategies.

COVERAGE

- Employment and Labor Laws
- Personnel Policies
- Organizational Learning
- Human Relations Movement
- Entrepreneurialism
- Collaborative Method
- Diversity in the Workplace
- Recruitment Process
- Performance Improvement
- Outsourcing HR

The Advances in Human Resources Management and Organizational Development (AHRMOD) Book Series (ISSN 2327-3372) is published by IGI Global, 701 E. Chocolate Avenue, Hershey, PA 17033-1240, USA, www.igi-global.com. This series is composed of titles available for purchase individually; each title is edited to be contextually exclusive from any other title within the series. For pricing and ordering information please visit http://www.igi-global.com/book-series/advances-human-resources-management-organizational/73670. Postmaster: Send all address changes to above address.

Titles in this Series

For a list of additional titles in this series, please visit:
http://www.igi-global.com/book-series/advances-human-resources-management-organizational/73670

Future Advancements for CSR and the Sustainable Development Goals in a Post-COVID-19 World
Andrea Pérez (University of Cantabria, Spain)
Business Science Reference • © 2022 • 355pp • H/C (ISBN: 9781799880653) • US $225.00

Building Competencies for Organizational Success Emerging Research and Opportunities
Donta S. Harper (University of Washington, USA)
Business Science Reference • © 2021 • 217pp • H/C (ISBN: 9781799865162) • US $195.00

Role of Leadership in Facilitating Healing and Renewal in Times of Organizational Trauma and Change
Lynda Byrd-Poller (Thomas Nelson Community College, USA) Jennifer L. Farmer (Renewed Mindset LLC, USA) and Valerie Ford (ISP Global Communications LLC, USA)
Business Science Reference • © 2021 • 291pp • H/C (ISBN: 9781799870166) • US $195.00

Impact of Infodemic on Organizational Performance
Muhammad Waseem Bari (Government College University, Faisalabad, Pakistan) and Emilia Alaverdov (Georgian Technical University, Georgia)
Business Science Reference • © 2021 • 380pp • H/C (ISBN: 9781799871644) • US $195.00

Handbook of Research on Advancements in Organizational Data Collection and Measurements Strategies for Addressing Attitudes, Beliefs, and Behaviors
Mihai C. Bocarnea (Regent University, USA) Bruce E. Winston (Regent University, USA) and Debra Dean (Regent University, USA)
Business Science Reference • © 2021 • 400pp • H/C (ISBN: 9781799876656) • US $295.00

Effective Strategies for Communicating Insights in Business
Ross Jackson (Wittenberg University, USA) and Amanda Reboulet (Jacoulet, USA)
Business Science Reference • © 2021 • 261pp • H/C (ISBN: 9781799839644) • US $195.00

For an entire list of titles in this series, please visit:
http://www.igi-global.com/book-series/advances-human-resources-management-organizational/73670

IGI Global
PUBLISHER of TIMELY KNOWLEDGE

701 East Chocolate Avenue, Hershey, PA 17033, USA
Tel: 717-533-8845 x100 • Fax: 717-533-8661
E-Mail: cust@igi-global.com • www.igi-global.com

Table of Contents

Foreword

Much has been said and written about the unprecedented times sparked by a simple coronavirus. The speed and spread of radical change took the world by surprise as citizens and institutions (from healthcare providers to schools to businesses to governments) struggled to understand and adapt. Throughout the pandemic, as it continued far longer than anyone hoped, was a fervent desire to return to the way life "used to be." But those times are gone, and there is no path backward.

When there is no path, smart people look to the body of work documenting prior experience (or they "google it"), and for our modern-day pandemic, there was no playbook. If the 1919 Spanish flu pandemic was the most recent corollary, subsequent changes to media, travel, agriculture, and industry would have rendered it useless. In 2020, organizations had no option but to invent their own playbook to manage the change that was thrust upon them, and to coin a phrase, "fly the plane while they were building it."

In early 2020, the use of Zoom for meetings took off – as organizations mandated remote work. Best practices, and a meme or two, addressed the challenges of barking dogs and frozen webcams. Essential workers kept the lights on while management teams learned how to lead from a distance and how to trust a workforce they could no longer see all day. Employees came to many realizations about their preferences for commuting (or not), cost of living, proximity to family, and flexibility for caregiving. The pandemic interrupted and forever changed both employee and employer assumptions about the nature of work.

At the time of this writing, organizations have grappled with and made decisions about how to keep workplaces safe and healthy, working through differences in opinion on topics from wearing face coverings to mandating vaccines. They have learned how to manage remotely, how to hire remotely, how to onboard remotely, and how to provide many services remotely. And now they must take all that they've learned and build a "new normal" – a post-pandemic workplace.

The pandemic is still so fresh, and evolving, that there has been a lack of time to create a body of research and experience. The challenge becomes even greater when one considers how distinct and varied organizations are. There can be no "one size fits all" solution. Consider that Twitter has already said a portion of their workforce can work remotely forever. Contrast that with organizations such as mine, where much of the work simply must be done onsite in physical labs with machinery, chemicals, or scientific samples that must be handled with care. The spectrum of organizations trying to build their playbooks demands a range of options.

To further complicate the challenge, look no farther than to the leaders responsible for the organizations and institutions. Leaders are individuals, and each is uniquely part of the opportunity and part of the challenge. Some take strong stances, while others equivocate. Some lead by consensus, some by decree. Some operate with a global mindset, while others are driven by more local motivations. Devising the appropriate strategy for a hybrid workplace of the future rests on the shoulders of very different leaders with very different challenges and very different workforces.

This book takes both an academic, research, and experiential look at the various issues that are central to developing the hybrid workplace of the future: trustworthiness, performance, productivity, developing leaders, managing change, motivating employees. The data, experiences, and narratives contained here will play a pivotal role in helping leaders understand these issues as they define the vision for their institutions. How will this all play out? It is far too early to tell. The world is still reeling from ongoing waves of infection, the emergence of new variants, doubt about length of protections afforded by vaccines, and either a resistance to or a shortage of vaccine to inoculate the world in a manner that would kick COVID to the proverbial curb. It is hard to see the bottom of a pond when someone is throwing stones into it causing ripples to obscure the view. And the pebbles keep hitting our collective global pond.

But there are indications that global business, academic, government, and non-profit organizations will figure it out. As an early career employee at Accenture in the 90s, I witnessed an innovation they called "hoteling," where workers who were primarily remote booked workspace in the office for the few days when they needed it, providing flexibility, and reducing the organization's real estate footprint. Thirty years later, the idea of hoteling is new again. But to that workforce, and countless others since then, hoteling is old hat, on a global basis, no less. There is more training in emotional intelligence, and in diversity/equity/inclusion, now than ever before, and that will benefit leaders who need to tap into those skills.

Much has been done in the sphere of measurement and metrics, and data science and advanced computing enables organizations to understand their organizations' performance, culture, and reputation in far better ways than in the past. The Harris Poll's Reputation Quotient (https://theharrispoll.com/axios-harrispoll-100/) and the Edelman Trust Barometer (https://www.edelman.com/trust/2021-trust-barometer) provide information and insight useful in gauging both competitive position, areas of weakness or strength, and progress over time.

There is no better time than now to look at the information collected in the pages that follow. Organizations of all sizes, shapes and missions are amidst the greatest reconfiguration of work in history. Every company or institution is about to renegotiate the written or unwritten contracts they made when their current employees signed on. Fundamental assumptions about the nature of work – when, where and how it would be performed – have been shaken by the pandemic. Leaders must make decisions and set a vision and a path forward for their organizations. And each employee will in turn decide whether the new employment package, with its job duties, work location, commute, compensation, benefits, and flexibility, meets their needs. That reality is ahead, and this book aims to help organizations understand the challenges and set the direction their workforces need to be successful.

There are many issues to consider, many perspectives to address. Michael Brown is a pioneer in this new world – starting the conversations, doing the research, defining new approaches, and ultimately shaping the future of work. While much has been learned, there is much yet to come, and a framework for success is offered. I encourage you to turn the page and get started.

Leslie Krohn
Argonne National Laboratory, USA

Leslie Krohn *is chief communications officer for Argonne National Laboratory in Lemont, IL. She is known for her talents as a strategic, transformational global communications leader, having worked for Nielsen, GE Healthcare and Financial Services, and Accenture.*

Preface

This book is useful for people and organizations seeking answers to COVID-related issues of teleworking. It can assist organizations that are considering the larger issues of crisis response that require teleworking as a primary solution. There are insights into many teleworking issues that existed long before the COVID-induced situations. So, this is a new look at teleworking, an examination of important factors, and a plan for improvement in the short and long term.

This examination does not confine itself to pandemic response; however, the starting point is the astronomical changes caused by COVID-19. It offers verification of the benefits available through telework and addresses resistance to the use of remote work as an organizational focus. It examines whether organizations have made decisions to mandate or encourage teleworking formally and informally, making the possibility of participation available to the whole organization.

To help you navigate this important learning adventure, the book is split into three sections. Section 1: Examining Telework and Contributing Factors, Section 2: Examining Telework and Contributing Factors, and Section 3: Analyzing the Data to Facilitate Fact-Based Decisions.

The first section contains Chapters 1 through 5. The section begins with a close look at teleworking and how it is accepted or dismissed in organizations. It continues to address how COVID has changed our world leading us deep into telework or remote work. It allows us to deal with various issues like balancing family and work, trustworthiness, performance, and accountability, but this is just the start. The section then moves through discussions of a preferred leadership theory, trustworthiness, and performance.

Section 2 deals with leadership responsibility, development, and engagement with employees. Leader acceptance or resistance of telework is examined in terms of motivation, performance, and productivity. No examination of this kind would be complete without considering emotional intelligence and issues of radical change. This section is intended to give leaders and their employees tools by which they can have robust discussions about the pros and cons of telework.

Section 3 provides data in the form of teleworking research. Several sources and methods are used to shed light on how all parties may view remote work. Three hypotheses are examined, allowing us to focus on working adults and how they feel about telework. The section ends with recommended approaches for the use of telework or for understanding resistance to the use of telework.

In the concluding chapter, a strategic approach is offered that encourages participation and that can assist in achieving, understanding, and building buy-in for teleworking. Let us take a closer look at each chapter.

Chapter 1, "Teleworking," examines teleworking and the important relationships that must be created and/or nurtured in successful organizations. It further develops a basic principle for the entire book: LMX.

Chapter 2, "Our Changing World," shows how COVID-19 has dramatically changed our world in terms of telework specifically and remote life in general. We are still learning new things about balancing family and work, trustworthiness, performance, and accountability issues, important changes and discoveries about the way the world goes to work, and discussions of the dynamic ways people communicate. The discussion that follows centers on qualitative interviews concerning telework, an evaluation of employee engagement now and in the future, and ideas and actions that should prove helpful to organizations.

Chapter 3 is "Leader-Member Exchange (LMX) Theory." Defined in the introduction, LMX is a relationship-based approach for managing teams. The chapter also highlights the teleworking best practices of communication, flexibility, standards, and team building.

Chapter 4 is "Trustworthiness." We can use trustworthiness and trust interchangeably because they both relate to LMX and its importance. Trustworthiness, then, is the quality of a person, or a thing, that inspires reliability. The existence of trustworthiness is shown when qualities like being respectful, honest, consistent, positive, and selfless. Leaders who can admit mistakes, acknowledge weakness, applaud strength, and help each other, and promote those qualities in the workforce, will be capable of building trust.

Chapter 5 is "Performance." The current examination of COVID-19-related issues is important because the pandemic grew so fast that it outpaced current research and literature. Contemporary literature has primarily been focused on teleworking and non-teleworking employees. As we focus on the supervisors and leaders, we must evaluate key requirements of the value of performance and productivity in the conversation. This will lead to mitigation strategies and shared understanding that are vital to improving performance.

Chapter 6, "Leadership," is about creating relationships and effective relationships are crucial to successful telework. So, leadership development relies on nurturing those relationships as you determine and/or strengthen leadership style. Development continues when there is a trusting connection, when there are clear roles and responsibilities, and when a quality environment is maintained. Leaders must engage with their staffs and all parties need to see this engagement the same way to be effective.

Chapter 7 is "Motivation." Any analysis of performance and leader resistance must also examine employee motivation. The chapter examines the history and background of telework and trustworthiness and other constructs to trace the development of workplace motivation theories. The development examination is followed by a comprehensive framework intended to compare some important theories of work motivation.

Chapter 8 is "Productivity." As we continue to examine and work to achieve trust and improved performance, our focus must remain on analyzing telework benefits gained, and risks involved. The success factors involved in helping organizations are productivity, employee risk, achievement, and accountability. Combining productivity and improved performance in an analytical undertaking can lead to a complete picture of success or failure.

Chapter 9, "Emotional Intelligence (EI)," evaluates EI research, introduces the concept of Engaged Interaction, and explains how leaders can use EI for self-improvement. EI leads people to gain awareness by recognizing personal emotions and those of others. The concept of Engaged Interaction is achieved when all parties participate in flexible, full-range communication, making sure to listen, hear, and understand. This open and flexible communication must continue until interaction and shared understanding are achieved. Leaders can combine EI, Engaged Interaction, and strategic flexibility to improve operations and team building.

Chapter 10 is "Radical Change." As we examine teleworking rules and best practices, we see people deal every day with the requirement to account for their time, performance, and efficiency. Radical change involves behavioral indicators that can prove invaluable to starting or improving teleworking. The effect of emotion on radical change dynamics can be best understood by looking at the change process as separate components. There are three critical steps required to achieve radical change: receptivity, mobilization, and learning.

In Chapter 11, "Teleworking Research," a March 2021 survey is used to consider three hypotheses relating to working adults. Hypothesis 1 is that teleworking perceptions of leaders and employees are related in terms of promoting increased trust and improved performance. Hypothesis 2 is that a structured plan with associated resources to sustain long-term telework situations will be positively associated with program effectiveness. Hypothesis 3 is that a structured plan with associated resources to sustain long-term telework situations will be positively associated with improved performance.

Chapter 12, "Recommended Approaches," looks at several approaches that could improve teleworking through increased trustworthiness and performance. Any of the approaches, or any combination of their features, should be beneficial.

Chapter 13 is "Conclusion." Overall, this book suggests using a strategic approach that encourages participation and that is required to achieve, understand, and build buy-in for teleworking. The strategic approach mentioned here will be enhanced with the resources provided in this book: how to develop leaders, motivating employees, increasing productivity, using EI, managing radical change, and learning from the research provided.

Now there is a full examination that suggests a solid plan for telework. The analyses here should be helpful to organizations regardless of their position on telework: do not support telework, support some level of telework, or intend to use telework to the fullest extent possible. Employee feelings about telework is important regardless of the organization's position on telework. The book talks about 32% of hiring managers reported they saw an increased in productivity through telework. One survey showed that 115 of 133 respondents had favorable impressions of telework. We also learn that 23% of workers would stay remote if they could and that 44% of workers want to continue working remotely. Organizations that listen to their workers' desires will take these findings as a signal to take a close look at remote work.

This book is about what one can learn by keeping our eyes and ears open in a world that keeps changing. When the Coronavirus, the virus that causes the Coronavirus Disease (COVID-19), first hit the United States, it was just an imposing danger that had to be dealt with. Around the world, people experienced panic, uncertainty, and desperation among the myriad of emotions and conditions we saw everywhere around us. Some people wanted to know why it happened and where it came from. Others wanted to know how we could survive the pandemic. Others wanted to know how long COVID-19 would continue its grip on the world.

I had all those thoughts at various times. But after a year of telework and separation from family and friends, my concern was something else. I wanted to know how we deal with the next pandemic or crisis and how we make the best from what we have learned from the current pandemic—being forced into a lengthy period of physical separation from others, which included extended telework for many of America's workers. I started to put my questions into a document. Like many writers, I wanted to capture whatever thoughts and questions I had just in case I was discovering something useful.

I started by asking about the social and technical factors that are important for leaders when teleworking or other remote work situations are created or increased in response to a crisis such as a pandemic. I wondered what tradeoffs are at play in terms of trustworthiness, performance, productivity, employee risk, achievement, accountability, emotional intelligence, and radical change. There were other questions. How do you deal with leaders and managers who find it hard to support telework? How do you improve teleworking for employers and employees alike to create trustworthiness and improve performance, effectiveness, and efficiency for all involved? In search of a national strategy, this project seeks to address implications for everyday situations. I believe this examination is necessary because teleworking and its successful use needed attention even before the current pandemic.

This project addresses the need for and existence of a shared understanding where leaders and employees openly discuss the challenges presented by teleworking. The project also explores whether there are impediments or obstacles that organizations could remove or reduce to enable employees to accomplish the same amount of work they are currently doing in the office, but in a shorter duration of time while teleworking.

This work conducts a deeper evaluation of telework than is currently available in relevant literature so that we can understand how to build strengths and mitigate weaknesses in trustworthiness and performance as they are applied in organizational development. For the most part, this project is guided by one overarching hypothesis:

> *Perceptions of leaders and employees about telework are related in terms of promoting increased trustworthiness and improved performance.*

There were many issues to sort through as the hypothesis was developed. The natural first thoughts had to do with how COVID-19 forced the nation into separation and even isolation. This project does not delve into the details of the pandemic and how it grew. It deals with the aftermath and how people came to cope with the disease and its effects. To do that, it was necessary to examine telework, how it has been done in the past, how people experienced it during the pandemic, and what telework might look like in the future.

Figure 1. Teleworking success relies on allowing people to work where they feel most comfortable without compromising the organization's need to be productive.

Research about work conditions and approaches involves many things. As I take you through this examination, we will keep the lens on two vital telework considerations: trustworthiness and performance. Trustworthiness can be defined as the quality of a person, or a thing, that inspires reliability. Key trustworthiness qualities include being respectful, honest, consistent, positive, and selfless. The performance part of this examination deals with how well employees, and the organization, perform when telework is involved. Further, we will gain an understanding of what is required to set employees up for success and the ways in which leaders and managers can be shown that telework can be a viable solution leading to continued or increased productivity.

There are three data points that guide our current examination of telework, trustworthiness, and performance. They are:

1. The Telework Act of 2010 (Services, 2011) (related reference: the 2021 Department of Defense Inspector General (DOD IG) report on technology and communications)
2. Telework, Trustworthiness, and Telework Survey, March 2021
3. Personal interviews

The first data point is the Telework Act of 2010 (Services, 2011), which established requirements for continuity of service, cost reduction, work-life balance, and employment for people with disabilities goals for federal entities. The 2021 DOD IG report, Evaluation of Access to Department of Defense Information Technology and Communications During the Coronavirus Disease-2019 Pandemic (IG, 2021) is mentioned because the Federal is the largest employer and there are insights to be gained from a broad view. DOD wanted to understand how well components did in providing access to information technology and communications during COVID-19.

The second data point is a survey I conducted with Dr. Denise Siegfeldt of the Florida Institute of Technology. The survey was intended to identify problems that exist with telework and to analyze what can be done to remedy these issues and allow employees to be productive. The study was also intended to contribute to the teleworking body of knowledge. The survey collected 135 responses before being closed. Two responses were deleted from the database because the participants did not agree to question 1, which asked respondents to consent to the terms of the survey.

The third data point is created from 13 interviews in which I asked the participants their impressions and experiences about how telework is conducted. The interviews asked participants to describe positive aspects and to discuss areas that needed improvement. The interviews were then synthesized into several common areas: distractions, fatigue, accountability, communication, productivity, technology, coping, work hours, resources, and plan approaches.

The three data points contribute to the examination of the current state of teleworking. President Barack Obama signed the Telework Enhancement Act of 2010 into law. Federal entities were directed to aspire to the goals set out in the legislation to address service, cost, job satisfaction, and service to those with disabilities.

A 2012 Government Accounting Office (GAO) review delivered three recommendations for OPM reporting in 2014. First, GAO suggested that the Office of Personnel Management (OPM) should assist agencies in setting goals if the agencies were not ready to set telework goals. Second, GAO recommended that OPM's reporting should demonstrate a methodology for assessing or verifying the savings provided by telework, accompanied by a statement of the amount saved. Thirdm "GAO recommended OPM work with the CHCO (Chief Human Capital Officers) Council and its leadership to develop documented agreements and a timetable to complete an automated tracking system or other reliable data gathering method that can be validated by OPM" (Cook, DeMarco, Doherty, & Jones, 2013, p. 15).

Federal telework programs are established primarily to meet agency mission and operational needs. Telework saves money by helping government reduce real estate and energy costs and promote management efficiencies; makes us more resilient in severe weather and other emergencies; improves the quality of employee work-life; and increases employment opportunities for persons with disabilities.

Advances in information technology have paved the way for increased telework. However, telework is not a new concept and is not necessarily dependent on the use of technology. The key is for managers and employees to clearly define the work expectations and objectives, and then to give employees the tools and flexibility needed to get the job done. (Services, 2011, p. 2)

REFERENCES

Cook, J., DeMarco, J., Doherty, W., & Jones, Y. (2013). OPM's 2012 Telework Report Shows Vast Opportunities for Improvement. *Public Management, 42*(4), 13.

DOD IG. (2021). *Evaluation of Access to Department of Defense Information Technology and Communications During the Coronavirus Disease-2019 Pandemic*. Alexandria, VA: DOD IG. Retrieved from https://media.defense.gov/2021/Apr/01/2002612366/-1/-1/1/DODIG-2021-065.PDF

Services, E. (2011). *Guide to Telework in the Federal Government*. Washington, DC: U.S. Office of Personnel Management (OPM) Retrieved from https://www.telework.gov/guidance-legislation/telework-guidance/telework-guide/guide-to-telework-in-the-federal-government.pdf

Acknowledgment

I have never had so much fun writing anything in my life. That includes my time as a sportswriter!

Thanks to Jim "Gunny" Goodwin. Every time I need a friend to help, you are there!

Section 1

Examining Telework and Contributing Factors

Chapter 1
Teleworking

ABSTRACT

This chapter examines teleworking and the important relationships that must be created and/or nurtured in successful organizations. The chapter also highlights teleworking best practices of communication, flexibility, standards, and team building. Communication requires managing both face-to-face and online situations, while flexibility helps in achieving work-life balance. Standards are required to build effective, collaborative relationships, and team building is enhanced when organizations can adjust to new or distributed operations. The best practices are driven by a set of rules for operating that should be developed collaboratively with all members of the team. Clear rules that are combined with supervisor and employee shared understanding should lead to success. To achieve that success, organizations must focus on the assumptions, approaches, personal vs. professional issues, e-leadership, and modeling discussed herein.

BACKGROUND

Teleworking affects many areas of the organization and virtually all its people in one way or another. Teleworking can only be effective if everyone in the organization supports the use of it. This does not mean that everyone must agree to teleworking or that every employee must be approved for telework. It means that the organization must commit to the use of the practice and achieve buy-in from all its members. When the workforce is split between those in the office and those at home, the need for communication is increased. Any

DOI: 10.4018/978-1-7998-8950-2.ch001

stressors in terms of resentment of the ability to telework, the division of labor based on who is in residence and who is not, or fairness in terms of how the decision to approve or disapprove telework is made can present problems that an organization may struggle to overcome. These are considerations that should always be top of mind for organizational leadership. We will examine teleworking best practices in this chapter.

Figure 1. Teleworking best practices are focused on communication, flexibility, standards, and team building.

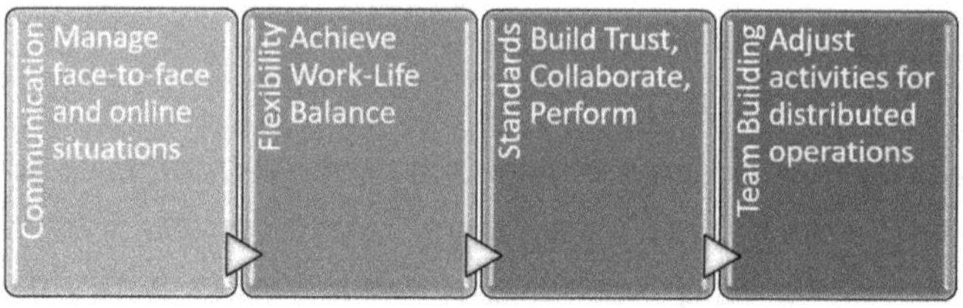

In Figure 1, I list important teleworking best practices collected from various literature sources in this book and my personal experience. These include communication, flexibility, standards, and team building. Supervisors must work with employees to improve or nurture communications both face-to-face and online. Effective communication should address four areas: assistance, viewpoint, standards, and team building. Supervisors should assist the person but should also manage the issue so that both are given the proper attention. People are our priority, but tasks must be completed.

New challenges or changes in operations may make it necessary for supervisors and employees to take a flexible approach to achieving work-life balance. Setting clear standards is the way to build the team and trust between the members, leading to improved collaboration, accountability, and performance. Finally, team activities should be tailored to distributed operations when possible so that all members have an equal chance to participate and be recognized.

The best practices mentioned here rely on a set of rules for operating. When the rules are clear and the supervisor and employee reach shared understanding of the decision to approve or disapprove telework, there is a greater chance for success. There are other issues that must be addressed if the organization is to successfully navigate the telework process. Let us look at teleworking assumptions, approaches, personal vs professional issues, e-leadership, and modeling.

Assumptions

There is an abundance of discovery and discussion about resistance to telework in later chapters of this book. To get started, it is important to address several assumptions to allow us to proceed with a robust examination of teleworking. Those assumptions include:

- Teleworking does not work universally
- Workers cannot be trusted to perform without in-person supervision
- Telework is just an excuse not to come to work
- Face-to-face interaction is more beneficial in achieving effective communication than is remote work

These are four common beliefs about telework that we can dispel. First, it is true that nothing works universally, but telework allows innovation and flexibility to address this issue. The resistance to using this work approach range from lack of trust to communication issues to accountability issues. The response to this assumption is that there are countless ways that the use of LMX principles can lead to agreements and adjustments that navigate through problems. Creating trusting relationships with your team and ensuring there is constant communication can help telework be effective for your organization.

The next assumption is that leaders and managers are skeptical that every worker can be trusted to be fully engaged and accountable for a full day's work. The challenges are very evident when there is a hot project or urgent need, and the employee does not respond in a reasonable amount of time. Or there is a missed deadline and the employee is not readily available to meet the suspense or explain the delay. The response to this assumption is that clear guidance and standards can address these challenges before they happen and mitigate the difficulty after the fact. Leaders should create a standard operating rhythm and specify when meetings happen and how tasks are to be turned in.

Another assumption is that telework is just an excuse not to come to work. While that is true in many ways, in many ways it is not. The response in the current examination is that teleworking can reduce employee costs, improve quality of work-life balance, demonstrate employer caring and flexibility, and make people happier. Research continues to demonstrate that allowing people to work where they are most happy delivers benefits in terms of performance, productivity, satisfaction, and retention. Leaders should understand that most people want to do good work, they just want to be as comfortable as possible doing it. One thing COVID-19 has uncovered is that many organizations and their people have discovered that telework can work, even in places that were sure it would not. For instance, Gallup tracked U.S. workers from March 30 to April 2, 2020, and found that the percentage of people whose employer offered flex time or remote work options had increased from 39% to 57%. In April 2020, Gallup polling found that 70% of workers were operating remotely, with that number reducing to 58% by September 2020 (Saad & Hickman, 2021). With these significant numbers of people working remotely, organizations would be well advised to find ways to that the experience is good for everyone involved.

Another assumption is that face-to-face interaction is more beneficial in achieving effective communication than is remote work. This is the notion that enforcing standards, onboarding new hires, and supervising are all better done in person. The response to this assumption is that "it depends." Success in these areas depends on the strength of the relationship between the parties and the ability for the work environment to be nurturing, regardless of where the parties are sitting or standing.

Leaders just need to bridge the gap to create effective messaging interactions regardless of the method. Take an interactionist view where you are both the leader and a full member of the communication. Blend your approach to get the best of both face-to-face and online communication and reinforce one with the other. Regardless of method you can use strategic flexibility, which measures environmental influences and adjusts the message for the best chance of success. Telework environmental influences can include technology issues, balancing family and work time, and task accountability, for instance.

Interactionism encourages leaders to strive for listening, hearing, and understanding by all parties regardless of whether they are in the room or a world away. In interactionism, social actors (senders) use the context of the interaction to adjust behavior to be complementary to the actions of other social actors (receivers) (Petras, 1968). This interactionist viewpoint allows us to leverage communication actions for the best outcomes as we interpret the situations we face and as we work to find telework behaviors that are beneficial to the organization's mission.

Leaders can view their telework activities in terms of networked individualism, where flexibility is at work when dealing with multiple and shifting work situations and members and even shifting sets of workgroups at times. Small group interactions can be used to keep members engaged, pairing teleworkers with in-office members, and ensuring regular communications. This personal touch can foster fellowship, respect, and tolerance. This is a way to achieve continuity and commitment that can be difficult in online environments.

Leaders can also build relationships with their teleworkers by using the "Question, W.A.I.T., Question," formula developed by Janine Driver in "You Say More Than You Think" that senders can use to find truth in communication (Driver & Aalst, 2010, pp. 175-177). W.A.I.T. stands for Why Am I Talking. The sender must wait and listen to what the receiver is saying before speaking again. The sender is responsible for asking pointed, specific questions to draw out information. Then the sender needs to W.A.I.T. and rely on listening skills to give the receiver the needed time to respond. Once the response is received, the sender validates or seeks more information. In this process, Formula One asks questions to assign the person a positive trait like trustworthiness. Once the receiver agrees and is finished responding, the sender validates the claim by seeking commonality, like saying "I'm trustworthy too." This approach allows continued conversation and helps with relationship building. There are two other "formulas," one that addresses information gathering in less confrontational negotiations, and one that detects deception and forces the receiver to confess. These are powerful tools that senders can use to engage receivers, share information, seek the truth, and improve work relationships.

Great leaders communicate effectively by identifying the target of their current message and by determining how the person or group wants to receive information. They follow with by ensuring they are getting feedback for their message. Now the leader can continue to monitor the dialogue and follow some simple rules of engagement: listen, learn, respect, and share. All communication should be clear, creative, and collaborative, characterized by well-crafted messages, crafted in a way that is entertaining and compelling. This collaborative approach to communication is important in creating messaging that has value for all participants.

Communication is also about relationships and information sharing. Leaders and members should agree on the purpose of the messaging activity and commit to an open and honest two-way exchange. Leaders must try to understand the member's information needs and attend to noise in the channel that includes emotions, relationships, and environment. Culture may also affect messages, leading to the need to develop skills to handle diversity of thought and action between the parties. Considering all the variables that can affect the interaction leads to an ability to ensure that the message is suitable for the organization's operations. Cultivate personal and group relationships as appropriate to get participants to think together and energize information sharing.

Keeping these assumptions in mind, we should take a closer look. We should as what are approaches that will deliver effective teleworking? Let us examine organizational approaches.

Organizational Approaches

Over the course of the COVID-19 pandemic, we have learned so much about how organizations view teleworking. Now we will take a deep look at how things have changed. There are many new viewpoints on teleworking, for instance, Chapter 2 will discuss, among other things, how one of the largest companies in the world, Siemens, announced a new corporate culture that is far-reaching in terms of giving employees the flexibility to work wherever they feel comfortable for a few days each week.

Many organizations simply take a commonsense approach to teleworking. They focus on schedule, communications, and goals to achieve effectiveness. How does this work exactly? They set up a schedule with employees to provide structure and adhere to core business hours when everyone can stay in contact. The schedule stresses regular breaks to achieve work-life balance. This reduces intrusions on the regular tempo of operations and allows people the maximum time to do the work they are assigned. Effective team communications also require discussions of distractions in the home and idea exchange about best practices to manage those distractions.

Some organizations have relaxed the conduct standards for virtual meetings to improve the telework experience. This was brought on by many behavioral and environmental factors, one of which is called "Zoom fatigue." Zoom fatigue has been defined by many users as the same as something called satiation.

According to the Oxford English Dictionary, satiation is the "*point at which satisfaction of a need or familiarity with a stimulus reduces or ends an organism's responsiveness or motivation.*" Satiation happens when someone has reached their emotional or mental capacity or goes beyond that capacity, and it relates to Zoom or other virtual meetings when people cannot handle one more minute of online interaction. Stress in this area can be caused when people feel the real or imagined requirement to be always in full view when meetings are conducted.

In other words, satiation is the point at which people are satisfied and want no more of what they have been craving. For instance, if it is hot in my room, I adjust the temperature to cool it down. It gets cool and I reach satiation, but then there is a problem. Now I am cold and my need changes to getting warm. But our focus is about that time when the temperature in the room is perfect for me, and I do not wish to be one degree warmer or cooler. This is like how people can feel about being in online meetings.

Satiation can impact performance and degrade motivation because people may feel that they never get a break. Increased close-up eye contact, inability to change positions in a long meeting, seeing your own image constantly, and concentrating for long periods of time without a break are stressors. It can also be stressful to multitask, managing every smile, every twitch, every clothing reshuffle, and even navigating trying to get a quick snack because you cannot take a break. People can become obsessed with how they present themselves in the virtual work environment.

In some cases, people misuse the camera or simply forget that it is on. Throughout the course of the COVID-19 pandemic, there have been multiple stories about people unintentionally exhibiting not-so-professional behavior: exposing themselves on camera, flushing the toilet during a meeting, or having an off-camera argument that comes across the transmission. Regardless of how these things happen, they signal the fatigue and stress that people experience in dealing with the possibility that they are always on camera. People must practice camera discipline. For instance, while it is convenient not to dress for a meeting when teleworking, it is good practice to make sure you are wearing clothing that you feel is appropriate and that other people would view as acceptable.

In scanning several online articles on the subject, which are prevalent in this atmosphere, there is much to learn. For instance, if there is any chance you would be embarrassed by what you are wearing, you should change clothes. Some recommend that you always mute the camera and microphone when you step away or engage in conversations external to the meeting. If it is not too difficult to reconnect, you might consider completely leaving the meeting, completing your other task, and then returning to the meeting. Many of the articles maintain that it far better to be absent than to experience an embarrassing or unprofessional outcome.

These issues can cause stress. Leaders and organizations can mitigate these feelings by identifying acceptable behavior and standards for virtual meetings, including appropriate dress, camera usage, and following set agendas. The standard can be set that people are permitted to show a photo or other image when they desire not to be on camera. There is a preference, of course, that when people are primary presenters, they should show themselves. However, most conversations can be carried on simply fine without seeing the person. Certainly, there can be issues of deciphering the full meaning of the conversation without visual cues, but there are ways to overcome this lack of visual communication. Asking questions, providing read-ahead material, or requesting a reduced follow on or one-on-one engagement can all help fill the void.

One method to establishing effective telework behaviors can be learned from companies that have established a culture of collaboration. These are the organizations that offer asynchronous work environments where work hours are not fixed but instead are flexible and are determined in large part by employees (Costa, 2021). This determination must come in coordination with leaders and supervisors, but it gives the employee greater latitude in matching taskings to personal responsibilities, hopefully leading to enhance work-life balance. This flexible approach lets colleagues communicate with others only when necessary, freeing everyone from constant distraction and allowing the kind of deep thinking that can improve performance and spark innovation. When employees are given the chance to participate in these determinations, the organization may find retention benefits or even increased loyalty.

Corporate Social Responsibility (CSR)

Considerations of CSR are important as organizations strive to achieve measurable benefits like innovation, rapid access to information given environmental constraints like a pandemic, and the pursuit of lower operating costs and that could lead to higher revenues. In my research on expectation, value, and return (EVR) on investment of time or effort, organizations need fluid communication and benefits that are easily understood (Brown Sr, 2013, pp. 95-97).

In terms of telework, organizations that accept its use must gain acceptance of participation from leaders and members. Participation can be a psychological process, and organizations should evaluate and take advantage of the benefits it can provide. To be effective, organizations must show all parties that their participation delivers a valuable return on investment of time and attention.

This is about finding organizational synergy. This is an approach where team communications achieve three central tasks. The first is identification of the nature and extent of social relationships important to the organization's culture, standards, and interactions. The second is understanding and nurturing the way people relate both in person and when working remotely, to ensure that the communication does not suffer in either instance. The third is to find ways to benefit from any increased cooperation, trustworthiness, or organizational efficiency.

Personal vs. Professional Issues

Failure to pay attention to employee challenges and concerns could lead to problems. For example, if an employee is not allowed to telework because of the nature of his or her position, the employee may feel that the employer is not concerned with their personal health or does not care as much about their health as they do about the health of others who were granted permission to telework. In the government, there can also be questions about determination of a reasonable accommodation for employees who are disabled or who have serious health concerns that do not have disability status. According to the Americans with Disabilities Act (ACA), "a reasonable accommodation is any change to the application or hiring process, to the job, to the way the job is done, or the work environment that allows a person with a disability who is qualified for the job to perform the essential functions of that job and enjoy equal employment opportunities. Accommodations are considered 'reasonable' if they do not create an undue hardship or a direct threat."

These and similar nuanced employer-employee issues must be addressed. The challenge is the unpredictability of specific employee challenges and concerns, as well as how these issues may change over time. An employee can be satisfied for months or years and then, for a personal or professional reason, become disenchanted. We are living this unpredictability now. More than a year ago, businesses apparently had a good hold on work-life balance. Then the COVID-19 pandemic forced most of the nation into work from home.

E-Leadership

One approach to navigating and addressing employees' personal and professional issues is through effective e-leadership. E-leadership involves using information technology to create social influence to produce a change in attitudes, feelings, behavior, performance, or thinking in one-to-one and one-to-many interactions (Avolio, Kahai, & Dodge, 2000, p. 617; Contreras,

Baykal, & Abid, 2020). Adjusting to these changes can assist teams to stimulate innovation, build trust and increase commitment to the organization. The effective e-leader can identify and employ a set of communication tools that are effective in meeting objectives, expectations, and goals.

E-leadership relies on sound IT practices and on discovery of future capabilities that will assist with continued improvement. E-leadership is successful when organizations can successfully blend technologies and traditional communication with information and communication technologies (ICT) mediated communication. ICT-mediated communication is using social software to conduct any form of communication where people interact and/ or influence each other using a network connection or the internet.

E-leadership helps organizations address workforces that are undergoing fast-paced changes such as the environmental challenges driven by COVID-19. But experts are also using it to adapt workforces to a variety of changes we see today. For instance, there was already evidence of potential vacancies in the highest skill areas before COVID-19, but now the nation is dealing with potential vacancies in service industries based on COVID-19, forcing people out of work or into remote work. The result are unemployed, skilled laborers struggling to find work, while organizations face finding skilled employees, often having to train employees with outdated skills or having to rethink their views on telework when faced with an abundance of highly qualified candidates who simply want to work at home.

Modeling

Modeling is observing or imitating the behavior of others to achieve personal or professional outcomes. Leaders and organizations should be open to finding and employing best practices that support organizational efforts, especially where telework is concerned. There are many things that we already know. Organizations can benefit by establishing in-office and remote schedules that share core hours. They can schedule at least one meeting per week during these core hours to get the whole staff together and satisfy face-to-face needs for feedback. They can allow time after the meeting for one-on-one interactions, as necessary. These ideas, if adopted, should be made a regular part of the operational rhythm.

Leaders can seek peak productivity by showing members that results are what matters. Leaders should let members who are working remotely choose their hours, making sure they pay attention to participation in core hours in some way. The way this is accomplished should be handled collaboratively between the leader and the member.

It is also a good idea to talk to remote workers about the ways trust can grow. Some of those ways are asking for help when needed, keeping their word, and by consistently delivering quality work. The leader can also announce their personal commitment to building trust. They can avoid micromanaging, ask for and sincerely consider input from the staff, and give thanks and other recognition when it is appropriate.

Many organizations have realized that the key to effective teleworking is to have a plan that both ensures organizational commitment is maintained and avoids professional isolation of the teleworker. Managing these two critical issues is invaluable to teleworking success.

FUTURE RESEARCH DIRECTIONS

The use of telework is growing and changing every day. At the time of this writing, the number of studies was exploding as the nation tried to come to terms with COVID and keeping workers safe and happy. I recommend that new research try to align employee desires with employer needs. It is easy to say there are hybrid answers, but it is much more difficult to try to examine and adjust to organizational and personal issues in the same initiatives. But this is the critical challenge today's researchers must take on.

CONCLUSION

Any approach to best practices must be verified by a set of rules for operating. Hopefully, the rules were developed collaboratively in the team. If there is synergy between these clear rules and leader and member shared understanding, the results should be successful. Keep in mind to focus on the assumptions, approaches, CSR, personal vs professional issues, e-leadership, and modeling discussed herein.

REFERENCES

Avolio, B. J., Kahai, S., & Dodge, G. E. (2000). E-leadership: Implications for theory, research, and practice. *The Leadership Quarterly*, *11*(4), 615–668. doi:10.1016/S1048-9843(00)00062-X

Brown, M. A. Sr. (2013). Social and CSR: Focus on Expectation, Value and Return. *PR News'. Corporate Social Responsibility Guidebook*, *6*, 95–97.

Contreras, F., Baykal, E., & Abid, G. (2020). E-Leadership and Teleworking in Times of COVID-19 and Beyond: What We Know and Where Do We Go. *Frontiers in Psychology*, *11*(3484), 590271. Advance online publication. doi:10.3389/fpsyg.2020.590271 PMID:33362656

Costa, M. L. (2021). *Businesses adopt 'asynchronous working' to fight remote-working fatigue and encourage cross-border collaboration*. Retrieved from https://digiday.com/marketing/asynchronous-working/amp/

Driver, J., & Aalst, M. v. (2010). *You say more than you think: the 7-day plan for using the new body language to get what you want*. Crown Publishers.

Petras, J. W. (1968). Social-psychological theory as a basis for a theory of ethics and value: The case of Charles Horton Cooley. *The Journal of Value Inquiry*, *2*(1), 9–21. doi:10.1007/BF00142455

Saad, L., & Hickman, A. (2021). Majority of U.S. Workers Continue to Punch. In *Virtually*. Gallup Panel.

Chapter 2
Our Changing World

ABSTRACT

COVID-19 has dramatically changed our world in terms of telework specifically and remote life in general. We are still learning new things about balancing family and work; trustworthiness, performance, and accountability issues; important changes and discoveries about the way the world goes to work; and discussions of the dynamic ways people communicate. This chapter examines reasons for resistance to telework to shed light on how COVID-19 has changed us. The discussion that follows centers on qualitative interviews concerning telework, an evaluation of employee engagement now and in the future, and ideas and actions that should prove helpful to organizations. Analyzing the interviews reveals several common threads: distractions, fatigue, accountability, communication, productivity, technology, coping, work hours, resources, and plan approaches.

BACKGROUND

Take a step back and consider how our world has changed in 2020 and 2021. It can be challenging to keep up with all the new experiences we have faced: quarantine, social distancing, wearing masks (and later two masks), and reliance on communication technology. By the time you read this, the world will be moving through vaccinations, children will return to the classroom, employees will return to the office, masks and social distancing requirements will become the exception, not the norm. And that's all just the tip of the spear as we return to, a new normal.

DOI: 10.4018/978-1-7998-8950-2.ch002

This chapter explores the large body of knowledge gained from the world's new experiences with telework specifically and remote life in general (Figure 1). Some common issues in discussions about telework are balancing family and work, LMX issues that involve trust, performance, and accountability, accepting changes and/or improvements in the way we work, and managing the ever-changing ways people communicate. These issues combine to demonstrate that people should resist the need to go back to the old way. If the current way is working, why not find a way to continue with the change? We should embrace current improvements. What are some reasons that organizations would resist continuing increased telework or embracing the new telework arrangement that COVID-19 created?

Figure 1. COVID-19 has had dynamic, direct effects on the world of work.

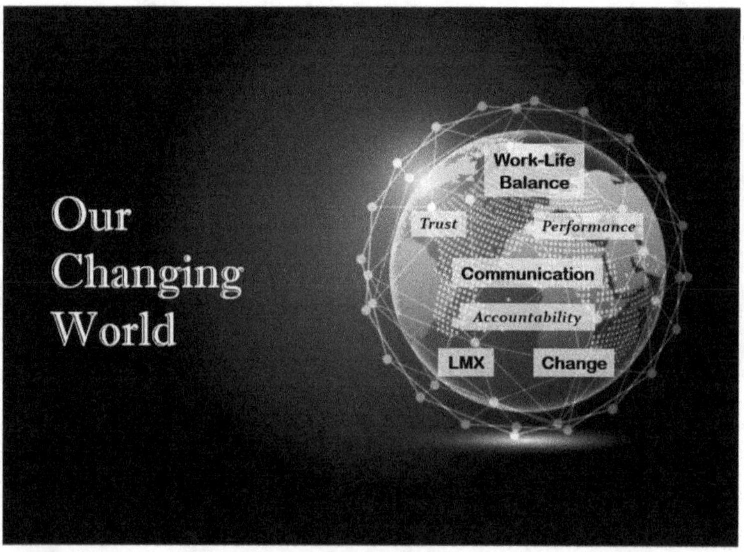

Telework Resistance Reasons

A review of relevant literature reveals at least 13 reasons that an organization or its leadership might resist the use of telework. My list is below, and I will discuss each one.

1. Most of our work is classified in nature
2. It will be hard to maintain our standards for secure operations

3. Our work cannot be done remotely (collaborative, interactive)
4. Teams cannot be built without face-to-face interaction
5. We cannot because we work face-to-face with the public
6. We cannot because we are a nonprofit
7. It will be hard to get a new hire up to speed and introduced to the team
8. Workers who need structure and supervision will fail
9. Communication is more effective in person
10. It will be hard to hold people accountable to work a full 8 hours a day
11. Everyone cannot telework, so using it can cause problems
12. We cannot do it
13. Our leaders say we cannot do it

1. Classified: Most of our Work is Classified in Nature

Yes, many organizations have an abundance of classified information and operations. What we learned from COVID-19 is that there are ways to get the work done. One of the ways that was already in place in military organizations was a secure courier to pick up and deliver secure information. You probably have examples of your own. Many organizations had to look at different ways to address classified information and their overarching cybersecurity concerns, but many organizations figured it out. Smart professionals from a variety of professions found innovative ways to address the classified question.

2. Standards: It Will be Hard to Maintain our Standards for Secure Operations

The biggest challenge to maintaining standards is not having a standard by which to measure. The grand move to telework caught some people and organizations without a structured way to handle a fully online existence. In these cases, organizations were forced into a trial-and-error environment to find the right solution for the task at hand. The lesson everyone should learn from this is that there must be a contingency plan that covers adoption of telework practices, increasing telework use, reducing telework use, and eliminating telework entirely. This all-inclusive approach forces an organization to assess all possibilities that may impact operations.

3. On-Site: Our work Cannot be Done Remotely

The medical community offers a great counter to this argument. Medical professionals and facilities have found countless ways to serve patients remotely using technology and common sense. For instance, one dentist office asks patients to come to call the office to check in for appointments once they arrive to the parking lot, then wait in their vehicles until they get a text. This reinforces social distancing. Also, many medical appointments can now be done virtually, and the doctor can determine whether face-to-face contact is necessary for proper care. Some doctors ask patients to keep a log of blood pressure readings, and there is new technology that diabetics can use to download the history of their daily glucose measurements for the doctor's use.

4. Team Building: Teams Cannot be Built Without Face-To-Face Interaction

There is no one right way to build a team. Team building requires communication, feedback, and structure. All of these can be accomplished remotely. People may become preoccupied by the myriad of environmental distractions brought about during telework. Undoubtedly, telework requires a renewed discipline to ignore these distractions while remaining focused on work-related matters. Viewed through a prism of the glass is half full, those same environmental challenges that can pull an employee's attention off work-related tasks also adds a greater depth of flexibility for employees to shift between work and personal responsibilities. One great benefit is that you can participate in two meetings back-to-back with no travel time. That feature can increase the number of meetings you can attend or the number of customers you can serve. Communicating and reinforcing behavior and accountability are great avenues to team building success.

5. The Public: We Cannot Because we Work Face-To-Face with the Public

Working with the public in fact became the very reason organizations had to master telework and other remote operations. The public could no longer come to the organization, so the organization had to figure out how to reach the public. The added challenge during the COVID-19 pandemic was that outreach and connection with the public now required a level of safety that had not been seen in decades. The ways in which organizations serve their public are too numerous to mention here, but they include curbside pickup, drive through vaccinations, and even instant oil changes that allow customers to wait in their vehicles during service.

6. Non-Profit: We Cannot Because we are a Nonprofit

In non-profits, especially small ones, timekeeping systems, and online communications may be challenging. The current system may not handle telework needs and can create unscheduled expenses. COVID-19 forced businesses of all kinds to take on this challenge for remote work, and many found ways to stay in operation. Regardless of the business status, nonprofit or otherwise, continued business operations through telework was necessary to remain profitable during the pandemic. American, and international, ingenuity may never have been tested this intensely.

7. Onboarding: It Will be Hard to get a New Hire up to Speed and Introduced to the Team

Having a good onboarding strategy built into your telework plan is the way to be successful. It is also good to have sponsors for newcomers who have experience in the office and teleworking. They can easily discuss any telework option and make sure training is provided as appropriate the newcomer to help them ease into the organization. Some organizations are building telework plans and training into the onboarding process, so everyone is at least capable of working from home, even if they are not currently authorized to do so.

8. Structure and Supervision: Workers who Need Structure and Supervision Will Fail

Effective communication, shared understanding, and structured plans are the ways to provide structure and supervision. Increased work-life balance and flexibility relies on more than just the proper work conditions. Managers should also consider that each employee may have different situations that conflicts with teleworking. Good two-way communication was required to work through these issues and get everyone working when it was impossible to have people in the office. Again, set the standard, make the employee accountable, reinforce desired behaviors, and correct negative behaviors.

9. Communicating: Communication is More Effective in Person

Face-to-face is the same as being in the same online room. If you need to see the person, just establish that the online meeting requires them to be visible. Only require the "visual" if it is absolutely necessary. Some people are just uncomfortable being on camera. The most important thing to emphasize is that effective communication requires clear messages, feedback, and follow up. Whether or not you see the person does not necessarily hinder those requirements.

10. Accountability: It Will be Hard to Hold People Accountable to Work a Full 8-Hour Day

Remember the old saying, "a watched pot never boils"? a solid telework plan and shared understanding about rules and responsibilities can address this reservation. Leaders must also understand that even an employee who is constantly in sight can delay or avoid getting work done. Whether they are working in front of the leader or at home, a clear set of standards and regular contact and communication are the keys to accountability. These are more important than where the employee sits. Often, this is a symptom of the issue, and the real concern is trust. In other words, leaders want to know "how can I trust that they are working?" That question will be answered by the relationship that leaders create with their members.

11. Problems: Everyone Cannot Telework, so Using it can Cause Problems

It is true that not everyone can telework. There are situations that just will not allow it. However, leaders can show commitment to their employees by giving everyone a chance to make the case for telework, and by being reasonable in assessing the opportunity. LMX requires that the organization discuss and partner with employees to find the right answer for all involved. A conversation about telework *before* a decision is made is invaluable in building trust and loyalty and shows that the organization cares about its people.

12. Negativity: We Cannot do it

Employers have figured out how to telework because of the pandemic. They had to. Many organizations survived the pandemic and even found increased opportunities to prosper. This is because organizations have found flexibility in determining when and where their employees perform, and in finding new approaches to improved work-life balance. A senior analyst at market research firm Forrester projects predicts that in the future about 60% of companies will provide their teams a hybrid work model, while 10% will be fully remote (Vasel, 2021). If you are a leader and you have been successful in allowing your workforce to telework at some frequency, I urge you to find ways to continue the practice. This will show your flexibility and loyalty to your staff.

13. Leadership Negativity: Our Leaders Say we Cannot do it

The same factors from #12 apply here, but with the added detriment of closed mindedness of organizational leadership. Leaders must be willing to use some form of the telework model. This helps prepare organizations to successfully transition to distributed operations during times of emergency and, just as important, enables ways to enrich the work environment for the workforce. We never know what will happen tomorrow but having a way for people to take care of their loved ones while still working is important. This is important as demonstrated in a survey that reported that 37% of employees would leave their current job in favor of one that allowed them to choose their work location at least part of the time (Gallup, p. 149). Using LMX theory, this shows responsibility, empathy, concern, and adaptability.

Gallup analyzed 12 elements of engagement on a recurring basis (Table 1), saying that taking care of employees requires more than conducting a basic employee survey (Gallup, 2007, p. 98). The list is grouped by the four levels of employees' performance development needs. Gallup uses this 12-element survey to understand and address employee development needs. The first three levels are intended to create a trusting environment and give support that enables all members of the team to get the most out of the fourth level. In this way, leaders motivate their team members, partner in improving performance, and witness how each level builds on the previous level (Gallup, 2007, p. 62). The ninth version of the Gallup research results demonstrate, again, that the best business outcomes are realized when employees are engaged.

In addition to analyzing the Gallup approach, I interviewed 13 people to capture and rank their thoughts and experiences on teleworking. This is an exceedingly small number of people to interview when we are discussing the vast universe of teleworking discovery. However, the questions were in part indicated by the survey on this topic that is reported in Chapter 11.

As you can see from the accompanying word cloud in Figure 2, work, time, home, people, teleworking (telework), and meetings were some of the most prevalent terms, or discussions, that came up. Let us examine a summary of the interviews that will continue to guide our analysis of telework, trustworthiness, and performance. The enduring theme in this book is that

LMX success relies on listening to and understanding the wants and needs of the workforce.

Table 1. Gallup engagement assessment

Gallup Employee Engagement Assessment Elements
Basic Needs
1. I know what is expected of me at work.
2. I have the materials and equipment I need to do my work right.
Individual Needs
3. At work, I have the opportunity to do what I do best every day.
4. In the last 7 days, I have received recognition or praise for doing good work.
5. My supervisor, or someone at work, seems to care about me as a person.
6. There is someone at work who encourages my development.
Teamwork Needs
7. At work, my opinions seem to count.
8. The mission or purpose of my company makes me feel my job is important.
9. My associates or fellow employees are committed to doing quality work.
10. I have a best friend at work.
Growth Needs
11. In the last six months, someone at work has talked to me about my progress.
12. This last year, I have had opportunities at work to learn and grow.

(Gallup, 2007)

A Gallup research effort found that 37% of employees would change jobs if they could find a new job that delivered an opportunity to "work where they want at least part of the time (Gallup, 2007, p. 149)," even if the new job offered flextime or similar compensation as the current job. About 53% of employees said a primary job-hunting consideration would be the opportunity to have greater work-life balance.

The interviews addressed a wide range of occupations to get a variety of opinion on telework, trustworthiness, and performance. The occupations of the participants included an Army civil servant, a retired Marine who is now a civil servant, an academia department head, a retired Air Force member who is also a retired attorney, a public relations professional, two business owners, a project management consultant, a mechanical systems engineer, a chief communications officer, two financial professionals, a director/strategic planner, and a college course designer. Please read on for the dynamic thoughts of our interviewees.

Figure 2. A word cloud illustrates the primary terms and considerations in teleworking.

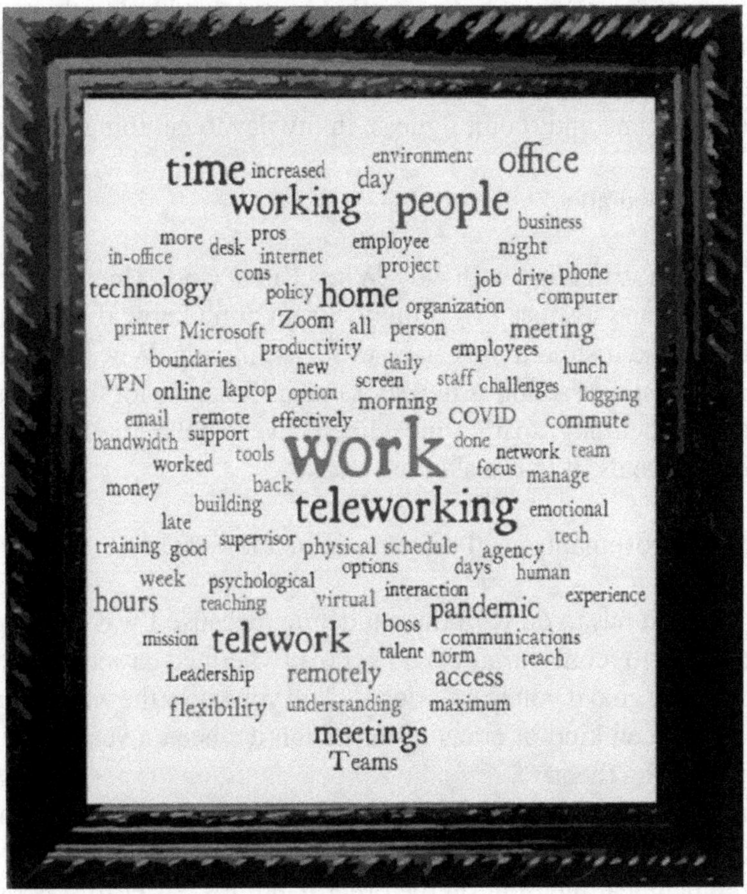

FULL INTERVIEWS

Tammy C.

Army Civil Servant

So, they've had us working from home 100%, probably around October-ish, they would have liked us to go in twice a week, but that didn't end up happening because I had two quarantines for family, so it's been 100%.

1. What are your teleworking experiences since the pandemic started?

Things like you realize just how much time you spend getting ready for work, commuting, and then getting settled in and that kind of thing. Just for the commute alone, I feel like I've gotten so much time back. You know me, I love me some people, but there's a lot less distractions as far as people go, so I have more time and room, I guess, in my day to get things done.

2. What is good about telework?

So, I've been struggling with why. When I'm at work, I'm pretty focused, and my theory, and it's just a working theory, I don't know if it's real, but to work through the distractions, I have to focus intently. When I'm at home, it's like my worst distraction is me, so it makes it harder for me to do jobs if they feel overwhelming, so it's almost like I have to deliberately break things down to small goals, if that makes any sense.

3. What improvements need to be made in telework?

And I think it has to do with the pandemic, because I was reading that it makes it harder to (concentrate). You get overwhelmed easier, or it makes it harder to reach a goal if you're emotional. And you know the whole pandemic thing has just been kind of crazy even though it's been a year, but anyway, that's my working theory.

On one hand, (telework) has got some really good things, but on the other hand, lunch ends up being (a challenge). I can make lunch at home so I'm eating so much healthier, but on the other hand, it's easier to stay on lunch hour longer, and I try my best not to do it, but sometimes I'll get distracted doing something at home. You know what I mean? Like laundry or something. And there's no stoppage because you are always at work. Like if I go over, I feel really bad for lunch, so instead I will stay late for work, finishing a project. And then I feel really (bad). The lines get blurred.

4. Is there anything else you want to tell me on this general subject?

It is oddly enough, its own kind of stress.

Dr. Brown: So, do you wonder about, without knowing how good or bad your organization is, the ethics of lunch and quitting time and accountability? Like when you get a question that is after hours so to speak? When does work stop?

You know, that's a really good question, because I'll see emails from my boss. He's really sympathetic and totally understanding about all this, but I've gotten it at 10 at night, or 7 at night. Maybe I was finishing up a podcast, so I was working later. So, at 7 at night, he's texting back and forth. So yeah, [laughter] exactly.

Dr. Brown: It is one thing if you have a good boss, but what if you have less than a good boss? The question becomes, first, should you answer or not? And can it wait until the morning? Will this be an issue?

So, when everything first started and we went home, I had put (Microsoft) Teams on my phone. And the problem wasn't at night, actually the problem was in the morning. I have a very strict morning schedule, meaning I don't start before 8 a.m. because I'm barely awake anyway. I struggle with morning stuff, and it would happen where things would come in to work on, because some people were up early there. The texts would start at like 6 in the morning, and I would start stressing out about all the things that needed to get done. And so, I ended up taking (Microsoft Teams) off the phone. So, I don't know the answers. And fortunately, my boss completely understands, and I have made it clear that it is no longer on my phone. So that's my line, and I'd like to think that I would draw boundaries with the boss who was saying, at 7 at night that they wanted me to look up something. I'd like to think that I would draw those boundaries. But I don't know because things have gotten oddly iffy.

Actually, if it's a project, it's one thing if you're sitting in the office, because we have a graphic designer who tends to work really slow. When that happens and you're in the office, it's (an easy) thing to say, "Oh, I can see what you're working on. Okay, that makes perfect sense." Whereas if everyone is at home and you're wondering, "Oh my gosh. What are you doing? It's taking so long." That makes a difference.

My boss is super kind and super really understanding, so I don't have quite the issues that some others may have. In time, you learn a lot more, what not to do, you know what I mean?

Jim G.

Retired Marine, Civil Servant

You have the challenge of getting the work done and of addressing technology fatigue. Because everything is virtual, you are doing all these meetings in front of your computer, whereas in the past you at least had some office presence. You can keep some of your capability, from your laptop or whatever your screen is, by doing person-to-person meetings. And for some people, of course, that ability can be more than for others. But you also need to get a break from your technology and you kind of get that needed interpersonal face-to-face interaction with another human being or else it can be an issue. I've been teleworking for a full year now from my kitchen table.

It's literally me in front of my laptop. I haven't actually seen my boss in person since last February. Yeah, and I started the job in January, so I saw him in person for about six weeks and then boom. For more than the year now, I haven't seen him in person. It's been all virtual or telephonic interaction.

1. What are your teleworking experiences since the pandemic started?

I'm looking at a lot of brothers in the National Capital Region, well I like to call it a kind of telework network. So, if I can wake up in the morning, roll out of bed, drink some coffee and log into my laptop, maybe I'd brush my hair or something, right? But because I can immediately get to work, that's golden for me. And in terms of productivity alone, being able to telework in general, this is certainly very conducive to being productive. It gives you back something that you can't get if you're working in an office, and that's time. And nowadays, time is everything, right? A lot of us work more and more hours, depending on what our position is, our role is, our agency is, etc. And in my role time is critical. I'm on call unofficially 24/7, just because of the nature of my agency's mission, which is "Federal Law Enforcement across the entire homeland." This means (that we are responsible for) all of the continental United States and all its territories. And of course, we have a lot of issues and things that need to be addressed in different time zones.

So, Portland, Oregon, is a great example. There's a lot of civil unrest there, a lot of attacks on our federal courthouse there, and when the news media comes calling and wants answers and information, that's on my office and my staff to be able to respond to that regardless of what time it is, day or night. So being able to telework gives to me a lot of that time back that I couldn't get when I was having to make the commute. Again, I think there's a geographical nuance to teleworking. Some folks maybe only work a few miles from their office, so teleworking may not be as advantageous in terms of getting time back. For me, it's critical. Before the pandemic, I was teleworking, I'd say, one day a week on average. So, four days a week at home, 16 days in the office per month. But the commute, both there and to the office in downtown, D.C., from where I'm at in Sterling, Virginia, and back. About three hours a day is what it would take for me from the time I walk out my front door to the time I was walking into my cubicle and vice versa. So, I've immediately gotten back three hours a day, every day. So, three times four is 12; that's 12 hours of work that I can get back in a work week.

2. What is good about telework?

Now, keep in mind, I'm not necessarily logging into my laptop at the time I would leave to go to the office. So 6:30 in the morning, I'm not necessarily logging in, but I would have to leave my house at 6:30 in the morning, I would arrive probably about 8:20, 8:30 in the morning, I'm at the office, and then I'd have to fire up, log in, etc. Then by 8:45, I'm actually in productivity mode. But here at home, I get up, I can hygiene, coffee, and go. I'm usually online by 7:30, 8 at the very latest. And on the reverse end, working late, you kind of have those (same transportation issues) again, nuanced to my geographical area. The later I wait to leave the office in the evening, the more crowded the trains get, the fewer the number of trains are. So, my commute can start extending and I have to plan when to cut my work off accordingly. And so that factor comes in. Now, when I'm teleworking, I can easily say, "You know what? This particular task is important, it's due tomorrow, I need to suck it up and work till 9 tonight." And I can do that. Now, I can put in a 14-hour day, not necessarily that I want to, but then that's the new norm.

But I can put in a 14-hour day to achieve a hot task that has to get done without sacrificing too much of my physical health, personal life, etc., because I'm here at home working.

3. What improvements need to be made in telework?

I think when this started a year ago, and the uncertainties of what technology we are using and getting the training to use the technology, that was a big issue. We use Microsoft Teams, and I had no idea how to use it; I didn't know what the heck it was. It was easy enough to click a button and realize, okay, they can see me, they can hear me, that's that. But I think probably the overarching change I would make is to get agencies to incorporate technology and telework training for all their employees from the get-go. And that doesn't just mean talking about it. You need structure. If another pandemic happens and we must work in the office for months on end or work from home for months on end, for example, it doesn't just mean, hey, here's the technology you need to be able to survive and get your job done and interact with other human beings. But also, it requires maybe some sort of emotional kind of counseling or workforce culture kind of counseling where companies engage with people to help their particular situation. That is because everything changes. You go from being in office and interacting with other humans and now you're teleworking all the time. That has a very real emotional and motivational impact on not just your work ethic per se, but your approach to how you operate on a day-to-day basis, frankly.

So, I think there definitely would need to be some kind of engagement or explanation about this is some of the long-term effects and the pros and cons of teleworking that science says is very real. Of course, who doesn't want to roll out of their bed, as we used to say, in their jelly-stained robe or in their pajamas and turn on their computer and sip coffee and then get to work? It's great; you get back so much time and as long as your technology is working, you're good. And that's the other thing I wanted to talk about. Working remotely is only as great as the technology allows. And for me personally, I have to rely on my own wireless network in order to be able to log VPN into my network for work and many times I have run into the issue of, okay, I've got my wife working from home, my kids working from home or going to school. Now we have a million devices on our "high speed internet" which I'm certain to question now after a year of teleworking. What am I paying the internet provider for? If you get too many devices on it can present a very real challenge. You try to be in a (Microsoft) Teams meeting or some kind of meeting where you've got multiple people, everyone's got their cameras on, and I've had many times where the technology starts to fade or just flat out fails.

Then I have to drop off a call or I can't keep up on a call because there's too much interference or the speed of the network is just too slow. This presents stresses and new challenges you have to deal with as an employee, and you have to able to recognize that you don't have your IT support always right there handy. Before the pandemic, I could literally pick up my laptop, walk 20 yards over to where our IT support desk is, plop it down, fill out a form and go, "Okay, I need help with this, this isn't working", and within an hour or two, they've done what they've had to do and I'm back online working. But now, if it's not something that IT can fix remotely, which does happen, then I am faced with the prospect of having to pick up, getting into my car and make the 25-mile drive to the office to get that IT support. This of course will kill pretty much my entire day, and then I lose time, right? So, there's that aspect of it as well. I definitely think there's the pros and cons of teleworking that are very obvious; you get time back; you get convenience back. A lot of people say they're more productive when they telework, others, maybe not so much. And then, of course, there are the cons of not having the human interaction, not being able to actually see somebody in person, and having trouble with the technology with difficulty in getting support.

4. Is there anything else you want to tell me on this general subject?

So, you got the surface level pros and cons, but I certainly think there's a deeper level to the pluses and minuses of teleworking. Telework fatigue is definitely, I think, a real thing, and I think for a lot of us incorporating practices into our daily life, forcing yourself to take a break, eating lunch, don't skip your meals, making sure you're not becoming a workaholic because it's convenient, easy to do. So, these sorts of things you have to kind of work harder at because you don't have those in-office cues that tell you, "Hey, it's time to go home or you're going to miss your train, right?"

And you have to understand that you might actually need an actual start time and end time at your house. For me, that's what I need to do. I need to say, "I'm going to make sure I'm on the computer by 7:00 or 7:30," and then I get off work at 4:30, 5, unless something's pressing. Otherwise, it's 10 at night and you're still working. And they're still calling you. I've seen a few situations where the boss says, "Hey, I sent you an email last night, but you didn't answer me." And "Yeah, it was at 11:30." I know I'm home but... So, the lines of those set boundaries of work becomes very, very blurred when you're teleworking. That is important because it is not just when you who is teleworking, everyone's teleworking, right? It's different when you're teleworking and your boss and everyone else is in the office because they're probably going to stop at a certain point. But when everyone's at home, typing away teleworking at all hours, long hours kind of start to become the new norm.

There is also the unspoken conversation about resources, so there are so many bosses who, regardless of whether they were pro-telework or anti-telework (at the outset), everybody was forced to be telework people unless employees were could only access their emails and other work from the office, as is the case with classified information.

There is also the difficult conversation about use of personal Wi-Fi. The organization is not providing that signal for you anymore; you're providing it. And they want it to be there when they need it to be there, and you're paying for it. Let's say you are also not issued a Blackberry. You're using your own cell phone, which I am, and so you're not getting paid for your Wi-Fi network or your phone, but you're providing your own work-related service based on that.

Dr. Brown: What about barriers to telework and communication? Like the conversation about coming back to work because telework is not effective or because we've conquered the pandemic?

That reminds me of a couple of work situations I've been seeing. When you're forced into teleworking, everyone's teleworking and you don't have the option to come into the office. You quickly find out who has the self-discipline to manage their time effectively to put in the hours and conversely to adjust to the work, right? Since people don't have those physical in-office cues to tell them, "Hey, the sun is setting, your train departure is coming up, and you have to leave no matter what." We don't have that anymore. But some people I've noticed, like some workers who rely on the Washington, D.C., metro system for transportation, have had a tough time adapting to telework. I say that not because they're lazy or they're easily distracted, but I get the sense that they're starting to fall in, or have fallen into, that trap of "I'm going to work all day and night." This is because they don't have to catch the train. They're online at 6 a.m. and they usually send emails out at 9 p.m. It's like they're literally tethered to their work phones or their work laptops 24/7. I know I'm on at all times unofficially, but unless somebody's calling my phone repeatedly to wake me up, I'm sleeping. At 11 at night, if you're sending me an email and waiting for me to reply, you're going to be waiting till 6:00, 6:30 in the morning at the minimum, when I'm awake.

You kind of get adjusted to working from wherever, whether it be home or wherever you're remotely working from. And then there's this fear of the unknown as an agency starts to try to figure out, "Alright, how are we going to approach this post-pandemic?" My agency, for example, which obviously it's a federal agency, is still trying to figure out how do we want to approach this? Do we want folks to come back in the office so many days a week, or do we want to allow certain individuals to work remotely 100% based on where they're at and what their jobs are? Classified material obviously drives a good bit of whether or not somebody has to come into a physical location. My agency has, you know, law enforcement officers. They can't work remotely. They stopped having that luxury at all. They have to do their jobs on the scene, so nothing's really changed for them, minus safety precautions that come along with the pandemic.

Dr. Brown: How do you deal with the conversation about telework opportunity? Certainly, the autocratic way of going about it is to say, I'm not discussing it with you, hey Jim, sit down.

If you're trying to build trust and get people who are accountable for their performance, you have to talk to them even if it's like, "Hey, there's no way I can allow you to telework." You have to communicate. For instance, "There's no way I can be successful, or the organization can be successful with you at home. We can look at some other things about flexibility." But you need to have that conversation.

Denise S.

Academia Department Head

1. What are your teleworking experiences since the pandemic started?

Starting the teleworking process was disruptive because much of the equipment that I was accustomed to using was at the office, such as the copier, scanner, and printing machine. At home, I had to resort to taking a picture of receipts and other documents from my phone camera and to send them to my work email address. I needed a printer, but it took 7 months before I was finally given permission to purchase one. The lack of a printer greatly hindered my ability to manage my site remotely, teach, and do research.

A lot of the documents that I needed to teach with were on the computer at the office, and I could not access them. I kept my teaching documents on my local computer drive whereas other materials related to students and faculty were on the organization shared drive. The issue of promotion and tenure came up, but my materials were in the locked building. I just completely gave up on that idea because not only did I not have access to my documents, but lack of a printer for 7 months represented a lot of lost time and effort that was needed to produce one or two articles. I know that a printer is not that expensive but there were other things that I had to purchase on my own at that time due to the building shutdown, like a desk appropriate for two monitors, an ergonomic chair for the desk, and certain cables for the computer – those things added up to over $500 out of my own pocket as Christmas was approaching.

I had been operating independently in the office, without any staff, when the Pandemic hit. Once the building was shut down due to people getting sick from what appeared to be COVID-19, I began telecommuting. I was extremely sick myself. Almost immediately, I, like others, were asked to document all of the work that we did, either daily or weekly. However, for me, doing the job of what was supposed to have been two people at a minimum, already took more time than I had during the regular workweek, and then being asked to document the work that I did was a huge burden. I found myself working 7 days a week and not even having time to pay my own bills.

Another thing that happened almost immediately was an increase in meetings using the Zoom platform. To me, much of the meeting time represented wasted time. There were a few people in the meeting who talked 90 percent of the time. I was already working alone before, so why did I have to make it obvious that I was working during the Pandemic by making appearances at the meetings. I am under the belief that stand up (5 minute) meetings can be very effective. Due to all of the increased time in Zoom meetings, online teaching, and all of the other work, I have found myself sitting in a chair at my desk, working for hours and hours at a time, including weekends. My back and shoulders hurt, and my legs are uncomfortable due to lack of moving around.

2. What is good about telework?

There are many good things about telework, including the ability to focus on certain aspects of work without many distractions. I don't have people stopping by to talk, for no particular reason, like typically took place at the office on a very frequent basis. There is also a cost savings for gas needed to drive back and forth to work. I am able to put dinner in the oven now, as many nights when at the office covering everything alone, my son would not have dinner, or it would be 10:30 p.m. before it was ready. I also don't end up having to drive home from work late at night on dark, cold nights from the office, because I am already at home doing that same work. I can let my dog and cat in and out of the house. Also, I can eat natural food more often rather than frozen (unhealthy) meals full of salt, and my blood pressure has come down.

3. What improvements need to be made in telework?

For the most part, I would prefer to be left alone to do my job. A reduction in unnecessary meetings would be welcome. If there could be more people performing the work and less people in place to just oversee, everyone's workload could be reduced. More access to system information would also be helpful because there are things that I need in order to function, that I have limited access to. It is a matter of "permissions." Finally, if there is a need to hold so many meetings by teleconference, at least let some of them be done by phone so that the staff can get outside once a month to walk. Seriously, I work 7 days a week and I rarely ever get to walk except to take the recycle bin and the trash bin to the road.

Sid P

Retired Air Force, Retired Attorney

1. What are your teleworking experiences since the pandemic started?

I am a retired attorney currently doing some adjunct teaching at two local colleges. I currently teach Intermediate Business Law at Lackawanna College and coach the intercollegiate Mock Trial Team at the University of Scranton. Neither would, I believe, be possible without remote classrooms - teleworking.

At Lackawanna College, I was teaching live and in person until COVID-19 stopped everything in mid-March 2020. After a two-week planning and adjustment period, we resumed class remotely through a Zoom-like platform called Canvas LMS. We were generally able to pick up where we left off, as all my students had both the hardware and the internet access to make that possible. For technical reasons, we were advised to have the students turn their cameras off - apparently it slowed the program down. I continued to lecture from my kitchen table, called on students, took questions, and administered both quizzes and exams. The course was not offered in the Fall, and this Spring, we have conducted the entire semester remotely without any noticeable hiccups.

The University of Scranton Mock Trial Team is an intercollegiate debate-like competition modeled in the form of a civil or criminal trial. Throughout this academic year, we have been exclusively on Zoom, for interviews, auditions, practices, and competitions. There are several members of the team, freshmen and sophomores who joined this year, whom I have never met in person! Remote work is the only thing that has made this season possible. Previously, we have competed in person with schools in the Northeastern U.S., a couple hours van drive for them or us. Now, with Zoom, we compete against national fields, all working under the same technological restraints and protocols. I also serve as a scoring or presiding judge regionally and nationally with the American Mock Trial Association, AMTA, our governing body, also all by Zoom.

2. What is good about telework?

Simply put, none of this would have been possible without remote learning access. Young people strike me as particularly adaptable to challenging circumstances and remote learning seems to fit them just fine. Last Fall, I taught an in-person class at the University of Scranton. Thirty students spread out in a large event space, masked, sanitizing-in, and sanitizing-out. It was probably the safest room they were in for the whole week. But in person, even from a distance, I could sense their tension and insecurity. That is not particularly possible online. I believe that, given the circumstances, most would have been more comfortable online.

3. What improvements need to be made in telework?

I think the main improvement that is actually achievable is broader and faster internet access. Students at Lackawanna College are generally from less-affluent family backgrounds. This was not true in my class last year, but I saw reports that some students had to drive to their local Dunkin' Donuts and sit in the car for their free Wi-Fi. It's a tribute to their dedication that they did so!

The real downside, in academia and I believe in business, is what could be called lack of context. There is something to be gained from face-to-face interpersonal activity. Looking at small squares on a screen, with either jumbled or artificial backgrounds, does not lend itself to personal connection. As I said, I have team members whom I have been coaching for seven months who I have not met. By this time in the school year, I know who they are, their family situations, their hobbies, etc. I don't know how - or if - that is fixable.

Jennifer G

Public Relations Professional

1. What are your teleworking experiences since the pandemic started?

My workday begins and ends with Microsoft Teams. It is the conduit through which we do everything--from uploading and exchanging files, to chatting with colleagues and holding meetings. I put in longer hours working from home, especially when I was working on a recent project. At the end of the day, I am exhausted and fatigued from so much screen time, plus the feeling that I am constantly "on."

2. What is good about telework?

The convenience, flexibility, and no commute!

3. What improvements need to be made in telework?

In the office, the work hours are respected; however, with teleworking, there is an implicit expectation that you should be on or always available, which makes it difficult to feel free to take a break. There should also be more emphasis on engagement and teamwork. When we are in the office, we have direct access to our colleagues to ask for their opinions or input, or to show them what we're working on. That's what is missing that makes teleworking so isolating and at times, frustrating.

4. Is there anything else you want to tell me on this general subject?

Frequent and consistent communication is the key to building or maintaining engagement and to fight the isolation that I and my colleagues have experienced.

Dr. Brown: Have there been any situations where a boss or customer assumed you were available "after hours," or when you were concerned that a request came outside of traditional working hours?

No requests have come in outside of traditional working hours. However, while working on the project I mentioned, it was implied that we had to work whatever hours were necessary to get the job done. During that time, I was working approximately 10-12 hours a day, with limited time available for breaks.

Tracy W

Business Owner

1. What are your teleworking experiences since the pandemic started?

To be candid, I have been working from a home office for many years, so the pandemic didn't alter my work habit necessarily. Although, I was unable to travel and visit clients on-site, which would have been problematic if it weren't for the fact that my clients also weren't on-site. Everyone had to participate in telework, which really brought us all together. Since the pandemic shifted my clients to join me in a telework/work-from-home experience, it greatly increased everyone's understanding of the benefits and challenges of doing so. It brought us together in a way that put us on equal footing. Our team (and others like us) weren't the only ones participating in meetings remotely. We all were! The experience has also shown me what I take for granted – a common sense work approach, necessary technology arrangements, planned communications, availability, and efficiency. So many high-tech professionals who had never worked remotely, and yet who were highly technical, asked our team for advice on set-up (and on) tips and tricks on how to work effectively. Our two decades of experience working remotely provided us with many opportunities to assist and help others do the same.

2. What is good about telework?

I love the flexibility of it. I really can work from anywhere, and 2020 put that to the test. Prior to the pandemic I would travel between Canada and the U.S. once a month, but once the border closed, I was forced to stay put. Nothing changed in terms of service to my customers, and our entire company was able to work as effectively as ever. And the great news is you can work with people all over the world. It increases your talent pool and your capabilities, which only further enhances your offering. In addition to the flexibility in terms of location and talent, it also enables us to provide virtually 24/7 service to our clients. That can be a blessing and a curse, of course, especially if you need to get some down time.

3. What improvements need to be made in telework?

I think there should be some clear boundaries with regard to time and access. Not only due to telework, but with everyone online and with a computer virtually on their wrist or in their hand, you are almost never disconnected. And with everyone working this way, it's almost accepted that you are working at all times. That understanding and those boundaries need to be built into the systems and processes that exist, as well as part of our conversation about work. Additionally, I'd love to see four-day work weeks become the norm, at least for some areas of work and for some roles. The expectation we put on ourselves and our customers be results driven not access driven. And of course, when it comes to accessibility, I've appreciated the closed captions in Zoom and the various other tools that exist, but we need to continue to do better to support and grow our capabilities with regard to accessibility, inclusion, and diversity.

4. Is there anything else you want to tell me on this general subject?

I'm pretty pumped that a lot of the world got to experience the way I've been working for almost two decades. With more people working remotely and participating in telework, it will help to improve the technologies and processes that are in place. Additionally, it will provide appreciation for in person, cubicle, and office work. I believe the future will include a hybrid of both in office and telework experiences, enabling organizations to access and retain the very best in talent, ultimately providing the best experience and solution for their customers.

Ugo I

Project Management Consultant

1. What are your teleworking experiences since the pandemic started?

I start work at about the same time each day but put in longer hours. Because I am not being "seen", I don't want people to feel like I'm taking it easy. My work output speaks for me, but I still feel that people like to watch you.

Generally speaking, I feel like I'm always on call. My computer is always on during the week. My coworkers and I enjoy greater flexibility and so messages keep flying late into the night. One person may sleep in and not start work until 10 a.m. and they may have to go out for a bit and generally end up working until 10 p.m.

On my part, there is often an urge to check my messages late at night. This is especially so even when I'm not working on anything major. I still have a lot of meetings to attend but do not get sidetracked with the occasional in office coworker chit chat.

2. What is good about telework?

I don't have to deal with the daily 2- or 2.5-hour commute to and from work. I like the flexibility. I can sleep in for an extra hour every morning. I am able to focus better. I tend to eat less.

3. What improvements need to be made in telework?

I don't know. My employer provided me with extra monitors, an additional mouse, and a second keyboard for use at home. Before the crisis, two days of telework was the norm. I think it should be expanded and staff should go into the office only once a week and no more than twice.

4. Is there anything else you want to tell me on this general subject?

I don't walk around or up and down stairs to attend meetings. This means that I sit more and gain weight easily. I was only just informed that we are allowed to take time out during the day to exercise or take a walk.

I don't miss team lunches or happy hours. I am not required to have my camera on for every meeting and so nobody sees my face when I am feeling overwhelmed or upset. I save money on fuel and there is reduced wear and tear on my car. Of course, I don't pay for parking in DC. Working from home helps me save money because I spend less. I used to travel for work, but I don't miss it.

Dr. Brown: Is the urge to check messages you mention self-imposed, or do you have real or suspected pressure from work?

The urge is on my part. My boss actually tells me not to extend myself unless there is a pressing work need. There are times when they tell me end the day early (say on a Friday) because I worked really hard earlier in the week.

Dr. Brown: I think I'm reading that your organization had been flexible and has made changes to improve over time. Is that right?

Yes, it is very flexible. 40 hours is expected, and I am free to work during the night if I like and sleep in the daytime. However, I must be at important meetings and so late-night work isn't ideal.

Jeannine B

Business Owner

1. What are your teleworking experiences since the pandemic started?

Fortunately, the pandemic did not change the way I do business. I am an entrepreneur with an online business, so nothing has really changed for me. I have one contract employee and a couple of freelancers I partner with, but we were already working in the virtual environment.

2. What is good about telework?

As a former government employee, I recall having the opportunity to telework on many occasions. Teleworking was convenient. Working from home eliminated my daily commute while also giving me the additional time required to complete various tasks. I also felt I had more control over my schedule. As an entrepreneur, I love offering my contract employee complete flexibility, and teleworking does just that for her. She gets the work done on her time and, as a result, produces even more than if I enforced a strict schedule. We meet in the virtual realm using tools like Zoom and Microsoft Teams.

3. What improvements need to be made in telework?

With the increase in teleworking, live virtual conferencing tools and other online applications have taken a bandwidth hit. This has caused a bit of an issue. Virtual calls get dropped more often, and email is lagging as well. I noticed my CRM application is having some connection and syncing problems too. To make teleworking most effective, internet service providers need to free up more bandwidth, and they need to keep the cost reasonable.

Eric R

Mechanical Systems Engineer

1. What are your teleworking experiences since the pandemic started?

Our department had to move to maximum telework around this time last year. We are currently still in maximum telework protocol. Although leadership is talking about a phased approach to return to work, there are no concrete published plans or dates. We still have classified meetings and laboratory work (tests and analyses) on base. In these cases, we have to inform our branch head and take our temperature with the instruments located at the main lobby. A small number of employees work in person because they cannot perform the required work via telework. The vast majority of employees work under a telework agreement.

2. What is good about telework?

Leadership reports that our department's productivity increased since we started teleworking. The specific workday hours rule was suspended. We can work different hours during the day instead of a specific schedule. Leadership expanded the capacity of teleconferencing numbers to ensure proper operation of the teleconference (meetings) calls.

3. What improvements need to be made in telework?

Our government computers and networks are not technologically advanced enough to keep up with others (OEM, vendors, etc.). The Navy computer network (NMCI) machines do not have cameras installed. We cannot fully participate in web calls (Microsoft Teams, WebEx, etc.). There is supposed to be a technical refresh to give us newer computers, but there are no set dates for the upgrade at this time. We are utilizing our personal cell phones to conduct official business. This situation was brought up at an All Hands Meeting recently. Leadership stated they were going to try to come up with a solution for this situation. Microsoft Teams and WebEx do not work correctly at times. There are two iterations of Microsoft Teams (CVR and Office 365). Meeting coordinators do not specify which (Microsoft) Teams they were utilizing. Many meetings have problems with people logging into the wrong version of (Microsoft) Teams.

During this time, my common-access card (CAC) expired. There were backlogs at all of the CAC offices and I had to continuously call to get a same day walk-in appointment. It seems to be getting better now. But I don't think things are back to normal.

4. Is there anything else you want to tell me on this general subject?

This was a quick switch to maximum telework. Overall, I think it was successful. Even the problems are getting addressed. Leadership is trying to work through these situations in a timely manner.

Leslie K

Chief Communications Officer

1. What are your teleworking experiences since the pandemic started?

Sure, so like most everybody else, on May 13, 2020, we issued an order, don't come to work the next week. I had worked from home occasionally but was really sort of set up for it. I had a laptop; I had a charger. Then I spent a couple of months trying to find the right room in my house for my kid to work, because I had a college kid who came home and had to Zoom school and I had a middle school kid who had to Zoom school. So, the competition was intense for bandwidth. I upgraded the bandwidth to the biggest pipe that I could get now and pretty soon I ended up with a really, really sore right arm and right shoulder, because of having the mouse in the wrong position. The good news was my employer had really good technology. We had Microsoft Teams on everybody's desktop, so once we had the connectivity, we were doing the actual work via (Microsoft) Teams. We used a system called BlueJeans as well (BlueJeans by Verizon is a company that provides an interoperable cloud-based video conferencing service that connects participants across a wide range of devices and conferencing platforms). That wasn't that hard. We did a lot of communications work, preparing people for that, making sure they knew how to get help and how to set up their desktops and how to access all the different various systems that they do from expense reports to payroll and time sheets and stuff like that.

We access a lot of different applications. So, the time sheets go in via a system called Dayforce, all of our HR records are on Workday, all those kinds of systems to approve invoices. People had to know how to access those tools, that was harder. Some of them you have to VPN in and some of them you don't. We had the challenge that some people didn't even know how to VPN in. So, there was a lot of communications helping people get comfortable in that remote environment, and that was the beginning of it, that was the first month. And after that, you started to get some people who were sitting in on folding chairs and card tables, and all of a sudden you start hearing about the physical strain of the teleworking. "My back hurts, my arm and my shoulder hurts, I'm getting headaches and all these kinds of things." And we luckily have a health and wellness clinic, and they set up ergonomic evaluations, they set up remote physical therapy visits, and so I actually did have them help me set up my workstation so I could have a standing desk at home. And so, I think we went through a period where people tried to get permission, government scenario, to take their chairs home; like their nice Herman Miller chair (Herman Miller, Inc., based in Zeeland, Michigan, is an American company that produces office furniture, equipment, and home furnishings).

So, the next six months were sort of full of that kind of, "How do I help adapt to the physical aspects of teleworking?" And then I think we went into this next phase, six months in, when people realized we're not coming back to work and it started to be that psychological phase of teleworking, where "Well, how do I connect with these people? How do I maintain relationships with these people? How do I build relationships with people I don't see anymore? How do I onboard new hires in a completely remote setting?" It kind of went from the technical to the physical to the psychological, in my opinion. And we are still in the world of psychological adaptation in teleworking.

2. What is good about telework?

I do think that what's good about it is the amount of time and money people are saving not commuting. People tell me all the time, "I can just get so much more work done if I don't have to drive to the office. There's no dead time in my schedule." But I think that comes with a challenge that there's no border between home and office anymore, and we hear that complaint all the time. There's no transition; it used to be you got in your car, you drank your coffee, you listen to NPR, and there was a transition in the morning. And in the evening, you could transition back to your home, and that definition has disappeared and that's challenging a lot of people, but I think people appreciate being able to kind of sleep in until 10 minutes before a call and then be at work in their PJs, if they want to.

3. What improvements need to be made in telework?

We have to think about the other challenges because that all moves into what we could improve. I hear constantly, and I've heard of some companies who have successfully adjust, but these meetings that just run into each other with no breaks all day long, people who never were in meetings all day, saying, "I'm in meetings all day and I don't have time to eat, and I don't have time to talk or walk the dog," or whatever. Some companies have said, "Every meeting that is a (scheduled) 30-minute meeting is 25 minutes, and every meeting that is a (scheduled) 60-minute meeting is 50 minutes," and they just build in transition time. I've heard of companies who have made meeting-less Fridays or no-meet Fridays. The only way that worked, in my opinion, is that everybody agrees to do it. Because the first person that schedules a meeting on a Friday pulls in people who don't want to be there or had planned not to be there or whatever causes problems for the organization. I commend them who have been able to do it because I think it takes an immense amount of intestinal fortitude, organizationally, but I think that is what is needed. You need some core hours from 9 a.m. to 4 p.m. or 10 a.m. to 2 p.m., and that's when you have meetings. And you have to give people time to do work. And our organization hasn't figured it out. I would love to see the best practices out of your research as to who has figured out a plan and how they implemented it, because I think that's one of the biggest improvements that's needed.

I will say, thank God for my CFO, and my head of safety, and the head of infrastructure, because there are some meetings that I sit on that none of us have any business being on, and so we make ample use of the chat feature all through the meeting to entertain ourselves. While the people who really need to be at the meeting with a couple of extra witnesses they don't need. And honestly, my CFO is a little more daring than I am on chat because you know, chat can be downloaded, so I watch what I say because I'm a communications person. But he will just rip into the current events, he'll rip into somebody's dog barking, he'll just have a running commentary, which is entertaining, right? And I'm appreciative of it and scared at the same time. You know, it's kind of fun.

It's called a pandemic, right? And there are people from the top saying, "maximum telework." And so, there's a reason, a purpose for doing it, and it's understood. People don't like it, but at least they understand it. And I think without that, I'm not sure teleworking would work. I think people would still be raising their eyebrows, going, "Well, why does he have teleworking? Why doesn't he have to commute to work? Why doesn't he have to show up?" So anyway...

Kevin W

Financial Professional

1. What are your teleworking experiences since the pandemic started?

I've found that clear communications are vital. From the perspective of both my supervisor and for me, this is a must. Now, I feel my supervisor has some added benefit because he has an employee that once sat in his seat. So, I know what is likely desired of leadership. I try to be proactive in leading from behind when given the opportunity. I imagine what he needs (expects), I attempt to empower myself, by anticipating needs, and I make every attempt to minimize uncertainty

I've asked questions that help me get a better idea of what is reasonable in this environment. The nature of our particular work hasn't changed. Financial Management work can be done off-site since we have to (work online to) access web-based systems even in a normal work environment. I attempt to communicate frequently based on need. I feel my management (supervisor) has allowed me the flexibility to achieve results; not necessarily focusing on hours or a schedule, although, this is the starting point. What is the impact?

- The workload has been manageable
- Guidance has been clear and realistic
- I've been able to manage my tasks
- I've been able to manage my time
- I've been able to juggle my work responsibilities and family commitments
- There are ways to address conflicts

With telework, stress is increased, but not unhealthy (kids in the home, they see or know you are in the office but that you are available); meeting may be in progress, project may be in progress, etc. With my older child, no problem (they are) self-sufficient; with my 5-year-old things are as I mentioned previously. Don't forget the spouse. It can be a combination of what is experienced with the children.

In terms of stress relieving, I'm in the home with them. I get to see them; they get to see me. Responses to their needs are more immediate and gratifying. I get to have lunch with the team daily!!!

2. What is good about telework?

Part-time teleworking (for unforeseen events such as weather, etc.) over the years was a good option, but efficiencies/effectiveness were realized.

Full-time teleworking has been great. I've been able to set up my home office (printing, scanning, home computer in combination with work computer, call forwarding, etc.), establishing a more flexible schedule based on mission needs (COVID-19 operations, etc.), communications tools (Microsoft Teams, etc.), and work output (products, reports, documentation, etc.)

Teleworking of any type helps to keep the target in sight. Keeps the mission progressing while operations are continued. Teleworking can positively impact work-life balancing, hence, if full-flexible work arrangements are embraced, advantages in diversity can be better realized.

3. What improvements need to be made in telework?

Productivity improvements: stakeholders will need to figure out best formula to solve what is sure to become a fixture in what is considered the new workplace environment.

Stakeholders will have to figure how digital discoveries, communication advances, and cloud tools can and will improve the bottom-line.

Management techniques will need to evolve. Employees, the other primary stakeholder, will probably get the deserved freedom they often seek (with ongoing challenges) self-governing, flexibility, constant change. Trust is a must!!!

Because of the nature of our business, National Defense, it is important to invest in digitization strategies (technology needs, available tech resources, tech policy, tech training, tech support, etc.)

4. Is there anything else you want to tell me on this general subject?

I'm excited about the future of teleworking; it is a win-win for both the organization and its employees. Organizational objectives can be realized while at the same time meeting the needs of employees.

Kevin G

Director, Strategic Planner

1. What are your teleworking experiences since the pandemic started?

We initially had a hybrid in the agency. We had some people who were more concerned, I think, physically, about their health or had other extenuating health concerns, so they opted for in home and working at home. The agency gave wide latitude for people to choose what they felt comfortable doing. Our physical layout here in this building enabled a lot of us to come in, because we have individual offices, not cubicles, so we are literally in our own office space, and we don't share. We don't have more than one person in an office. So, some of us opted to come in and those are the people who either had equipment issues, (needed access to) key equipment that they needed here, or they personally performed better with the regimen of going into work and being in an office environment and working/ And some of us quite frankly were afraid of being distracted or perhaps wandering a little bit because they didn't have the environment of the office to go to.

So, in our case we had a wide latitude of what to do. I personally chose to come into work every day, and from the moment we started that's what I did. In March, when everything shut down, I think the first day after the mass of nationwide shut down, I think everybody worked from home, and then after that, I opted to come into the office to work, and I worked all the way through the year. And I happen to be one of those people who I think just performed better when I had the routine. I had all my files and everything that I needed to do my work here. Although I could have made arrangements to access various things from home certainly, but it was just easier for me to come in here and get to it.

So, for the majority of 2020, I came in every day, five days a week and worked here. Now, I will say that toward the end of December, we had a little outbreak in the agency. We had three or four people who got sick, kind of one, two, three days in a row, and then everybody that had returned to the office or were working in the office was then requested to go work remotely. The management here said, "Everybody go home, get tested, and we're going to ride this out. Everybody just worked from home until we kind of get through this patch." And that's what we did. The last couple of weeks of December, around Christmas and New Year's, and then through January, everybody worked remotely. Then right around February, those of us who wanted to come back and felt good about it, we returned to work.

2. What is good about telework?

What's good about it is, it's a time saver, in the fact that you don't have to worry about the commute. So, you get that time back. Obviously, there's savings out of pocket because you're not filling up the gas tank, you're probably not going out for lunch. So, you're saving all those kinds of nickels and dimes, but they add up, so you come out saving. You're also having less stress in your life because you're not looking at the clock, or saying, "Okay, I have so much time to get a shower, I gotta get on the road, I gotta worry about traffic jams or whatever." You don't have the daily battle of slugging out (traveling) or commuting to and from work. Your stress level goes down. In my case, my wife and I we're dinks so we don't have any kids, so we didn't have that hurdle (Note: A dink is a partner in a well-off working couple with no children).

We didn't have rug rats coming in or busting in our Zoom calls. Although we did have dogs barking at every passing car and knock at the door of the postman. We had that to put up with, but we each kind of did it. She's got her office and I was working on the dining room table, so we kind of accommodated each other that way. In that sense, she was totally working from home from day one, and so I had my doubts, whether I'd be able to stay focused or when we get together and commiserate or sit down for a cup of coffee and just, "Oh, where did the hour go?" But we were very disciplined, we didn't have that problem. We booked our time, and we worked like a regular day. So, I would say from a financial standing point, you certainly saved. You weren't going out to eat, you were brown bagging it, right next to your kitchen. So, you saved all that. You saved wear and tear on your car, you saved cleaning and things like that because you didn't necessarily have to get a nice, starched shirt and put on a tie and all that.

3. What improvements need to be made in telework?

Well, wider broadband and improved access to high-speed Internet is going to have to be something that I think will have to be offered because it was just a problem. It was so random who had good connections and who had bad, and who hasn't been on a Zoom call, or my Internet connection is not good, and the dog ate my homework.

Maybe your microphone dropped off or something like that. I think that's going to be necessary. Probably some improvements in the camera and microphone, and just some of the fundamental things that you need to telework and be able to communicate with groups. Some of us are slaves to email and some of us work only within certain structures or formats here at work, Word docs, and everything goes into a file up on a server, and all that sort of stuff. But collaboration things such as working groups like Google Docs and then Slack (messaging platform), things like that, where people can kind of come and get used to a new way of working. I think those are going to have to be either better marketed or they're going to have to improve and get a little bit more idiot-proof because they can be daunting to somebody, especially older workers who are a little bit resistant or afraid of change. It could be challenging trying to get them to adopt Slack, for example, when they ask how do I get there? And who am I talking to?

Why can't we just use email? That type of thing. So probably some in-house training will have to be done, better tutorials and things along those lines. Now, that's just if you're working, I think, from a base unit or a laptop or whatever. But if you're working out on a mobile device, hand-held, then you're talking about a whole other different technology, and I think you're starting to see better cameras and better microphones and more hearing. Being able to do more right on your hand-held device is important. I think the technology just keeping pace is important. It just might have to be a little bit better introduced and cultivated amongst some portions in the workforce, really, namely older workers.

Denise M.

Finance Professional

1. What are your teleworking experiences since the pandemic started?

I do budget work for the Department of Defense-Air Force on a military base. I think when we started teleworking, I worked longer hours. My leadership would start contacting me earlier in the morning. If I did not respond quickly to an email, I would get a text, then a phone call. My supervisor would get a call to check and see why I did not answer the text or the phone. I was expected to be available longer hours in the day, than I normally worked in the office. It seemed like our leadership expected us to be available to answer emails and text messages 24 hours a day. They never said anything, but those calls came before I work up and continued well into the night. They felt to contact me anytime they had an emergency.

2. What is good about teleworking?

Teleworking gives you more time away from the office. And it eliminates many of the interruptions that you can have in the office. I think I got more paperwork and assignments done at home. I did not have the phone calls and visits from customers like I do when we are in the office. I could start and finish a project on the same day. That meant I was less stressed (out), and I could get things done. Now that I am back in the office, I may not get it done and I must bring it home. But that is overtime, not telework.

3. What improvements need to be made in telework?

If we are teleworking not by our own choice, I should be able to get some of the home office expenses paid. There should be some funding for office supplies at the minimum. I need paper, ink, file folders, etc., and those costs can add up. Telework also made me use my cell phone more when we had to check in every day to ensure that everyone was working.

4. Is there anything else you want to tell me on this general subject?

Before the pandemic, I applied for a new job that would give me a promotion. I was not accepted until after the pandemic started, so I made the change while COVID was active. I was ok not having a going away party, but it was kind of sad that my supervisor was the only one who reached out to me at that time. Normally people get an award for their years of service, and I have gotten awards for various things over the years. This time I did not get any award from my top leadership. I did not even get a phone call.

Starting a new job during a pandemic and finding that the staff is teleworking is just as hard. I did not get the proper information about my job, they were not totally clear about what was expected of me, and I did not get the proper training at the time I started. I had to do a lot of research and discovery on my own to allow me any success in the first four months. By the time we were back in the office and trying to close out the financial records for the end of the year, it was apparent that there was a large gap in what I needed to know. I still need training on many of the things I am expected to do. I thought I had the knowledge I needed, but now that the whole staff is back, I realize more training is needed to do the job well. I am missing a lot of information and training.

With the pandemic you are trying to get back to work, but it is hard to be comfortable because there seems to be more concern for those that have the attitude of "if you get (COVID) it you get it." We do not know who is safe to be around, with or without a mask. Meetings and events are just planned, but there is no prior interaction with the staff as a whole. No one asks us if we feel comfortable being in these environments, but you are expected to attend the meetings and events.

INTERVIEW ANALYSIS

Now, it is time to dissect and analyze everything the interviews tell us about teleworking today. An attempt to segment the key parts of the interviews is below. Some interview responses are paraphrased to allow for ease of reading.

The word cloud offered earlier is interesting, but a closer analysis reveals several common topics widely discussed throughout the interviews. They are distractions, fatigue, accountability, communication, productivity, technology, coping, work hours, resources, and plan approaches. The relevant text from the interview is arranged accordingly below.

Distractions

- There are a lot less distractions, so I have more time and room in my day to get things done. I am my own worst distraction, so I must deliberately break my day down to small goals.
- Eliminates many of the interruptions that you can have in the office. I could start and finish a project on the same day.

Fatigue

- There is an added challenge of getting work done while addressing technology fatigue. Since the entire workday is virtual, I am doing all these meetings in front of my computer, whereas in the I at least had some office presence. I also need to get a break from technology and get that needed interpersonal face-to-face interaction with another human being by going to the office. If not, fatigue continues to be an issue.

- Now that I am back in the office, I may not get it (the work) done and I have to bring it home. But that is overtime, not telework.

Accountability

- When working late at the office, I must think about transportation issues. The later I wait to leave the office in the evening, the more crowded the trains get, the fewer the number of trains in service are available. So, my commute can start extending and I must plan when to cut my work off. And so that factor comes in. Now, when I am teleworking, I can easily say, "You know what? This particular task is important, it's due tomorrow, I need to suck it up and work until 9 tonight." And I can do that. Now, I can put in a 14-hour day, not necessarily that I want to, but then that is the new norm. But I can put in a 14-hour day to achieve a hot task that has to get done without sacrificing too much of my physical health, personal life, etc.
- With the pandemic you are trying to get back to work, but it is hard to be comfortable because there seems to be more concern for those that have the attitude of "if you get (COVID) it you get it." We do not know who is safe to be around, with or without a mask. Meetings and events are just planned, but there is no prior interaction with the staff as a whole. No one asks us if we feel comfortable being in these environments, but you are expected to attend the meetings and events.

Communication

- Communication is easy if you are sitting in the office because it is easy to see someone working and accept that they are trying their best. On the other hand, if we are both at home communication gets harder because I may wonder what you are doing or why it takes so long for you to answer.
- It is literally me in front of my laptop. I have not actually seen my boss in person since last February. I started the job in January, so I saw him in person for about six weeks and then boom (we were on telework). For more than a year now, I have not seen him in person. It has been all virtual or telephonic interaction.

- Frequent and consistent communication is the key to building or maintaining engagement and to fight the isolation that I and my colleagues have experienced.
- We must think about the other challenges because that all moves into what we could improve. I hear constantly, and I have heard of some companies who have successfully adjusted, but these meetings that just run into each other with no breaks all day long, people who never were in meetings all day, saying, "I'm in meetings all day and I don't have time to eat, and I don't have time to talk or walk the dog," or whatever. Some companies have said, "Every meeting that is a (scheduled) 30-minute meeting is 25 minutes, and every meeting that is a (scheduled) 60-minute meeting is 50 minutes," and they just build in transition time. I have heard of companies who have made meeting-less Fridays or no-meet Fridays. The only way that worked, in my opinion, is that everybody agrees to do it. Because the first person that schedules a meeting on a Friday pulls in people who do not want to be there or had planned not to be there or whatever causes problems for the organization.
- It is called a pandemic, right? And there are people from the top saying, "maximum telework." And so, there is a reason, a purpose for doing it, and it is understood. People do not like it, but at least they understand it. And I think without that, I am not sure teleworking would work. I think people would still be raising their eyebrows, going, "Well, why does he have teleworking? Why doesn't he have to commute to work? Why doesn't he have to show up?"
- I have found that clear communications are vital. From the perspective of both my supervisor and for me, this is a must. I try to be proactive in leading from behind when given the opportunity. I imagine what he needs (expects), I attempt to empower myself, by anticipating needs, and I make every attempt to minimize uncertainty
- Before the pandemic, I applied for a new job that would give me a promotion. I was not accepted until after the pandemic started, so I made the change while COVID was active. I was ok not having a going away party, but it was kind of sad that my supervisor was the only one who reached out to me at that time. Normally people get an award for their years of service, and I have gotten awards for various things over the years. This time I did not get any award from my top leadership. I did not even get a phone call.

Productivity

- Telework is certainly very conducive to being productive. It gives you back something that you cannot get if you are working in an office, and that's time. And nowadays, time is everything, right? We have a lot of issues and things that need to be addressed in different time zones.
- Before the pandemic, I was teleworking one day a week on average. So, four days a week at home, 16 days in the office. But the commute, both there and to the office in downtown, D.C., from where I am at in Sterling, Virginia, and back. About three hours a day is what it would take for me from the time I walk out my front door to the time I was walking into my cubicle and vice versa. So, I have immediately gotten back three hours a day, every day. So, three times four is 12; that's 12 hours I can get back each week.
- Leadership reports that our department's productivity increased since we started teleworking. The specific workday hours rule was suspended. We can work different hours during the day instead of a specific schedule. Leadership expanded the capacity of teleconferencing numbers to ensure proper operation of the teleconference (meetings) calls.
- Productivity improvements: stakeholders will need to figure out the best formula to solve what is sure to become a fixture in what is considered the new workplace environment. Stakeholders will have to figure how digital discoveries, communication advances, and cloud tools can and will improve the bottom-line. Management techniques will need to evolve. Employees, the other primary stakeholder, will probably get the deserved freedom they often seek (with ongoing challenges) self-governing, flexibility, constant change. Trust is a must.

Technology

- I think when this started a year ago, and the uncertainties of what technology are we using and getting the training to use the technology, that was a big issue. I think probably the overarching change I would make is to get agencies to incorporate technology and telework training for all their employees from the get-go. And that does not just mean talking about it. You need structure.

- Working remotely is only as great as the technology allows. I must rely on my own wireless network and now with my wife and my daughter we have a million devices on our "high speed internet," and it is not as fast as I want. What am I paying the internet provider for? If you get too many devices on it can present a very real challenge. You try to be in a (Microsoft) Teams meeting where you have got multiple people, everyone has got their cameras on, and I have had many times where the technology starts to fade or just flat out fails. Then I need to drop off a call or I cannot keep up on a call because there is too much interference, or the speed of the network is just too slow. This presents stresses and new challenges you must deal with as an employee, and you must be able to recognize that you do not have your IT support always right there handy.
- Because of the nature of our business, National Defense, it is important to invest in digitization strategies (technology needs, available tech resources, tech policy, tech training, tech support, etc.).
- Well, wider broadband and improved access to high-speed Internet is going to have to be something that I think will have to be offered because it was just a problem. It was so random who had good connections and who had bad, and who has not been on a Zoom call, or my Internet connection is not good, and the dog ate my homework.
- Why can't we just use email? That type of thing. So probably some in-house training will have to be done, better tutorials and things along those lines. Being able to do more right on your hand-held device is important. I think the technology just keeping pace is important. It just might have to be a little bit better introduced and cultivated amongst some portions in the workforce, really, namely older workers.

Coping

- If another pandemic happens and we must work in the office for months on end or work from home for months on end, for example, it does not just mean, "Hey, here is the technology you need to be able to survive and get your job done and interact with other human beings." It also requires some sort of emotional kind of counseling or workforce culture kind of counseling where companies engage with people to help their situation. That is because everything changes. You go from this being in office and interacting with other humans and now you are teleworking all the time. That has a very real emotional and motivational impact on not just your work ethic per se, but your approach to how you operate on a day-to-day basis, frankly.

- I had been operating independently in the office, without any staff, when the Pandemic hit. Once the building was shut down due to people getting sick from what appeared to be COVID-19, I began telecommuting. I was extremely sick myself. Almost immediately, I, like others, were asked to document all the work that we did, either daily or weekly. However, for me, doing the job of what was supposed to have been two people at a minimum, already took more time than I had during the regular workweek, and then being asked to document the work that I did represented a huge burden. I found myself working 7 days a week and not even having time to pay my own bills.
- There are many good things about telework, including the ability to focus on certain aspects of work without many distractions. I also do not end up having to drive home from work late at night on dark, cold nights from the office, because I am already at home doing that same work. Also, I can eat natural food more often rather than frozen (unhealthy) meals full of salt, and my blood pressure has come down.
- Everyone had to participate in telework, which really brought us all together. Since the pandemic shifted my clients to join me in a telework/work-from-home experience, it greatly increased everyone's understanding of the benefits and challenges of doing so. It brought us together in a way that put us on equal footing. Our team (and others like us) were not the only ones participating in meetings remotely. We all were! The experience has also shown me what I take for granted – a common sense work approach, necessary technology arrangements, planned communications, availability, and efficiency.
- I do not have to deal with the daily 2- or 2.5-hour commute to and from work. I like the flexibility. I can sleep in for an extra hour every morning. I can focus better. I tend to eat less. I think telework should be expanded and staff should go into the office only once a week and no more than twice.
- Teleworking is convenient. Working from home eliminated my daily commute while also giving me the additional time required to complete various tasks. I also felt I had more control over my schedule. As an entrepreneur, I love offering my contract employee complete flexibility, and teleworking does just that for her. She gets the work done on her time and, as a result, produces even more than if I enforced

a strict schedule. We meet in the virtual realm using tools like Zoom and Microsoft Teams.

- With telework, stress is increased, but not unhealthy (kids in the home, they see or know you are in the office but that you are available); meeting may be in progress, project may be in progress, etc. With my older child, no problem (they are) self-sufficient; with my 5-year-old things are as I mentioned previously. Do not forget the spouse. It can be a combination of what is experienced with the children. In terms of stress relieving, I am in the home with them. I get to see them; they get to see me. Responses to their needs are more immediate and gratifying. I get to have lunch with the Team daily!!!
- We experience top-level pressure for political reasons that make it challenging. My leadership is reserved in some ways but overall, on board with teleworking and supportive.
- What is good is that it is a time saver, in the fact that you do not have to worry about the commute. So, you get that time back. Obviously, there's savings out of pocket because you are not filling up the gas tank, you are probably not going out for lunch. So, you are saving all those nickels and dimes, but they add up, so you come out saving. You are also having less stress in your life because you're not looking at the clock.

Work Hours

- There is no stoppage because you are always at work. If I work past the time I set, I feel bad for lunch, so instead I will stay late for work, finishing a project. And then I feel bad. The lines get blurred. It is, oddly enough, its own kind of stress.
- I try to draw boundaries with the boss who was saying, at 7 at night that they wanted me to look up something. I try to do that.
- Telework fatigue is a real thing. I think for a lot of us incorporating practices into our daily life, forcing yourself to take a break, eating lunch, do not skip your meals, making sure you are not becoming a workaholic because it is convenient, easy to do. So, these sorts of things you have to kind of work harder at because you do not have those in-office cues that tell you, "Hey, it's time to go home or you're going to miss your train," right? And you must understand that you might need an actual start time and end time at your house. So, the

lines of those set boundaries of work becomes very, very blurred when you are teleworking. That is important because it is not just when you who is teleworking, everyone's teleworking, right? It is different when you are teleworking and your boss and everyone else is in the office because they're probably going to stop at a certain point. But when everyone is at home, typing away teleworking at all hours, long hours kind of start to become the new norm.

- In the office, the work hours are respected; however, with teleworking, there is an implicit expectation that you should be on or always available, which makes it difficult to feel free to take a break. There should also be more emphasis on engagement and teamwork. When we are in the office, we have direct access to our colleagues to ask for their opinions or input, or to show them what we are working on. That is what is missing that makes teleworking so isolating and at times, frustrating.
- I think there should be some clear boundaries about time and access. Not only due to telework, but with everyone online and with a computer virtually on their wrist or in their hand, you are almost never disconnected. And with everyone working this way, it is almost accepted that you are always working. That understanding and those boundaries need to be built into the systems and processes that exist, as well as part of our conversation about work. Additionally, I would love to see four-day work weeks become the norm, at least for some areas of work and for some roles.
- I feel like I am always on call. My computer is always on during the week. My coworkers and I enjoy greater flexibility and so messages keep flying late into the night. One person may sleep in and not start work until 10 a.m. and they may have to go out for a bit and generally end up working until 10 p.m. On my part, there is often an urge to check my messages late at night. This is especially so even when I am not working on anything major.
- I do think that what is good about it is the amount of time and money people are saving not commuting. People tell me all the time, "I can just get so much more work done if I don't have to drive to the office. There's no dead time in my schedule." But I think that comes with a challenge that there is no border between home and office anymore, and we hear that complaint all the time. There is no transition; it used to be you got in your car, you drank your coffee, you listen to NPR, and there was a transition in the morning. And in the evening, you could

transition back to your home, and that definition has disappeared and that is challenging a lot of people, but I think people appreciate being able to kind of sleep in until 10 minutes before a call and then be at work in their PJs, if they want to.

- I was expected to be available longer hours in the day, than I normally worked in the office. It seemed like our leadership expected us to be available to answer emails and text messages 24 hours a day. They never said anything, but those calls came before I work up and continued well into the night. They felt to contact me anytime they had an emergency.

Resources

- The expectation we put on ourselves and our customers to be results driven and not access driven is important. When it comes to accessibility, I have appreciated the closed captions in Zoom and the various other tools that exist, but we need to continue to do better to support and grow our capabilities regarding accessibility, inclusion, and diversity.
- There is also the difficult conversation about use of personal Wi-Fi. The organization is not providing that signal for you anymore; you are providing it. And they want it to be there when they need it to be there, and you are paying for it. You are using your own cell phone and so you are not getting paid for your Wi-Fi network or your phone, but you are providing your own work-related service.
- Starting the teleworking process was disruptive because much of the equipment that I was accustomed to using was at the office, such as the copier, scanner, and printing machine. At home, I had to resort to taking a picture of receipts and other documents from my phone camera and to send them to my work email address. I needed a printer, but it took 7 months before I was finally given permission to purchase one. The lack of a printer greatly hindered my ability to manage my site remotely, teach, and do research.
- A reduction in unnecessary meetings would be welcome. If there could be more people performing the work and less people in place to just oversee, everyone's workload could be reduced. More access to system information would also be helpful because there are things that I need to function, that I have limited access to. It is a matter of "permissions." Finally, if there is a need to hold so many meetings by teleconference,

at least let some of them be done by phone so that the staff can get outside once a month to walk.

- We were generally able to pick up where we left off, as all my students had both the hardware and the internet access to make that possible. For technical reasons, we were advised to have the students turn their cameras off - apparently it slowed the program down. I continued to lecture from my kitchen table, called on students, took questions, and administered both quizzes and exams. The course was not offered in the Fall, and this Spring, we have conducted the entire semester remotely without any noticeable hiccups.
- I think the main improvement that is achievable is broader and faster internet access.
- With the increase in teleworking, live virtual conferencing tools and other online applications have taken a bandwidth hit. This has caused a bit of an issue. Virtual calls get dropped more often, and email is lagging as well. I noticed my CRM application is having some connection and syncing problems too. To make teleworking most effective, internet service providers need to free up more bandwidth, and they need to keep the cost reasonable.
- Our government computers and networks are not technologically advanced enough to keep up with others (OEM, vendors, etc.). The NMCI machines do not have cameras installed. We cannot fully participate in web calls (Microsoft Teams, WebEx, etc.). There is supposed to be a technical refresh to give us newer computers, but there are no set dates for the upgrade at this time. We are utilizing our personal cell phones to conduct official business. This situation was brought up at an All Hands Meeting recently. Leadership stated they were going to try to come up with a solution for this situation. Microsoft Teams and WebEx do not work correctly at times.
- If we are teleworking not by our own choice, I should be able to get some of the home office expenses paid. There should be some funding for office supplies at the minimum. I need paper, ink, file folders, etc., and those costs can add up. Telework also made me use my cell phone more when we had to check in every day to ensure that everyone was working.

Plan

- If you are trying to build trust and get people who are accountable for their performance, you must talk to them even if it is to say there is no way they can be allowed to telework. You must communicate. For instance, maybe say, "There's no way I can be successful, or the organization can be successful, with you at home. We can look at some other things about flexibility." But you need to have that conversation.
- None of this would have been possible without remote learning access. Young people strike me as particularly adaptable to challenging circumstances and remote learning seems to fit them simply fine. Last Fall, I taught an in-person class with 30 students spread out in a large event space, masked, sanitizing-in, and sanitizing-out. It was probably the safest room they were in for the whole week. But in person, even from a distance, I could sense their tension and insecurity. That is not particularly possible online. I believe that, given the circumstances, most would have been more comfortable online.
- The real downside, in academia and I believe in business, is what could be called lack of context. There is something to be gained from face-to-face interpersonal activity. Looking at small squares on a screen, with either jumbled or artificial backgrounds, does not lend itself to personal connection. As I said, I have team members whom I have been coaching for seven months who I have not met. By this time in the school year, I know who they are, their family situations, their hobbies, etc. I do not know how - or if - that is fixable.
- Our department had to move to maximum telework around this time last year. Although leadership is talking about a phased approach to return to work, there are no concrete published plans or dates. We still have classified meetings and laboratory work (tests and analyses) on base. In these cases, we must inform our branch head and take our temperature with the instruments located at the main lobby. A small number of employees work in person because they cannot perform the required work via telework. Many employees work under a telework agreement.
- Sure, so like most everybody else, on May 13, 2020, we issued an order, do not come to work the next week. I had worked from home occasionally but was really sort of set up for it. I had a laptop; I had a charger. Then I spent a couple of months trying to find the right room

in the house and trying to find the right room in my house for my kid to work, because I had a college kid who came home and had to Zoom school and I had a middle school kid who had to Zoom school. So, the competition was intense for bandwidth. I upgraded the bandwidth to the biggest pipe that I could get now and soon I ended up with a really, sore right arm and right shoulder, because of having the mouse in the wrong position. The good news was my employer had good technology. We had Microsoft Teams on everybody's desktop, so once we had the connectivity, we were doing the actual work via (Microsoft) Teams. We used a system called Blue Jeans as well (Blue Jeans by Verizon is a company that provides an interoperable cloud-based video conferencing service that connects participants across a wide range of devices and conferencing platforms). That was not that hard. We did a lot of communications work, preparing people for that, making sure they knew how to get help and how to set up their desktops and how to access all the different various systems that they do from expense reports to payroll and time sheets and stuff like that.

- So, the next six months were sort of full of that kind of, "How do I help adapt to the physical aspects of teleworking?" And then I think we went into this next phase, six months in, when people realized we are not coming back to work and it started to be that psychological phase of teleworking, where "Well, how do I connect with these people? How do I maintain relationships with these people? How do I build relationships with people I do not see anymore? How do I onboard new hires in a completely remote setting?" It kind of went from the technical to the physical to the psychological, in my opinion. And we are still in the world of psychological adaptation in teleworking.
- Part-time teleworking (for unforeseen events such as weather, etc.) over the years was a good option, but efficiencies/effectiveness were realized. Full-time teleworking has been great. I have been able to set up my home office (printing, scanning, home computer in combination with work computer, call forwarding, etc.), establishing a more flexible schedule based on mission needs (COVID-19 operations, etc.), communications tools (Microsoft Teams, etc.), and work output (products, reports, documentation, etc.). Teleworking of any type helps to keep the target in sight. Keeps the mission progressing while operations are continued. Teleworking can positively impact work-life balancing, hence, if full-flexible work arrangements are embraced, advantages in diversity can be better realized.

- I am excited about the future of teleworking; it is a win-win for both the organization and its employees. Organizational objectives can be realized while at the same time meeting the needs of employees.
- We initially had a hybrid in the agency. We had some people who were more concerned, I think, physically, about their health or had other extenuating health concerns, so they opted for in home and working at home. The agency gave wide latitude for people to choose what they felt comfortable doing. Our physical layout here in this building enabled a lot of us to come in, because we have individual offices, not cubicles, so we are literally in our own office space, and we do not share. We do not have more than one person in an office. So, some of us opted to come in and those are the people who either had equipment issues, (needed access to) key equipment that they needed here, or they personally performed better with the regimen of going into work and being in an office environment and working/ And some of us quite frankly were afraid of being distracted or perhaps wandering a little bit because they did not have the environment of the office to go to.
- So, in our case we had a wide latitude of what to do. I personally chose to come into work every day, and from the moment we started that is what I did. In March, when everything shut down, I think the first day after the mass of nationwide shut down, I think everybody worked from home, and then after that, I opted to come into the office to work, and I worked all the way through the year. And I happen to be one of those people who I think just performed better when I had the routine. I had all my files and everything that I needed to do my work here. Although I could have planned to access various things from home certainly, but it was just easier for me to come in here and get to it.
- So, for the majority of 2020, I came in every day, five days a week and worked here. Now, I will say that toward the end of December, we had a little outbreak in the agency. We had three or four people who got sick, kind of one, two, three days in a row, and then everybody that had returned to the office or were working in the office was then requested to go work remotely. The management here said, "Everybody go home, get tested, and we're going to ride this out. Everybody just works from home until we kind of get through this patch." And that is what we did. The last couple of weeks of December, around Christmas and New Year's, and then through January, everybody worked remotely. Then right around February, those of us who wanted to come back and felt good about it, we returned to work.

EMPLOYEE ENGAGEMENT AND THE FUTURE

The interview details we have just examined tell us a great deal about how people are thinking about and experiencing telework. An article by an Upwork Chief Economist is useful in analyzing the information and in assessing the future of telework (Ozimek, 2020). The author analyzed what we already know; there was a forced movement to remote work generated by COVID-19. The study that resulted investigated the current state of remote work and drew conclusions about the long-term impacts.

Upwork looked at a combined 1,500 hiring managers to get answers. Executives, vice presidents, and managers shared their views and plans that guided their remote work decisions. Let us examine the key issues found in my 13 interviews under the lens of the Upwork findings. Again, those issues are distractions, fatigue, accountability, communication, productivity, technology, coping, work hours, resources, and plan approaches.

The Upwork research supported findings of key telework issues, including distractions, fatigue, communication, coping, and work hours. The research found that the largest report of perceived benefits, shared by 40% or more of the survey participants, were listed as "…lack of commute, fewer unnecessary meetings, and reduced distractions at the office… (Ozimek, 2020, p. 2)." Upwork supports what we have learned about technology and resources issues, reporting that technological issues were the single biggest drawback encountered. "One third of hiring managers found that productivity had increased as a result of remote work, a greater share than found productivity decreased (Ozimek, 2020, p. 2)." Finally, the Upwork study signals opportunity to convince more leaders to accept and support remote work. Upwork's survey demonstrated that remote work was less problematic than expected as reported by 56% of hiring managers. Only one in 10 reported remote work had gone worse than expected.

FUTURE RESEARCH DIRECTIONS

Future research should be focused on telework and how it can address the issues of balancing family and work, LMX issues that involve trust, performance, and accountability, accepting changes and/or improvements in the way we work, and managing the ever-changing ways people communicate. How can employers get value added from addressing these non-traditional employee concerns? It is important to point the research at problems employers face with people who are resisting the need to go back to the office. An Aug. 31, 2021, New York Times article, *Return to Office Hits a Snag: Young Resisters,* reported about a recent survey that reported that 55% of millennials questioned the need to return to the office, while the number was 45% for Generation X and 36% for Baby Boomers. Even if one only considers the Baby Boomers number, this is an indication that almost 4 in 10 workers question returning to the office. These are considerations that must be addressed in some way.

Everyone has questions and concerns. Employees have real questions about why they cannot continue to work at home when they have been productive for something like a year. Employers struggle with the need to have the workforce in one location so they can get the benefits of accountability and collaboration. These are the issues that must be examined for all concerned.

CONCLUSION

Of interest, the Upwork study demonstrates that despite the many worker responses as to why remote work was difficult, there is optimism that productivity has increased and will continue to do so. The survey confirms the commonality of such problems as technology challenges (36.2%), increased distractions at home (32.0%), reduced team cohesion (30.5%), difficulties in communication (30.3%), teams becoming less organized (23.3%), and less productivity (22.5%). Only 14.8% of respondents reported no issues. However, 32.2% of hiring managers reported an increase in productivity as opposed to only 22.5% who reported a decrease. The author states, "That one third finds remote work increases productivity, despite the rapid pace of change and struggles with technology, is a very optimistic result for future adoption and future productivity (Ozimek, 2020, p. 5)."

We can use these results to assist us in working through positive and negative aspects of telework.

REFERENCES

Gallup. (2007). *State of the American Workplace*. Gallup.com.

OzimekA. (2020). The future of remote work. Available at SSRN 3638597.

Vasel, K. (2021). *'I don't have to choose between lifestyle and career.' How remote work changed these people's lives.* Retrieved from https://www.cnn.com/2021/03/15/success/remote-work-changed-lives-pandemic/index.html

Chapter 3
LMX Theory

ABSTRACT

This chapter develops the background and use of a basic principle for the entire book: LMX. Defined in the introduction, LMX is a relationship-based approach for managing teams. It drives leader effectiveness through developing dyadic relationships with members, and even using these dyads to build effective groups. Leaders measure the dyadic relationships in terms of the level of loyalty, support, respect, and trust. The leader treats each member as a unique individual as a singular relationship is built. In role making, leaders tend to put people into groups: in-group or out-group. LMX is a powerful way to create and nurture relationships between the leader and each member supervised. It shines the light on leadership communication and demonstrates how trust, respect, and loyalty can improve work relationships.

BACKGROUND

The Leader-Member Exchange Theory (LMX) was discovered in the 1970s to focus on work relationships. A seminal article by Fred Dansereau, George Graen, and William Haga (1975) evolved LMX from vertical dyad linkage (VDL) theory. LMX employs the vertical dyadic interaction between leaders and members. The LMX term is used herein to signify the crucial team relationships that contribute to or detract from effective telework programs. This notion ties to the recommended emphasis on improving LMX quality to reduce the impact on negative effects of teleworking such as professional isolation (de Vries, Tummers, & Bekkers, 2019).

DOI: 10.4018/978-1-7998-8950-2.ch003

Figure 1. Leader-Member Exchange Theory (LMX) focuses on dyadic (two-way) relationships with members, and on using those dyads to build effective groups.

LMX theory is well suited to developing new teams or to team building during a major change. For the purposes of the current discussion, the major change is telework. COVID-19 forced a majority of the country into telework or some kind of remote situation, and today organizations and their employees are struggling with what to do about telework. Every day there is a post online or a TV news report or a board meeting or a conference that addresses why organizations do or do not want to telework, why employees will or will not come back to work, and whether telework can provide increased productivity or other benefits over an extended period of use. The world is dealing with these issues and this work suggests using LMX to guide the necessary communication and operations in pursuit of an answer.

It allows rapid evaluation of people's current skills and promotes a convenient way to segment them into groups where the work is done. Putting the team into two groups, each possessing similar skills and abilities, is a way to get people working and possibly avoid some of the team-forming tensions that may arise using other leadership techniques. This segmentation is placing people into in-groups and out-groups, which we will discuss a little later in this chapter. LMX can be highly effective in these situations, but leaders must remember to avoid making the segmentation a permanent arrangement so that a member who shows progress can join the group that is performing the best. Also, as leaders grow their people and build their teams, they should look at mixing the groups to increase capability and allow within-group mentoring. Again, this will be explored later in the chapter.

So, LMX drives leader effectiveness through developing dyadic (two-way) relationships with members, and even using these dyads to build effective groups. Leaders measure the dyadic relationships in terms of the level of loyalty, support, respect, and trust. All of the business success factors – decision making, access to resources, responsibility, and member performance – are influenced by the quality of the dyadic relationships (Janse, 2019).

According to the theory, relationship building between leaders and their subordinates progresses through three stages: role taking, role making, and routinization. Role taking happens when members first join the group. This occurs when members demonstrate their skills and abilities and when the leader forms first impressions. Role making is when the leader creates a role for the new member, or when the member may assume a certain role based on their capabilities. Routinization is when a mutual commitment to the mission and objectives of the work unit gets shaped and reinforced.

Interestingly, an LMX research project analyzed differences in high- and low-quality relationships. High-quality is about the effectiveness gained by social exchanges and reciprocity where there is mutual trust and members are valued by leaders as great work relationships can develop. The low-quality relationships are considered strictly contractual and are characterized by members doing only what is required in their prescribed job while leaders provide members only what is needed to perform (de Vries et al., 2019, p. 577). For example, the relationship may be based on a limited-scope contract and once it is performed there is no more interaction. The leader does not seek more production of this project and the member does not receive, or expect to receive, a bonus for completing it.

The LMX focus can also be seen in an article from 2014 that discussed the risks of professional and social isolation in some telework programs (Denison et al., 2014). Concerns are identified in terms of culture, effective mentoring, and lack of face-to-face contact between employee and manager. Part of the concern could be that telework is driving organizational culture while people are trying to realign their lives and surroundings to accommodate increased telework. Remote mentoring may not be as effective as in person mentoring, leading to fewer people interested in, or having access to, opportunities for leadership roles. Even if this is only a perceived problem on the part of the employee, there is a reality in terms of dealing with that perception. Additionally, the reduction in face-to-face contact in the organization based on teleworking makes it hard to develop and maintain critical relationships, especially those between members and leaders.

A key part of the theory is that the leader treats each member as a unique individual as a singular relationship is built. In role making, leaders tend to put people into groups: in-group or out-group. This sometimes happens subconsciously. The leader has the most trust in the members of the in-group and ensures the group has challenging and interesting work. The in-group gets the attention they need to succeed and can get additional training and advancement. The leader may feel personal similarities to members of the in-group.

On the other hand, members of the out-group tend not to have the leader's trust. This could be because leaders view their work as sub-par, perhaps not as good as the productivity of the in-group members or because there has been an issue that prevents developing the leader's trust. The result is that the out-group has less access to the manager. While the in-group members get complex assignments and autonomy, the out-group members get basic assignments and are highly scrutinized. As a result, the out-group does not receive the same opportunities for growth or advancement as may be afforded to the in-group.

Routinization establishes routines, norms, and expectations. Once placed in groups, members learn the routine of the organization and the standards by which they will work with their leader. This routinization allows members to work with leaders to build trust, persistence, empathy, patience, and respect. This can be a challenging time for organizations because leaders will tend to spend time with and give opportunities to the in-group. On the other hand, the leader might simply hope that the out-group does not create difficulty for the organization. This in-group and out-group placement is natural in many ways because leaders need to be successful, and they do this by finding their most promising team members and using these employees' talents to achieve success.

Some experts believe LMX theory has an inherent weakness in that it assumes that all team members are equally worthy of in-group status. In other words, everyone deserves trust, prestigious projects, and opportunities for promotion or recognition. That supposed weakness may be mitigated when some are assigned to the out-group. However, it is easy to see that in high-performing teams that recruit top-notch candidates that there is no out-group on the team. Even in these situations, there may be a need to have an out-group if members cannot keep up with the in-group tempo or if their behavior and/or productivity become sub-par.

LMX relies on an assumption that everyone on a team is hard-working, honest, and talented. Use of the theory creates trustworthiness and accountability between the leader and the member in the telework arrangement. These are important issues that this examination will continue to probe throughout this work.

Equally important is the theory's assumption that not all talented people are equal in the eyes of their leaders, thus accounting for a lower percentage of an organization's foundation. Of course, not everyone is a great worker, but this view through the prism of LMX that not all talented people account for the same amount of productivity view of LMX can be a strength. To capitalize on the benefits of LMX, leaders should prioritize identification of the in-group and the out-group. However, once identified, the leader's greatest challenge is to work with the members of the out-group to try to move them to the in-group.

Leaders tend to make in-group members advisers or assistants. Those distinctions give those members the inside track on interesting task assignments, assumption of the most prestigious responsibilities, gaining the leader's ear when decisions are made, and receiving the privilege of learning new and important information before out-group members. Giving the in-group these "enhancements" is not necessarily a bad approach, but the practice could be harmful over time if not tempered with fairness and verification of job performance by all.

The most effective use of LMX is to collaborate and communicate with out-group members to feature their strengths and improve on their weaknesses. The best outcome would be that at any given time the in-group/out-group organization would change to an in-group/train-group/out-group organization. The train-group would be the people who have worked with their leader to identify an improvement plan and who are actively working on the identified improvements. It is necessary to avoid unfairness and unconscious bias and search for ways to offer similar opportunities for advancement regardless of group, creating an atmosphere where relationships can grow and prosper. LMX is a way to give everyone a chance at improved organizational benefits.

LMX is a powerful way to create and nurture relationships between the leader and each member supervised. It shines the light on leadership communication and demonstrates how trust, respect, and loyalty can improve work relationships. Leaders must be careful, however, not to show favoritism to the in-group over the out-group. If the leader does not work to elevate out-group members to the in-group, problems arise. This is because the in-group usually enjoys higher job satisfaction and good promotion rates. Their careers are helped by increased mentoring. Leaders must take responsibility to develop out-group members. When this does not happen, the result for these members can be lower salaries, high attrition rates, and missed promotion opportunities.

Table 1. LMX-7 Questionnaire

Recommended Measure of LMX (LMX 7)

1. Do you know where you stand with your leader ... do you usually know how satisfied your leader is with what you do? (Does your member usually know)

Rarely	Occasionally	Sometimes	Fairly Often	Very Often

2. How well does your leader understand your job problems and needs? (How well do you understand)

Not a Bit	A Little	A Fair Amount	Quite a Bit	A Great Deal

3. How well does your leader recognize your potential? (How well do you recognize)

Not at All	A Little	Moderately	Mostly	Fully

4. Regardless of how much formal authority he/she has built into his/her position, what are the chances that your leader would use his/her power to help you solve problems in your work? (What are the changes that you would)

None	Small	Moderate	High	Very High

5. Again, regardless of the amount of formal authority your leader has, what are the chances that he/she would "bail you out," at his/her expense? (What are the chances that you would)

None	Small	Moderate	High	Very High

6. I have enough confidence in my leader that I would defend and justify his/her decision if he/she were not present to do so? (Your member would)

Strongly Disagree	Disagree	Neutral	Agree	Strongly Agree

7. How would you characterize your working relationship with your leader? (Your member)

Extremely Ineffective	Worse Than Average	Average	Better Than Average	Extremely Effective

Notes: Continuous scale of sum of 5-point items (1 left to 5 right). Leader's form consists of the same seven items asked about member of (leader in parentheses). Expected agreement between leader and member reports is positive and strong and used as index of quality of data.

(Graen & Uhl-Bien, 1995, p. 237)

The LMX-7 Questionnaire (Table 1) can help in evaluating members and how they interact with leaders. Leaders and members use the 7-item instrument to describe the amount of mutual respect, trust, and obligation that are exchanged in the LMX relationship. Researchers debate whether the construct should be considered unidimensional or multidimensional, but there is nonetheless value in using the questionnaire to measure the quality of working relationships.

Additionally, two researchers analyzed the effects of LMX presence and the way in which it affects the salience of fairness concerns (Erdogan & Bauer, 2015, p. 645). Employees consciously or subconsciously seek fairness and a lack of it can affect levels of trust, worker productivity, team communication, etc. The referenced study examined how employees felt about how LMX practices are distributed within the group, which was viewed in the light of LMX differentiation. LMX differentiation is the way a leader forms a quality exchange relationship and the way in which those relationships differ across dyads in a work group.

The study demonstrated how employees react to their own relationship quality and compares it to how they view other employees' relationship quality, thereby showing the importance of the distribution of in-group and out-group status. The study introduced relative LMX. Relative LMX is a computation of one employee's LMX quality as compared with the average LMX within the team. This means employees can get job satisfaction from having a high-quality exchange compared to that of other team members. The research further contends that when controls are emplaced to assure LMX quality, "relative LMX is positively related to self-efficacy, performance, citizenship behaviors (Hu & Liden, 2013), and psychological contract fulfillment (Henderson, Wayne, Shore, Bommer, & Tetrick, 2008; Vidyarthi, Liden, Anand, Erdogan, & Ghosh, 2010).

LMX differentiation, fairness, and relative LMX are awareness concerns for anyone using LMX theory. The way that one employee's LMX compares to that of other team members requires attention, in terms of both actual activities and perceived standards or practices. Paying attention to these issues will contribute to team building by effectively managing dyads in the way LMX prescribes. Leaders who successfully use LMX theory benefit from workers with initiative and drive, effective networks that extend capabilities, and teams that take risks toward higher productivity. This relationship can offer members greater access to resources and increased opportunities for advancement. People want to follow these leaders and these leaders want members who are driven.

FUTURE RESEARCH DIRECTIONS

LMX Theory can be a powerful tool for those who understand it. More research specific to telework is needed to examine how LMX differentiation, fairness, and relative LMX relate to current challenges. Research is needed to help organizations understand how different employees react to actual activities and perceived standards or practices. This relative LMX can be applied to team building efforts to strengthen the skills and interactions that result.

LMX is about managing dyads and more. It is about injecting successful dyadic interactions into the entire organization. Again, since this has not been examined in this light, now is the time to research this area.

CONCLUSION

LMX can be applied successfully by leaders and members alike to maximum efficiency and organizational growth. They can accept the challenge of using LMX to foster continuous improvement by finding ways to train and develop out-group members into in-group members. By accomplishing extra tasks, taking on new challenges, aligning with the leader, and delivering consistently positive results, members can apply LMX to their best advantage. Leaders can facilitate this cross-pollination by finding projects where the in-group and out-group are temporarily realigned on a project that has a longer timeline and/or presents less risk to the organization. For instance, if a reorganization is pending, these adjusted groups could be asked to create an employee survey to find out what worries people about the change. This could go a long way to addressing any resistance to change.

REFERENCES

Dansereau, F. Jr, Graen, G., & Haga, W. J. (1975). A vertical dyad linkage approach to leadership within formal organizations: A longitudinal investigation of the role making process. *Organizational Behavior and Human Performance*, *13*(1), 46–78. doi:10.1016/0030-5073(75)90005-7

de Vries, H., Tummers, L., & Bekkers, V. (2019). The Benefits of Teleworking in the Public Sector: Reality or Rhetoric? *Review of Public Personnel Administration*, *39*(4), 570–593. doi:10.1177/0734371X18760124

Denison, M. B., Banks, D., Bosley, E., Hyduke, B., James, K., Lefkowitz, E., ... Prochaska, G. (2014). Effective engagement strategies for an increasingly dispersed workforce. *Public Management*, *43*(3), 62.

Erdogan, B., & Bauer, T. N. (2015). Leader–Member Exchange Theory. In J. D. Wright (Ed.), *International Encyclopedia of the Social & Behavioral Sciences* (2nd ed., pp. 641–647). Elsevier. doi:10.1016/B978-0-08-097086-8.22010-2

Graen, G. B., & Uhl-Bien, M. (1995). Relationship-based approach to leadership: Development of leader-member exchange (LMX) theory of leadership over 25 years: Applying a multi-level multi-domain perspective. *The Leadership Quarterly*, *6*(2), 219–247. doi:10.1016/1048-9843(95)90036-5

Henderson, D., Wayne, S., Shore, L., Bommer, W., & Tetrick, L. (2008). Leader-Member Exchange, Differentiation, and Psychological Contract Fulfillment: A Multilevel Examination. *The Journal of Applied Psychology*, *93*(6), 1208–1219. doi:10.1037/a0012678 PMID:19025243

Hu, J., & Liden, R. (2013). Relative Leader–Member Exchange Within Team Contexts: How and when Social Comparison Impacts Individual Effectiveness. *Personnel Psychology*, *66*(1), 127–172. Advance online publication. doi:10.1111/peps.12008

Janse, B. (2019). Leader-Member Exchange Theory (LMX). *Toolshero*. Retrieved from Retrieved May 11, 2021: https://www.toolshero.com/management/leader-member-exchange-theory-lmx/

Vidyarthi, P. R., Liden, R. C., Anand, S., Erdogan, B., & Ghosh, S. (2010). Where do I stand? Examining the effects of leader–member exchange social comparison on employee work behaviors. *The Journal of Applied Psychology*, *95*(5), 849–861. doi:10.1037/a0020033 PMID:20718513

Chapter 4
Trustworthiness

ABSTRACT

We can use trustworthiness and trust interchangeably because they both relate to the importance of LMX. Trustworthiness, then, is the quality of a person, or a thing, that inspires reliability. The existence of trustworthiness is shown through qualities like being respectful, honest, consistent, positive, and selfless. Leaders who can admit mistakes, acknowledge weakness, applaud strength, and help each other, and who can promote those qualities in the workforce, will be capable of building trust. Mutual trust is important, and everyone has a lot at stake with trust issues because of the inherent risks. Those risks are about putting one's faith or a pending decision in the hands of someone in whom you have not yet developed confidence in, or in whom there are limits to that confidence. Leaders who follow telework policies developed in response to COVID-19 must build trust with subordinates and superiors alike. Trust can then grow as emotions are shared, real understanding developed, and core issues are addressed professionally.

BACKGROUND

Trustworthiness can grow if leaders and members can admit mistakes, acknowledge weakness, applaud strength, and help each other improve the telework experience in a way that allows both sides to prosper. Organizations can also refer to telework legislation (Services, 2011). Leaders can increase their own trustworthiness by trusting their team. Both leaders and members have much at stake because trust is a contract that comes with risks. The risks

DOI: 10.4018/978-1-7998-8950-2.ch004

involve putting one's faith or a pending decision in the hands of someone in whom you have not yet developed confidence in, or in whom there are limits to that confidence.

Table 1 lists several factors that contribute to building trustworthiness which can be a complicated pursuit of enduring relationships. This is the expectation that a person will act in an honorable and mutually beneficial way.

Table 1. Keys to building trust

Building Trust
Receiver Adjustment: Building trust takes time, so senders must be patient as receivers adjust to messages and the communication process. Recognition is one way to help the receiver accept the interaction. Careful conversations to help with adjustments are important.
Sender/Leader Power: Collaborate and make the decision or course of action more suggestion vs. a direct order. Provide choices and explain the rationale for any decisions made.
Security: Work to manage risk and raise comfort levels. Take the time to help people understand and adjust to the activity.
Risk Tolerance: Acknowledge and confront risk. Explain what is at stake, analyze options, and provide a safety net. If things go wrong, do not place blame. Work through the difficulty together.
Match Interests: Trust comes from shared values, shared interests, and shared responsibility. Take everyone's point of view into consideration and accommodate when possible. The overall goal should drive common actions and shape the culture of the relationship and/or group to the best outcome.
Personality Match: Find common ground in terms of values, beliefs, and even cultural background. Emphasize "we" more than "I."
Care about Others: Make sure your actions in communicating are good for all involved. You might have to sacrifice your own wants and desires at times to allow other interests to prevail for the good of the communication. Be fair in your actions and make sure the process is fair. Try to focus on a win-win outcome wherever possible and be prepared to compromise when that is not possible.
Capability: Use your skill and competence to manage the communication or complete the task. Senders sometimes must relinquish control to address issues that threaten progress.
Integrity and Predictability: Use the adage "under promise and over deliver." Be honest in your successes and failures and share information about the values that drive the communication effort and sender actions.
Communicate-Communicate-Communicate: Communication should be timely and candid. The best relationships are formed without constraints or thinking outside the box.

(Brown Sr, 2016, p. 183)

One avenue to address telework rules and responsibilities is through a foundation of trustworthiness, where we seek to understand what creates and/or contributes to relationship-building decisions. The existence of trustworthiness promotes the development of dependence, satisfaction, and commitment. This leads to communication-friendly relationships. Trusting relationships in organizations involve an ongoing decision to give most people the benefit of the doubt, and it can even be extended to people we do not know through direct interaction (M. Brown, Sr., 2011). Current research indicates that new ways of communicating "alter the patterns of interdependencies and the nature and extent of uncertainty (McEvily, Perrone, & Zaheer, 2003a)." These new ways make people rely more on the decisions and actions of others, creating both dependency and vulnerability. Leaders must understand and master the use of these factors because they are crucial to building and maintaining trustworthiness.

Trustworthiness, then, is important in pandemic-related activities, like face mask wearing, social distancing, vaccination, and other initiatives. Many researchers have taken up the topic of trust in the 1990s and early 2000s (Bachmann, Knights, & Sydow, 2001; Denise M. Rousseau, Sim B. Sitkin, Ronald S. Burt, & Colin Camerer, 1998) and books (Gambetta, 1988a; Kramer, 1996; Lane & Bachmann, 1998). However, while examinations of trust in and between organizations seem to have increased (C. Brown, Smith, Arduengo, & Taylor, 2016; Brown Sr, 2017; Frank Messina, 2011; Kaplan & Haenlein, 2010; McAllister, Lewicki, & Chaturvedi, 2006), the challenges that organizations and leaders face today indicate the need for renewed evaluation. New research on trust can be valuable in understanding how it factors into the ways our world has changed because of COVID-19.

Trustworthiness in today's organizational context has even more importance because crisis and technology have forced changes in the way people relate to one another. The differences caused in person-to-person exchanges and coordination of work across time and distance are crucial factors in how trustworthiness is formed and nurtured. In knowledge-intensive organizations, for example, change can force people to be both more dependent and more vulnerable to the actions and decisions of others. These are important considerations in building and maintaining trustworthiness.

Organizational science scholars continue to make important advances that promote understanding of the meaning of trustworthiness and how it relates to the way organizations operate. One relevant focus area represented a wide range of methodological approaches, a diverse set of theoretical disciplines, a variety of levels of analysis, and a blend of empirical models (McEvily et al., 2003a). Two scientific papers authored are important for the current focus on trust. Becerra and Gupta (2003) probed the influence of organizational context on trust, emphasizing how the influence of social structure in an organization is contingent on communication frequency. They argue that frequency of communication is related to emphasis, in that as frequency increases the emphasis shifts from the trustor's to the trustee's individual and contextual characteristics. The relationship among senior managers of a multinational organization is the basis for testing the hypotheses. Findings point to a view of trust production in organizations that consists of individual, dyadic, and contextual components.

Examining the trust construct as it relates to performance in organizations requires an examination of two central issues. The first involves trust as a means for dealing with uncertainty. The second focuses on trust and acceptance of vulnerability (Newell & Swan, 2000). Luhman (1988, p. 103) argues that trust occurs in situations of risk and uncertainty: "A system requires trust as an input condition in order to stimulate supportive activities in situations of uncertainty or risk." In the context of COVID-19 and its effects, vulnerability, risk, and uncertainty are all factors that should be examined when evaluating the use of telework.

Luhmann's notion suggests that trust is an attitudinal mechanism that allows individuals to subjectively assess whether to expose themselves to situations where there may not be an acceptable trade-off in terms of possible damage versus received advantage. The attitude develops when individuals feel vulnerable. Viewed through Luhmann's suggestion of trust as a determination of risk vs. reward, the attitudinal mechanisms related to work environments during the COVID-19 pandemic could be how people view their contributions given they do not have direct or face-to-face contact with supervisors or fellow team members. This may also be indicative of employees' concerns about how they can maintain connections with other members of the team.

Trustworthiness is also a multi-dimensional concept where values, attitudes and emotions or moods interact (Newell & Swan, 2000). There are three reasons someone may be able to develop trust (Sako, 1992):

1. Because of a contractual agreement that binds the parties in the relationship
2. Because of a belief in the competencies of those involved
3. Because of a belief in the goodwill of those involved

There are other dimensions to consider as well. The research of Dirks and Ferrin provide additional areas of inquiry that may be helpful in addressing COVID-19 or some future pandemic or crisis. The information gained could be very useful because other inquiries cover trust in organizational settings, using rewards to increase and decrease trust, and examining the effects of third-party relationships on interpersonal trust (Dirks & Ferrin, 2001; D. L. Ferrin & Dirks, 2003; D.L. Ferrin, Dirks, & Shah, 2006). A typology distinguishing between deterrence-based trust, knowledge-based trust and identification-based trust was developed in 1992 (Shapiro, Sheppard, & Cheraskin). A developmental focus was argued by Zucker (1986), establishing three central mechanisms of trust production: process-based, characteristic-based, and institutional-based. Process-based trust focuses on reciprocal, recurring exchange. Characteristic-based trust is defined by social similarity. Institutional-based trust is determined by expectations embedded in societal norms and structures.

We know trustworthiness can grow between people as they share emotions in addressing real issues; the research supports this notion. Stephen Covey, American educator, author and keynote speaker, said, "Trust is the highest form of human motivation. It brings out the very best in people (Frank Messina, 2011, p. 219)." Trustworthiness can minimize or eliminate uncertainty in communication because it allows each party to believe that the other will behave in a way that is beneficial. When the result of the communication is shared value and common understanding, a bond is created.

Building trustworthiness brings benefits in terms of understanding personal versus organizational views. If everyone involved in the discussion is willing to admit mistakes, acknowledge weaknesses, applaud strengths, and lean on each other for help, they can benefit from an extraordinarily strong sense of trust.

Trustworthiness is obviously a primary consideration in this examination of telework. Our focus is based on five types: history, third-party interaction, and rules-based (Kramer, 1999) and deterrence-based and knowledge-based. The types can be explained this way (Kramer, 1999, pp. 575-579; Lewicki & Bunker, 1995, p. 142; McAllister et al., 2006):

- During interactions, history-dependent processes guide an individual's perception of someone's trust and their willingness to engage in trusting behavior
- Third-party testimonials and second-hand information are major players in building trust, because they may have information consistent with what the decision maker wants to hear (the key is whether the third-party relays information that is truthful and relevant)
- Rules-based trust requires shared understanding among leaders and members in terms of the system of rules that establish the standards of appropriate behavior

- Deterrence-based trust relies on consistency of behavior, or the notion that "people will do what they say they are going to do," and is sustained by the threat of punishment (Lewicki & Bunker, 1995)
- Predictability leads to knowledge-based trust because there is enough information about someone to understand them and reasonably predict their likely behavior (Lewicki & Bunker, 1995)

Trustworthiness is important for every organization and every leader should strive for continuous engagement that builds and maintains it. A great way to create and nurture trustworthiness is to instill in every member an understanding of their value to the group and to achieving organizational goals, ensuring all members have chances to participate. This is especially important in teleworking programs when the team tends to be splintered and communications may be challenged at best.

Effective collaboration can lead to trustworthiness by building an environment that allows people to share work, understand each person's situation, and enforce engaged responses during group communications (Leinonen, Järvelä, & Häkkinen, 2005; Nardi & Whittaker, 2002). Effective management of telework schedules and routines helps leaders achieve shared understanding among team members. Telework arrangements work best when the organization can create learning and interaction when working remotely.

It is important to understand the differences in viewpoints of the organization, the leader, and the member. Leaders must also deal with the various challenges that may arise from telework arrangements. For instance, personal values and expectations can cause problems if they are not addressed in open and honest communication at the beginning of the telework arrangement. Organizations must find common ground with employees to communicate when the parties are wrapped up in their own points of view.

Leaders must manage the hierarchy of the organization with effective communication at all levels. Make sure each employee knows their value by including all team members in organization-level communication, and by following up and getting feedback when someone is excluded from interactions for whatever reason.

Collaboration, personal values and expectations, and issues of hierarchy are all potential barriers to communication. These barriers can be exacerbated by the remote activities where communication is slower, and when we do not have the benefit of important face-to-face feedback. Organizations that establish and rely on a unifying philosophy of open and honest communication are usually well equipped to deal with these barriers. The organization must have established processes for negotiation of goals and roles as the work evolves.

Armed with this foundation of trustworthiness, we should examine telework as it relates to trust and reliability. In 2016, researchers observed that federal government managers denied their workers opportunities to telework despite the existence of an Executive Office mandate encouraging telework (C. Brown et al., 2016). This information comes from a hermeneutic phenomenological study of qualitative data from the lives of 12 federal government managers who did not allow teleworking. The study identified themes related to trust with 5 of the 8 trust-related themes focusing on lack of trust.

As telework grows in organizations, new dynamics and therefore communication challenges arise. Shared understanding is crucial to the endeavor and there is an increasing amount of research to assist with these new interactions. Many researchers have addressed various trust issues and examinations in and between organizations which are insightful for telework analyses (Bachmann, 2001; Beauregard, Basile, & Canonico, 2019; C. Brown et al., 2016; Day & Burbach, 2015; Gambetta, 1988b; Jackson, Wilson, & Borden, 2020; Marx, Reimann, & Diewald, 2021; Denise M Rousseau, Sim B Sitkin, Ronald S Burt, & Colin Camerer, 1998). Additional information is available in a special journal issue that published seven papers that represent a wide range of methodological approaches, a diverse set of theoretical disciplines, a variety of levels of analysis, and a blend of empirical models (McEvily, Perrone, & Zaheer, 2003b). These views explain how trust may grow between people as they share emotions in addressing real issues. Also, leaders who follow telework policies developed in response to COVID-19 build trustworthiness around them. Trustworthiness can also grow when people share emotions in addressing real issues.

Social learning theory tells us that behavioral change can come as the result of vicarious learning through modeling. Done well, that learning can build or enhance trustworthiness. If this type of learning is successfully accomplished, the result can be trustworthiness creation and/or improvement. An examination of the nature of an observed model during vicarious learning can influence the probability that an observer will imitate the modeled behavior and have a chance to be successful (Manz & Sims, 1981). The model with the most interpersonal attraction will command the most attention (Bandura, 1977a). Credible models are people perceived as being successful and who exert greater influence than non-credible models (Bandura, 1969, 1977a). There is evidence in the literature that effectiveness increases for modeling-based training programs in which the models presented have achieved high status and competence (Goldstein & Sorcher, 1974; Rosenbaum, 1978; Weiss, 1978). The belief is that subordinate employees showed greater similarity in behavior to superiors who were viewed as being competent and successful, indicating great possibilities for building trust. These benefits, behavior change, personal success, improved professional status, and modeling-based training, can be achieved during the LMX efforts by leaders mentioned throughout Chapter 3.

In 2009, researchers analyzed the importance of trust and its consequences for management (Gursakal, Oguzlar, Aydin, & Tuzunturk) with a network analysis to determine which employees trust other employees on a personal level. The researchers found that trust can create effective cooperation within enterprises, thereby having a positive influence on performance, growth, and survival.

FUTURE RESEARCH DIRECTIONS

Research on trust is not new and there are new studies every day. Future research should add to examinations of trustworthiness and telework as primary considerations. We see the need for this in everyday pandemic-related activities, like face mask wearing, social distancing, vaccination, and other initiatives. One burning question for researchers is why is there such emotional reactions to decisions of mask-wearing and vaccination? We see some political issues, but researchers must go beyond that to seek root causes.

Researchers should be examining the standards for who can telework and who cannot? Another consideration in trust and telework is whether employees can negotiate flexibility in their work arrangements. One example of the dilemma is Yahoo CEO Marissa Mayer who, according to a 2013 Reuters article, built a nursery adjacent to her office but told employees they could not work from home. That caused much controversy. So, researchers should be looking at how these kind of trust issues play out in telework conversations and negotiations.

CONCLUSION

Throughout this chapter, we have used trust and trustworthiness as key factors in creating quality work relationships that contribute to organizational cohesion and success. The creation and nurturing of trustworthiness are an ongoing responsibility that rests with everyone in the organization. Leaders and members must behave in ways that contribute to trust – honesty, open communication, good ethics, and good performance. So, leaders must demonstrate their trustworthiness at every opportunity. This can present modeling opportunities for members as they try to emulate the standards set by the boss. Members must also exhibit trustworthiness at the highest level to demonstrate they are key assets to the operations of the organization. Trustworthiness must be combined with an exchange between leaders and members that promotes performance, which is the focus of the next chapter.

REFERENCES

Bachmann, R. (2001). Trust, power and control in trans-organizational relations. *Organization Studies*, *22*(2), 337–365. doi:10.1177/0170840601222007

Bachmann, R., Knights, D., & Sydow, J. (2001). Special Issue: Trust and control in organizational relations. *Organization Studies*, *22*(2). Advance online publication. doi:10.1177/0170840601222007

Bandura, A. (1969). *Principles of behavior modification*. Holt, Rinehart and Winston.

Bandura, A. (1977a). *Social Learning Theory*. Prentice-Hall.

Beauregard, T. A., Basile, K. A., & Canonico, E. (2019). *Telework: Outcomes and facilitators for employees*. Academic Press.

Becerra, M., & Gupta, A. K. (2003). Perceived trustworthiness within the organization: The moderating impact of communication frequency on trustor and trustee effects. *Organization Science*, *14*(1), 32–44. doi:10.1287/orsc.14.1.32.12815

Brown, C., Smith, P. R., Arduengo, N., & Taylor, M. (2016). Trusting telework in the federal government. *Qualitative Report*, *21*, 87.

Brown, M., Sr. (2011). *Social networking and individual performance: Examining predictors of participation* (Ph.D.), Old Dominion University. Retrieved from http://proquest.umi.com/pqdweb?did=2355291551&Fmt=7&clientId=3505&RQT=309&VName=PQD

Brown, M. A. Sr. (2016). *Solutions for High-touch Communications in a High-tech World*. IGI Global.

Brown, M. A. Sr. (2017). *Motivationally Intelligent Leadership: Emerging Research and Opportunities: Emerging Research and Opportunities*. IGI Global.

Day, F. C., & Burbach, M. E. (2015). Does organization sector matter in leading teleworker teams? A comparative case study. *International Journal of Business Research and Development*, *3*(4). Advance online publication. doi:10.24102/ijbrd.v3i4.547

Dirks, K. T., & Ferrin, D. L. (2001). The role of trust in organizational settings. *Organization Science*, *12*(4), 450–467. doi:10.1287/orsc.12.4.450.10640

Ferrin, D. L., & Dirks, K. T. (2003). The use of rewards to increase and decrease trust: Mediating processes and differential effects. *Organization Science*, *14*(1), 18–31. doi:10.1287/orsc.14.1.18.12809

Ferrin, D. L., Dirks, K. T., & Shah, P. P. (2006). Direct and indirect effects of third-party relationships on interpersonal trust. *The Journal of Applied Psychology*, *91*(4), 870–883. doi:10.1037/0021-9010.91.4.870 PMID:16834511

Frank Messina, E. D. (2011). *Two-And-A-Half Minutes To "Effective"*. Daily Thoughts for Improving Your Effectiveness in the Areas of Communications, Coaching, and Delegation.

Gambetta, D. (1988a). *Trust: making and breaking cooperative relations*. B. Blackwell.

Gambetta, D. (1988b). *Trust: Making and breaking cooperative relations*. Academic Press.

Goldstein, A. P., & Sorcher, M. (1974). *Changing Supervisory Behavior*. Pergammon.

Gursakal, N., Oguzlar, A., Aydin, Z. B., & Tuzunturk, S. (2009). Measuring trust in an intra-organisational context using Social Network Analysis. *International Journal of Management and Enterprise Development*, *6*(4), 494–512. doi:10.1504/IJMED.2009.024238

Jackson, K. S., Wilson, D., & Borden, D. (2020). Telework: Achievements and Blunders. *Journal of Government Financial Management*, *69*(1), 58–59.

Kaplan, A. M., & Haenlein, M. (2010). Users of the world, unite! The challenges and opportunities of Social Media. *Business Horizons*, *53*(1), 59–68. doi:10.1016/j.bushor.2009.09.003

Kramer, R. M. (1996). *Trust in organizations: Frontiers of theory and research*. Sage Publications.

Kramer, R. M. (1999). Trust and distrust in organizations: Emerging perspectives, enduring questions. *Annual Review of Psychology*, *50*(1), 569–598. doi:10.1146/annurev.psych.50.1.569 PMID:15012464

Lane, C., & Bachmann, R. (1998). *Trust within and between organizations: Conceptual issues and empirical applications*. Oxford University Press.

Leinonen, P., Järvelä, S., & Häkkinen, P. (2005). Conceptualizing the Awareness of Collaboration: A Qualitative Study of a Global Virtual Team. *Comput Supported Coop Work Computer Supported Cooperative Work*, *14*(4), 301–322. doi:10.100710606-005-9002-z

Lewicki, R. J., & Bunker, B. B. (1995). Trust in relationships. *Administrative Science Quarterly*, *5*(1), 583–601.

Luhmann, N. (1988). Familiarity, confidence, trust: Problems and alternatives. In D. Gambetta (Ed.), *Trust: Making and breaking cooperative relations*. Basil Blackwell.

Manz, C. C., & Sims, H. P. Jr. (1981). Vicarious Learning: The Influence of Modeling on Organizational Behavior. *Academy of Management Review*, *6*(1), 105–113. doi:10.5465/amr.1981.4288021

Marx, C. K., Reimann, M., & Diewald, M. (2021). Do Work–Life Measures Really Matter? The Impact of Flexible Working Hours and Home-Based Teleworking in Preventing Voluntary Employee Exits. *Social Sciences*, *10*(1), 9. doi:10.3390ocsci10010009

McAllister, D. J., Lewicki, R. J., & Chaturvedi, S. (2006). *Trust in developing relationships: from theory to measurement.* Paper presented at the Academy of Management Proceedings. 10.5465/ambpp.2006.22897235

McEvily, B., Perrone, V., & Zaheer, A. (2003a). Introduction to the special issue on trust in an organizational context. *Organization Science*, *14*(1), 1–4. doi:10.1287/orsc.14.1.1.12812

McEvily, B., Perrone, V., & Zaheer, A. (2003b). Trust as an organizing principle. *Organization Science*, *14*(1), 91–103. doi:10.1287/orsc.14.1.91.12814

Nardi, B. A., & Whittaker, S. (2002). The place of face-to-face communication in distributed work. *Distributed Work*, 83-110.

Newell, S., & Swan, J. (2000). Trust and inter-organizational networking. *Human Relations*, *53*(10), 1287–1328. doi:10.1177/a014106

Rosenbaum, B. L. (1978). New uses for behavioral modeling. *The Personnel Administrator*, 27–28.

Rousseau, D. M., Sitkin, S. B., Burt, R. S., & Camerer, C. (1998). Not so different after all: A cross-discipline view of trust. *Academy of Management. Academy of Management Review*, *23*(3), 393–404. doi:10.5465/amr.1998.926617

Rousseau, D. M., Sitkin, S. B., Burt, R. S., & Camerer, C. (1998). Not so different after all: A cross-discipline view of trust. *Academy of Management Review*, *23*(3), 393–404. doi:10.5465/amr.1998.926617

Sako, M. (1992). *Prices, quality, and trust: Inter-firm relations in Britain and Japan*. Cambridge University Press. doi:10.1017/CBO9780511520723

Services, E. (2011). *Guide to Telework in the Federal Government*. Washington, DC: U.S. Office of Personnel Management (OPM) Retrieved from https://www.telework.gov/guidance-legislation/telework-guidance/telework-guide/guide-to-telework-in-the-federal-government.pdf

Shapiro, D. L., Sheppard, B. H., & Cheraskin, L. (1992). Business on a handshake. *Negotiation Journal*, *8*(4), 365–377. doi:10.1111/j.1571-9979.1992.tb00679.x

Weiss, H. M. (1978). Social learning of work values in organizations. *The Journal of Applied Psychology*, *63*(6), 711–718. doi:10.1037/0021-9010.63.6.711

Zucker, L. G. (1986). Production of trust: Institutional sources of economic structure. In B. M. Staw & L. L. Cummings (Eds.), *Research in organisational behaviour* (Vol. 8). JAI.

Chapter 5
Performance

ABSTRACT

The current examination of Covid-related issues is important because the pandemic grew so fast that it outpaced current research and literature. To date, according to the literature examined herein, there is a shortage of studies about telework. Also, existing studies have not yet gone far enough to consider the enormous contribution and involvement of supervisors and leaders as they relate to telework. Contemporary literature has primarily compared and contrasted teleworking and non-teleworking employees. As we focus on supervisors and leaders, we must evaluate key requirements of the value of performance in the conversation. This will lead to mitigation strategies and shared understanding that are vital to improving performance. As the authors conduct this evaluation, there will be lots of information about how leaders can help members. They will also understand how to take advantage of the benefits of teleworking. They will also highlight situations where leaders may be reluctant to use telework, understand the reasons for reluctance, and begin the discussion to improve acceptance of telework.

BACKGROUND

The previous chapter examined trustworthiness and the interactions that build, and sometimes degrade, trustworthiness. As we start to look at performance and how it factors into our examination, we should keep in mind that by performing well, workers provide value to the organization. Much of the discussion here will address how that value could be rewarded with the use of some level

DOI: 10.4018/978-1-7998-8950-2.ch005

of telework. We will call the dyadic relationship either supervisor-employee or leader-member. For our discussion, these are interchangeable terms, but some of the referenced literature does not refer to leader-member or LMX.

Key requirements in reaping the benefits available from the value of telework are assessments of employee performance. Performance is the act of accomplishing or carrying out a function, action, or task.

According to Contingency Theory, organizations must respond to new and changing environmental conditions by redesigning their internal processing capabilities through structures and technology (Rice, 1992). The theory concedes that there is not one organizational design that ensures performance over another design. Performance is contingent on an appropriate match between contextual variables, such as task demands, and organizational arrangements, such as communication structures and media. In other words, the kind and availability of resources is crucial to achieving success in your organization.

Leaders who can master the challenges of goal alignment, providing oversight, avoidance of communications meltdown, coordinating multiple players, managing the tension between competition and collaboration, and overcoming data deficits and capacity shortages will be most successful in managing the challenges of telework. Issues of mission and strategy take on extra importance in the teleworking world. Leaders must determine what individual performance goals they hope to accomplish and then socialize how these goals address what members should be doing to accomplish mission objectives.

These intentions must be effectively communicated at all levels of the organization when telework is involved. This is because you cannot grab everyone for a quick meeting to adjust course like you would in the office. In this way, telework focuses organizations on starting with mission and then determining the process. This allows the necessary change from the tradition of deciding on a process and then trying to fit it to a mission.

A good organizational climate is helpful to this undertaking. Organizational climate focuses on current perceptions of people in a work environment and their observable personal relationships that affect their performance (Hatala & Fleming, 2007). Understanding organizational climate sheds light on an individual's perceptions of leader support, opportunity to use new training, level of peer support, supervisor sanctions, and positive or negative personal outcomes resulting from application of training on the job (Hatala & Fleming, 2007). Leaders must pay attention to these variables when pursuing performance that makes teleworking effective.

When examining performance, it is important to compare the leader and member views of telework to see if mitigation strategies and a shared understanding can make this a win for all involved. The current literature seems to focus more on employees and their needed adjustments than on supervisors. Examine the words of two researchers in 2020:

> *Nevertheless, as the focus of the studies in the contemporary literature was on teleworking and non-teleworking employees, only a few studies sought to recognize and account for supervisors in the telework context. Thus, there is a gap in the literature (Park & Cho, 2020, p. 5).*

The Park and Cho (2020) research effort focused on what the researchers believed to be an often-neglected group: supervisors. The study compared non-teleworking and teleworking supervisor behaviors to allow an examination of the factors affecting the organizational impact of telework. This examination focused on supervisor perceptions. Organizations that employ telework need supervisors who can effectively direct remote operations, implement policy, and manage the day-to-day practices to achieve the best performance.

Agreeing to let employees telework can be risky for leaders. They are taking the risk to surrender some control of their workforce in terms of presence and communication. While this is necessary for telework programs to be viable, it is nonetheless a risk. As much as we put trust in others, some people do not do well without close supervision. For various reasons, some people struggle with communication when they are in person, and it does not necessarily get better in a remote setting.

Let us examine a confrontational situation to illustrate this part of the discussion.

> *IN-PERSON SCENARIO: An in-office employee has just turned in their product to the supervisor, and the supervisor makes no secret of their displeasure with the product. The employee hears the supervisor telling someone in leadership that they are disappointed in what was turned in. The supervisor goes on to mention they will "grab" the employee and make sure it is correct the next time it is submitted. The employee is trying to figure out how to delay the next conversation with the supervisor as they try to understand where they went wrong. The employee was trying to do a good job and thought they had a grasp on what the supervisor wanted. The employee was comfortable with the draft because it was not a final product. It was intended to generate initial feedback before course finalizing the product.*

Continued on following page

REMOTE SCENARIO (differences from the previous scenario are in italics): A remote employee has just turned in their product to the supervisor, and the supervisor is not pleased with the product. The supervisor shares with someone in leadership that they are disappointed in what was turned in. The supervisor goes on to mention they will "grab" the employee and make sure it is correct the next time it is submitted. The supervisor sends an e-mail to the employee saying they need to talk about the issues with the submission. The employee is sure this is a negative conversation and does not immediately answer the email, trying to understand what the problem might be. The supervisor waits 10 minutes, does not get a reply, and calls the employee's cell phone. The employee does not answer the cell phone because there is now stress about what this might turn into. *The employee was trying to do a good job and thought they had a grasp on what the supervisor wanted. The employee was comfortable with the draft because it was not a final product. It was just intended to get feedback before course correcting or starting over.*

In both scenarios, the eventual meeting or discussion begins with high levels of stress on both sides. The supervisor is feeling the stress of loss of control and the belief that they are getting substandard performance. The employee is feeling the stress of doing what they thought was good work only to find out they are wrong or misguided in their product. However, the important thing is to focus on communication in both scenarios. Focus on communication throughout the assigning and turning in of the work. Leaders should avoid making this about control, real or imagined. In both scenarios, supervisors and employees share the need to communicate clearly. For instance, did the supervisor provide clear instructions, was there a chance for clarifying questions to be asked, did leaders provide resources adequate to do the work, and was the required product specified as a draft, an almost complete proposal, or a final delivery?

Also in both scenarios, when it was apparent that the product was not sufficient, did the follow-on conversation focus on the person, the work, or both? In these instances, it is recommended that supervisors evaluate the task and collaborate with the person. Constructive criticism should be directed at the work that was done, avoiding making an emotional judgement of the person. Once the work is redirected, if possible, and subsequently completed, any emotional issues can be addressed independent of the work. Be sure that any emotional discussion is professional and is about the person only. Despite the assumption that either of these situations could end up in a negative confrontation, both should result in communication that includes feedback and leads to shared understanding. Following these suggestions can help with these kinds of issues in the future.

The way you correct and/or criticize is important to performance. Done right, it ensures that both sides keep an open mind, and that communication is easy and free flowing. Done wrong, it makes adversaries of the people involved. This can be a problem with those who guard their true feelings and who become less willing to communicate anything other than the minimum requirement. Always focus on the work, not the person. If you want to incite or inspire a positive change, avoid criticizing people directly. When talking to a service professional about their customer service skills, it is better to discuss word choices and body language that may come across as aggressive or unfriendly to customers. This is a much better way to engage than telling the person that they do not seem to be friendly or, even worse, that they seem to be unhappy with their job and that the customers are picking up on it.

Another example is when you have an employee who has trouble making deadlines. The direct, negative way to handle it is to suggest the person is less than professional or lazy or just cannot handle the job. The caring, positive way is to discuss with the person how they approach deadlines. Find out if they are using calendar reminders, ask if they set personal deadlines that are 1 to 2 days before the actual suspense, or offer to work a deadline with them so you can share your approach to getting it done. These are ways to not only get the person to perform better, but to help them feel good, or continue to feel good, about themselves.

Creating a Quality Environment

Your quality environment relies on being effective in five areas: people, purpose, support, contributions, and appreciation.

People

Start with managing the mix of people in your team. The leader must work on team building whether they are managing the existing team through a pandemic or establishing a new team. There might even be a need to make some hiring and/or firing decisions to adjust the team and make sure it is fully manned. Whatever happens, working on how team members interact is critical. Pay attention to the dynamic relationships that are changed, created, or destroyed by the pandemic with the understanding that the work must be done regardless of any professional or personal feelings.

There is no need to allow likes and dislikes to affect the team's performance, but it is important to understand that they exist. It is even more important to understand how they affect team activities. For instance, it is probably not a good idea to put two people who dislike each other together on a project. That can be a recipe for disaster, but the fact that people dislike each other could influence them to strictly focus on the task at hand to get it finished. On the other hand, putting two people who like each other on the same project might not work out either. They could be so busy enjoying their relationship that they do not finish their work. If it happens that neither wants to tell the other that the work done on the project does not meet quality standards, the situation becomes even more challenging. The result could be that they turn in a sub-par product.

It is just as important to take special care when adding new members to the team. Effective onboarding programs are important to success. Pay attention to group dynamics and make decisions accordingly whenever possible. Some teams simply lay out the team norms and hope the new member can catch on. A better approach is to onboard the whole team, so everyone starts with the same baseline. This may be difficult in large, complex organizations, but there are ways to make it work.

Purpose

Leaders must keep teams focused on one overarching purpose. This means that the group is on a singular mission to perform at a high level. The team understands the vision and the desired end state, and they are ready to support it and one another. This approach should build team pride by getting buy-in for the bottom line. Once there is buy-in, trustworthiness can really increase. When people know the desired behaviors and standards they move from uncertainty to commitment to trustworthiness.

This is hard work and everyone should understand the "Enemies of Trust (Galford & Drapeau, 2003)" and work to conquer them. Galford and Drapeau provided a list of trust-building enemies; the list includes inconsistent messages and standards, misguided protection or loyalty to problematic employees, false feedback, failure to trust others, 'elephants in the parlor,' rumor spreading, and consistent organizational underperformance. Elephants in the parlor refers to painful or politically charged issues that are evident in the organization but are not being addressed. There is no easy way to address all these things, but they must be addressed with acknowledgement or action, or both, to create an interactive culture of trustworthiness. Once a trusting team is created, the sky is the limit for individual and team accomplishments.

Support

As the group gathers to pursue one purpose, success is enhanced by mutual support. Team members trust each other and make sacrifices, big or small, to ensure goal achievement and ease of working together. Many times, the team will find its own way to solving the challenges of dislikes and likes mentioned earlier. This is a form of social capital. Social capital can be defined as the value and cooperation that is created by social networks and other human relationships.

Contributions

Members make contributions every day and leaders must ensure that those contributions matter. If contributions are recognized in public, members will be more inclined to perform. Similarly, if creative thought and risk taking are allowed, members may achieve even greater contributions. Creating a collaborative environment where people can enlarge their thoughts and stretch their skills can be wildly effective for organizations.

Leaders can also help by ensuring an interactive culture where discussion and disagreement are welcome topics for discussion. This helps avoid the "we've never done it that way" comment, for instance, that can stifle creativity. Finally, leaders can make sure every member gets a chance to contribute their voice. When members are uncomfortable speaking in the larger group, leaders should find ways to still get that rich information contribution.

Leaders can show members that their talents and contributions are appreciated in many ways. They can tell them on the spot or tell the CEO or other top leadership. Leaders can allow unscheduled breaks or a day off to recognize a member, or they can invest in the member through training or advancement opportunities. By showing members how they are making a difference and giving them flexibility to work the best way they see fit, leaders are providing their own, valuable contributions.

Appreciation

Finally, groups thrive on appreciation. Show everyone in the group that you appreciate their efforts and contributions. This can come through formal recognition or pay raises, but those things may not be most valuable to your members. A daily "thank you," a kind "good job," or a public "good work" often are more important and valued to group members than anything else you can do. That may be because there is no nomination package to prepare, no awards board to meet, and no annual competition to wait for. Show appreciation when the good work happens. Show appreciation when you feel it!

Effectiveness

There are still mixed results when analyzing the effectiveness of telework that must be addressed before making the leader-member suggestions contained herein. The literature discusses the various actual or proposed improvements in individual and/or organizational level outcomes. For instance, using telework is said to increase organizational productivity by delivering improved flexibility and performance (Belzunegui-Eraso & Erro-Garcés, 2020; Choudhury, Foroughi, & Larson, 2020).

The COVID-19 pandemic revealed that many companies were already teleworking, were already including specific clauses in their collective agreements and plans, or were finding new, more effective ways to facilitate teleworking. The pandemic also led to the discovery that the collective agreement that anticipates the need to mass telework in a crisis to address security and health considerations probably does not exist, or is the exception rather than the rule (Belzunegui-Eraso & Erro-Garcés, 2020, p. 14). The literature also points to the possibilities for reduced healthcare cost in terms of savings on use of sick leave and for growing the talent pool by utilizing people who reside outside the organization's geographical area (Bughin & Cincera, 2020; Rainisch, Undurraga, & Chowell, 2020; Tavares, 2017).

Telework use has the potential for other organizational benefits. Organizational commitment might be increased if the flexibility and convenience of telework creates increased levels of commitment on the part of employees (Beauregard, Basile, & Canonico, 2019; Marx, Reimann, & Diewald, 2021). Employees might have increased loyalty to the organization when telework allows them to balance family considerations and work with innovations like work from home, work at regional satellite facilities, or flexible commuting strategies (Alamillo, 2020; Ravalet & Rérat, 2019).

A telework program could be part of an organization's high-quality workforce approach if it uses this type of flexible work program as a recruiting and retention tool (Jackson, Wilson, & Borden, 2020). Teleworkers may be sick less or exhibit lower levels of stress as they manage their own schedules at home, usually resulting in a lower absentee rate (Snyder, 2012, pp. 11-14).

There is ample evidence for the benefits of telework. For example, the 2012 Federal Employee Viewpoint Survey (FEVS) results showed significant employee benefits (Denison et al., 2014). The FEVS showed that "both employee engagement and global satisfaction were seven percentage points higher for those who teleworked (Denison et al., 2014, p. 63)."

The literature also tells us that not every implementation or adoption of telework goes well or delivers benefits. There are many instances where employees believe that telework is a job benefit. The perceived denial of that benefit, whether real or assumed, produces dissatisfaction, turnover, and even litigation in some cases (Cook, DeMarco, Doherty, & Jones, 2013; O'Keeffe, 2008; Singh & Verma, 2020; Weisberg & Porell, 2011). Some teleworkers report that they feel isolated because of the reduced contact with others and difficult communication with coworkers and supervisors (Smith, Patmos, & Pitts, 2018). Teamwork can be affected when the team meets together to share ideas or solve problems and teleworkers are excluded either accidentally or by design (Even, 2020). This is related to the feeling among some teleworkers that they miss out on impromptu information meetings, idle office gossip, or other informal interactions that contribute to organizational communication in general (Cascio, 2000; Greer & Payne, 2014; Nakrošienė, Bučiūnienė, & Goštautaitė, 2019).

What is the overall difference in work motivation and job satisfaction between teleworkers and non-teleworkers? There is a mix of beliefs about the real benefits of teleworking. For instance, instead of using telework to retain high-quality workers, James Caillier (2012) argued that professional development opportunities, job satisfaction, and promotion are factors that have a greater impact on turnover intentions than teleworking. On the other hand, the research suggests that the isolation that frequent teleworkers feel can be mitigated by meetings and parties to promote face-to-face opportunities. The research also suggests that a desirable social exchange could be gained by offering teleworking to all eligible employees, leaving the decision to take advantage of the program to them. Research also points to the fact that people who chose not to accept telework agreements were more highly motivated than those who were denied the opportunity to telework. In concert with this kind of discussion, researchers provided the following recommendations (Denison et al., 2014, p. 65).

Let us look at the notion of LMX in terms of organizational motivation initiatives. Remember, much of the United States and the world were forced into new and/or increased teleworking arrangements by COVID-19. Some organizations and their people already had programs in place, some started successful programs or improved on what they were already doing, and some struggled because they either avoided telework or just could not make it work. All of this happened so quickly that researchers and organizational development experts are still trying to understand exactly what happened, what it means, and what is next. One way to make sense of what is happening is to look to motivation.

Table 1. Methods to develop telework incentives

Developing Telework Incentives
• Develop a telework implementation and maturation plan that includes conducting pilots on telework programs prior to full scale implementation.
• Assess program improvements needed by completing a gap analysis on criteria including teleworker engagement, IT infrastructure support, and acceptability of training programs.
• Create ongoing and robust communications and evaluation plans.
• Provide counseling about the opportunities and challenges of teleworking prior to an employee beginning to telework, after teleworking commences, and at least annually thereafter to enhance employee satisfaction and to gauge potential feelings of professional and social isolation.
• Provide frequent engagement programs fostering interaction among teleworking employees and among teleworking employees and on-site employees.
• Establish managerial and employee training programs centered around virtual team development and trust as well as development of listening and learning skills in a virtual environment.
• Ensure robust succession planning for management by allowing teleworking employees the same upward mobility opportunities as on-site office employees starting with career details and progressing up to managerial positions and senior leadership positions.
• Ensure appropriate IT investments are made to stay current with technological improvements and support next generation virtual teams by enabling a variety of types of communication.
• Measure engagement via equitable measurements of qualitative and quantitative program metrics.

Chapter 7 takes an in-depth look at motivation, primarily from personal leader and/or member levels. This chapter tries to give you a focus at the organizational level. Motivation is the degree to which an organization can create a climate where individuals want and choose to engage in specified behaviors that the organization deems beneficial (Mitchell, 1982). But there are many definitions of motivation. The organization can focus on the technical definition where motivation is the psychological processes that cause the arousal, direction, and persistence of behavior (Atkinson, 1964; Campbell, Dunnette, Lawler, & Weick, 1970; Huse & Bowditch, 1977; Kast & Rosenzweig, 1979; Korman, 1974; Luthans, 1977). The definition can also include emphasis on goal direction or some voluntary aspect. So, motivation can be viewed as psychological processes that cause the arousal, direction, and persistence of voluntary actions that are goal directed (Mitchell, 1982).

Mitchell (1982) thus provides a clear definition of motivation that is appropriate for this project. Motivation should be intentional, multifaceted, and tailored to the needs of the organizational team. The best way to motivate is to pay attention to individual desires.

If leaders know what matters to their members, telework can present opportunities that members see as beneficial. This examination has mentioned many of them, such as safety from a pandemic, ability to improve work-life balance, solve or mitigate child-care issues, or reduce travel costs to name a few. Leaders who are not already in tune with their members should search for commonalities and motivating perspectives if they are to fully leverage telework benefits in service to organizational ideals.

An easy way to enrich someone's job is to determine what is important to her or him and use that information to enhance the value of the job. Studies show that job enrichment has been shown to improve the fit between the worker and the organization (Herzberg, 1966). The intended benefits of telework that are discussed throughout this work can contribute to job enrichment. Beyond that, job enrichment through telework can give people a chance to be comfortable in the new work arrangement, motivating them to do worthy work and to make significant contributions to the organization. The belief is that job enrichment may result in happy teleworkers who feel empowered to control their own actions and work situation.

Leaders can achieve job enrichment through telework success by focusing on four themes identified by a 2020 study of best practices for avoiding social and organizational isolation in employees (Even). The study reviewed 20 relevant articles. That discovery found that (1) frequent teleworkers have a high degree of feelings of isolation, (2) some teleworkers feel they are forgotten or dismissed in terms of operations, (3) teleworkers may have belonging issues related to the isolation of the practice, and (4) "E-leaders must provide active, mutual, continuous communication through socializing activities to enhance cohesion and feelings of togetherness (Even, 2020, pp. 11-12; Lilian, 2014). To satisfy the mission with high-quality communication, leaders must foster shared roles and identities. Leaders must be supported with training that focuses on best practices and collaboration with employees to achieve the best results.

Leader Resistance

We have talked a lot about ways leaders can help employees and take advantage of the benefits of teleworking. Let us take a closer look at situations where leaders may be reluctant to use telework.

Courtney Brown's (2013) study showed that participants who were against the use of telework were influenced by their own past counter-productive behavior. Also, participants whose work history and performance were not the best often assumed that other employees would have the same problems. The study warned that these assumptions were dangerous to the organization. Leaders must consider each employee individually when considering approval for telework. The lack of trust may come from many things, generational differences for instance, but leaders must avoid problems through flexibility and adaptability. Prohibiting telework based on past negative experience does a disservice to members and goes against the principles of situational leadership which can be insightful.

When using situational theory, the leader uses cues in the situation and adapts the style for the best result. The cues are typically the type of task, the kind of group, the timeline, and other factors that would indicate how to best get the job done. Management experts Paul Hersey and Ken Blanchard developed this theory in 1969 (Bates, 2016, p. 44), stating that the best leaders employ a range of different styles depending on the environment.

Leaders may be affected by negative perceptions of individual performance because it can be difficult or impossible to observe or monitor members working when you cannot see them, or when they do not share your work location. Leaders traditionally want to observe their workers in person, manipulating co-worker interactions and relationships. Leaders may also have a pessimistic view of how available and attentive workers are throughout the course of the day. There may also be a history of workers not responding when there is an urgent or short-notice task that must be done. When this is the case, there should be standard organizational practices that are helpful to both sides.

Best practices that are reciprocal are outlined in a study of outcomes and facilitators for employers where the organization has a proven, formal process for selecting and preparing employees for telework and where the organization effectively manages flexible work practices (Beauregard et al., 2019, p. 1). This type of remedy relies on a culture of trustworthiness and openness that has adequate communications, IT equipment, and support. There is also benefit in having "an adapted physical workplace to allow teleworkers to work and interact with their colleagues when they come to the office (Beauregard et al., 2019, p. 42)."

Leader resistance can be mitigated through good collaboration with members. Members who understand that there are risks and rewards for leaders can help the process.

> *Telework is a great federal government initiative and provides significant work-life balance for federal employees. While there are measurable benefits in teleworking, employees must understand that telework is a privilege. At the same time, supervisors must learn to leverage telework, personnel and workloads to ensure work processes, deliverables and customer service are not compromised. — Kimberly S. Jackson (2020)*

In a study examining whether flexible working hours and home-based teleworking were attractive to all employees, the researchers wanted to know how the decision to leave a company was affected. The study focused on flexible work times and on home-based teleworking in large German firms, using these constructs because they affected the whole work force. The study concluded that measures of flexibility can reduce negative impacts on retention, possibly keeping employees with the organization (Marx et al., 2021, p. 15). Organizations that demonstrate their flexibility in addressing employee work-life balance might achieve increased employee loyalty. Workers who feel that their employer cares may increase their focus on company and think less about finding the next ideal job.

The LMX approach can also assist the team in teleworking efforts. Members are consistently interested in making the adjustment to remote work and leaders continue to work to find shared success between the member and the organization. The relevance for members is accountability and the relevance for leaders is responsibility. Members are accountable to do the work for which they are responsible. Leaders are responsible for setting processes and communication methods to empower member accountability.

The telework plan must be created, people must be educated, and shared understanding must be achieved. This is better achieved through interactive communications where both sides can demonstrate and discuss their understanding of the rules. Where there are disconnects, leaders must take the time to clarify and, when necessary, adjust or amplify the guidance.

There are key issues in effective teleworking that are equally important to leaders and members, and each has a different connection to the various associated issues discussed earlier. Leaders and members can work together to improve face-to-face opportunities, reduce social isolation, and manage distractions at home. The telework plan should set the stage for regular, purposeful connections to assist with performance. Leaders should provide acknowledgement and praise as necessary but should also make course corrections when necessary. One-on-one communication is essential to LMX success.

Providing the resources necessary to conduct efficient telework operations and establishing team communication preferences are critical success requirements. Finally, a consistent routine is necessary to keeping everyone equally informed.

The Figures 1 and 2 demonstrate the specific responsibilities of leaders and members.

Figure 1. Leader (Supervisor) Responsibility

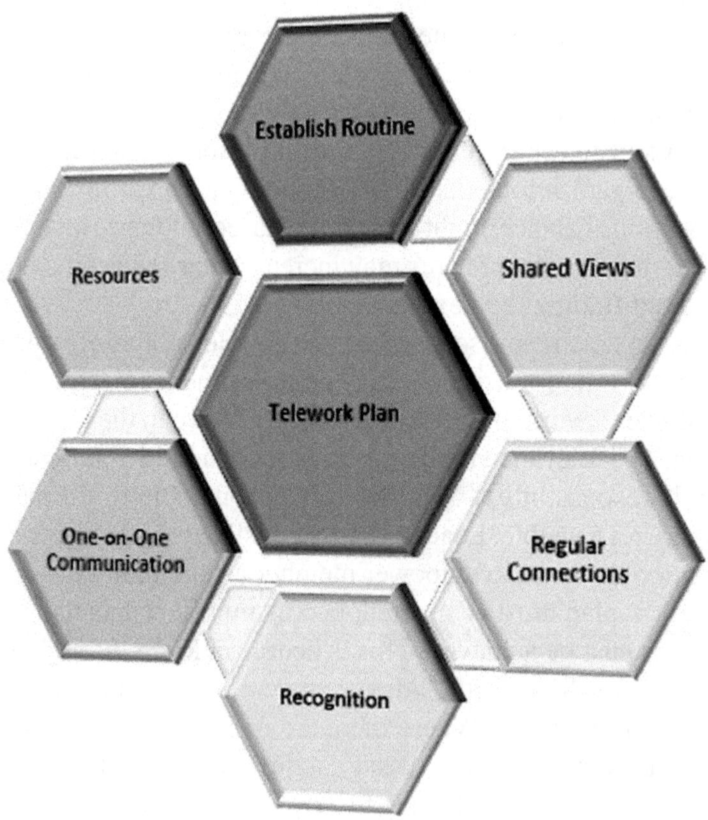

The leader provides the primary support and ensures the effectiveness of the telework plan. This is done in several ways. It begins with a shared view of how the plan works throughout the organization. This shared view is communicated through regular, purposeful connections. Leaders support members' need for visibility, ensuring participation in regular team connections. Success can be achieved by providing acknowledgement and praise when appropriate, and by protecting and promoting one-on-one communication between supervisor and subordinate at every opportunity. Leaders are responsible to set conditions that allow regular verification of member accountability. Setting a consistent routine for getting the work done and continuing to build and nurture team dynamics is crucial to continued success.

Figure 2. Member (Employee) Accountability

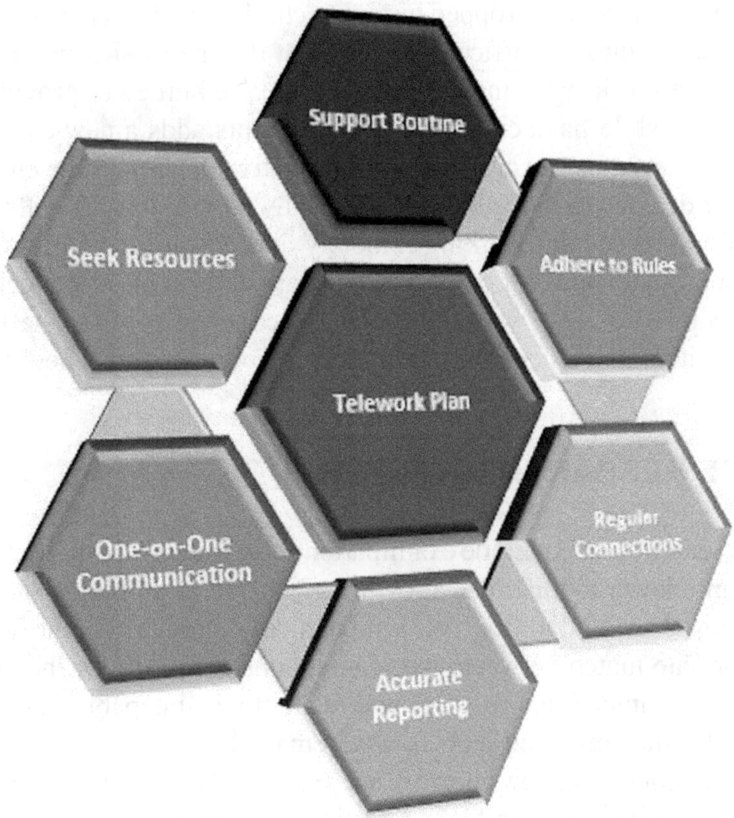

Members contribute to plan effectiveness by performing their tasks well and adhering to their designated team role. They must understand and share the intent of the plan, which is communicated through regular, purposeful connections. Effectiveness and efficiency are served by accurate reporting of progress and accomplishments to supervisors and other leadership.

Members want to stay visible while teleworking and must learn the plan and follow it. Members should participate in regular team connections and should look for every opportunity to have one-on-one communication, especially with their supervisor. Member accountability is verified when accurately reporting performance or progress.

Once members work with the organization to identify resources necessary for teleworking, they must ensure they are fully responsible for the work they are charged with. Members must adjust their home situation at home to allow them to follow the organization's stated routine or activity. For example, an employee who normally dropped his or her child off at daycare at 8 a.m. daily before heading into the office may find that that he or she may no longer need daycare services for their child. As such, the burden of providing care for the child while balancing work commitments adds a new dynamic the employee must negotiate and resolve. Alternatively, perhaps the employee's supervisor decides to move the in-office daily 9:30 a.m. staff call to 8 a.m. since all employees are working remotely and no longer require the extra time to commute. Now our employee must either drop his or her child off at daycare before 8 a.m. or wait until after the conclusion of the staff call (or come up with some other solution to meet the organization's new routine).

FUTURE RESEARCH DIRECTIONS

Future research should include examinations of performance metrics that can be used in telework situations, allowing a balance of employer satisfaction and employee accountability. This kind of analysis requires identification of an appropriate match between operational considerations for the employer such as communication structures and technological capability, contextual variables for the employee such as task demands.

Organizations that allow telework need to identify individual performance goals and ensure that measurable expectations are communicated to employees. There seems to be a lack of research and discovery about telework as it pertains to performance.

CONCLUSION

If leaders and members can be effective in understanding each other's teleworking challenges and responsibilities, it will be easier to get a shared understanding going forward. That shared understanding helps in countless ways. First, it can mitigate problems of leader or member resistance to teleworking for any reasons that may arise. Effective mitigation strategies open the door for real conversations about ways to improve organizational efficiency and employee work-life balance.

Second, removing roadblocks allows everyone to focus on the benefits of teleworking. This creates an atmosphere of trustworthiness. That trustworthiness makes it harder to become discouraged by problems or challenges. It allows people to be innovators and problem solvers and focuses on how to get to "yes." If COVID-19 taught us anything, it is that there are numerous positions for and against telework in today's organizations. That means there is ample room for compromise and collaboration to find effective solutions.

Third, there are no wrong answers. That means we must all keep open minds and be honest communicators to allow real discourse about the way ahead. Yes, COVID-19 thrust the world into forced telework, but it has also driven us to find the best ways to make it work. There were few opportunities to completely avoid the telework solution because the health of entire workforces depended on its use. That meant we found ways to make it work. It also meant we accepted trial-and-error to find the right method or combination. We solved many "telework cannot work" declarations and proved keeping people working and simultaneously safe were not mutually exclusive. While we lost many jobs and companies, we also witnessed companies that found new ways to survive and even prosper in a socially distanced world.

What does that mean for performance? It means we were flexible, creative, and forgiving in finding what works best. Throughout the journey of the book, we find instances where it worked despite the challenges. Now, the hope is that the world can capture the goodness of telework and find a new normal. That new normal will be somewhere between old normal and pandemic strange. The new day should be exciting.

REFERENCES

Alamillo, J. (2020). *Teleworking Benefits for Los Angeles County Employees*. California State University.

Atkinson, J. W. (1964). *An Introduction to Motivation*. Van Nostrand.

Bates, C. (2016). A methodology study of Hersey and Blanchard situational leadership theory. *Int J Adv Eng Technol Manage Appl Sci, 3*(11), 42–48.

Beauregard, T. A., Basile, K. A., & Canonico, E. (2019). *Telework: Outcomes and facilitators for employees*. Academic Press.

Belzunegui-Eraso, A., & Erro-Garcés, A. (2020). Teleworking in the Context of the Covid-19 Crisis. *Sustainability, 12*(9), 3662. doi:10.3390u12093662

Bughin, J. R., & Cincera, M. (2020). *FOG and teleworking: Some labor economics of covid-19*. Academic Press.

Caillier, J. G. (2012). The Impact of Teleworking on Work Motivation in a U.S. Federal Government Agency. *American Review of Public Administration, 42*(4), 461–480. doi:10.1177/0275074011409394

Campbell, J. P., Dunnette, M. D., Lawler, E. E. III, & Weick, K. E. Jr. (1970). *Managerial Behavior, Performance and Effectiveness*. McGraw-Hill.

Cascio, W. F. (2000). Managing a virtual workplace. *The Academy of Management Perspectives, 14*(3), 81–90. doi:10.5465/ame.2000.4468068

Choudhury, P., Foroughi, C., & Larson, B. Z. (2020). Work-from-Anywhere: The Productivity Effects of Geographic Flexibility. *Academy of Management Proceedings, 2020*(1), 21199. doi:10.5465/AMBPP.2020.225

Cook, J., DeMarco, J., Doherty, W., & Jones, Y. (2013). OPM's 2012 Telework Report Shows Vast Opportunities for Improvement. *Public Management, 42*(4), 13.

Denison, M. B., Banks, D., Bosley, E., Hyduke, B., James, K., Lefkowitz, E., ... Prochaska, G. (2014). Effective engagement strategies for an increasingly dispersed workforce. *Public Management, 43*(3), 62.

EvenA. (2020). The Evolution of Work: Best Practices for Avoiding Social and Organizational Isolation in Telework Employees. *Available at* SSRN 3543122. doi:10.2139/ssrn.3543122

Galford, R. M., & Drapeau, A. S. (2003). The Enemies of Trust. *Harvard Business Review*. Retrieved from https://hbr.org/2003/02/the-enemies-of-trust

Greer, T. W., & Payne, S. C. (2014). Overcoming telework challenges: Outcomes of successful telework strategies. *The Psychologist Manager Journal*, *17*(2), 87–111. doi:10.1037/mgr0000014

Hatala, J. P., & Fleming, P. R. (2007). Making Transfer Climate Visible: Utilizing Social Network Analysis to Facilitate the Transfer of Training. *Human Resource Development Review*, *6*(1), 33–63. doi:10.1177/1534484306297116

Herzberg, F. (1966). *Work and the nature of man*. World Pub. Co.

Huse, E. F., & Bowditch, J. L. (1977). *Behavior in Organizations: A Systems Approach to Managing*. Addison-Wesley.

Jackson, K. S., Wilson, D., & Borden, D. (2020). Telework: Achievements and Blunders. *Journal of Government Financial Management*, *69*(1), 58–59.

Kast, E. F., & Rosenzweig, J. E. (1979). *Organization and Management: A Systems Approach*. McGraw-Hill.

Korman, A. K. (1974). *The Psychology of Motivation*. Prentice-Hall.

Lilian, S. C. (2014). Virtual teams: Opportunities and challenges for e-leaders. *Procedia: Social and Behavioral Sciences*, *110*, 1251–1261. doi:10.1016/j.sbspro.2013.12.972

Luthans, F. (1977). *Organizational Behavior*. McGraw-Hill.

Marx, C. K., Reimann, M., & Diewald, M. (2021). Do Work–Life Measures Really Matter? The Impact of Flexible Working Hours and Home-Based Teleworking in Preventing Voluntary Employee Exits. *Social Sciences*, *10*(1), 9. doi:10.3390ocsci10010009

Mitchell, T. R. (1982). Motivation: New Directions for Theory, Research, and Practice. *Academy of Management Review*, *7*(1), 80–88. doi:10.5465/amr.1982.4285467

Nakrošienė, A., Bučiūnienė, I., & Goštautaitė, B. (2019). Working from home: Characteristics and outcomes of telework. *International Journal of Manpower*, *40*(1), 87–101. doi:10.1108/IJM-07-2017-0172

O'Keeffe, S. W. (2008). Shifting federal telework into drive. *Public Management*, *37*(1), 47.

Park, S., & Cho, Y. (2020). Does telework status affect the behavior and perception of supervisors? Examining task behavior and perception in the telework context. *International Journal of Human Resource Management*, 1–26. doi:10.1080/09585192.2020.1777183

Rainisch, G., Undurraga, E. A., & Chowell, G. (2020). A dynamic modeling tool for estimating healthcare demand from the COVID19 epidemic and evaluating population-wide interventions. *International Journal of Infectious Diseases*, *96*, 376–383. doi:10.1016/j.ijid.2020.05.043 PMID:32425631

Ravalet, E., & Rérat, P. (2019). Teleworking: Decreasing mobility or increasing tolerance of commuting distances? *Built Environment*, *45*(4), 582–602. doi:10.2148/benv.45.4.582

Rice, R. E. (1992). Task Analyzability, Use of New Media, and Effectiveness: A Multi-Site Exploration of Media Richness. *Organization Science*, *3*(4), 475–500. doi:10.1287/orsc.3.4.475

Singh, H. K., & Verma, S. (2020). *Understanding the Challenges of Mandatory Telework Adoption and Its Effect on Employee Engagement.* Paper presented at the International Working Conference on Transfer and Diffusion of IT.

Smith, S. A., Patmos, A., & Pitts, M. J. (2018). Communication and teleworking: A study of communication channel satisfaction, personality, and job satisfaction for teleworking employees. *International Journal of Business Communication*, *55*(1), 44–68. doi:10.1177/2329488415589101

Snyder, K. (2012). Enhancing telework: A guide to virtual leadership. *Public Management*, *41*(1), 11–14.

Tavares, A. I. (2017). Telework and health effects review. *International Journal of Healthcare*, *3*(2), 30. doi:10.5430/ijh.v3n2p30

Weisberg, A., & Porell, M. (2011). Moving telework from compliance to competitiveness. *Public Management*, *40*(1), 12.

Section 2

Understanding Leadership and Related Factors to Telework

Chapter 6 Leadership

ABSTRACT

Leadership development happens when one can determine and/or strengthen leadership style. Development continues when there is a trusting connection, when there are clear roles and responsibilities, and when an environment that facilitates quality communication is maintained. This chapter examines a study that shows a disconnect in opinions from employees, CEOs, and human resources professionals who were all asked the same questions about how people view their organization. Top-level leaders were overly optimistic about the frequency with which their employees were being recognized for their contributions. Conversely, human resources professionals were pessimistic about frequent recognition while employees seemed to be divided about the frequency and appropriateness of recognition. The authors find a variety of team qualities as they peruse thousands of leadership, management, and self-improvement books. This chapter narrows the focus to engagement, the setting of leader and manager roles, and developing members.

BACKGROUND

Leadership style is important to telework success, especially when person-to-person and team communications are done remotely. To ensure leaders are ready for the challenge, develop them through creating, identifying, or refining their leadership style. The leadership style should guide all efforts and assist with course corrections when things do not go exactly as planned with your team. Developing this leadership style requires several, ongoing steps.

DOI: 10.4018/978-1-7998-8950-2.ch006

First, determine and/or strengthen leadership style. Second, demonstrate the importance of a trusting connection. Third, establish roles and responsibilities. Fourth, create a quality environment.

Figure 1. Requirements for Building Leaders

The leadership requirements figure above is a roadmap for success. Each leader has a style whether they are aware of it or not. The first step should be to determine what is your leadership style. There are formal and informal ways to do this. One formal way is to consult The Leadership Practices Inventory® at www.lpileadershippracticesinventory.com. According to the website, the inventory "assessment not only measures the frequency with which you engage in exemplary leadership behaviors leadership skills, but it also inspires the breakthrough insights needed to build positive relationships and achieve the extraordinary. This 360-degree assessment helps organizations create change towards a more motivated and productive workforce by building a culture of leadership."

Informally, you can use the Table 1 below to determine your leadership style. There are many lists available containing seven or more styles, but this text uses the three identified by Kurt Lewin and his team of researchers in 1939: authoritarian, participative, and delegative (Bhargavi & Yaseen, 2016, p. 90).

Identify and perfect your style so that you can provide clear and consistent leadership in your organization. Explain your style to others at every opportunity so that those you lead and those you work with understand your point of view and motivation. Review your style often and make course corrections when necessary. Work to improve yourself at every opportunity.

Table 1. Leadership Styles

Style	Advantages	Disadvantages
Authoritarian - Autocratic (directive) • You make all the decisions • Little or no discussion with workers • Team expected to obey orders	• Decisions will be quick • Greater control in crisis situations • Value achieved when decision is the right one • Provide direction to encourage workers	• Difficulty motivating workers • Miss out on worker experience and ideas that could be helpful
Participative - Democratic (collaborative) • You discuss plans with workers who can influence decisions	• Workers have a voice • Workers may feel motivated and committed • Worker ideas and skills could be helpful	• Decisions will be slower • May be difficult if quick decisions are needed
Delegative - Laissez Faire: "leave to do" • You decide upon the objectives and leave it up to the workers to achieve them	• Works for independent, motivated workers	• Workers may lack direction • Workers may take advantage • May not suit all workers

NOTE: Many leadership experts also refer to transformational and servant leadership. Transformational leaders are active, communicating any changes to members and focusing on motivation. Servant leaders shine the light on members, while leaders work behind the scenes.

As you work on your leadership style, keep in mind that there is no one best way to lead and focus the team's attention on a goal or a direction. Help the team use their experience to cope with uncertainty in the environment. Good leadership requires five overarching actions that should color any approach: open dialogue, interactive communication, multiple approaches, reevaluation and/or reassessment activities, and course corrections. Ensure the dialogue is open and honest to stimulate discussion and decision making. Employ multiple methods and venues such as meetings, task groups, special duties, or off-site focus sessions, to inspire team cohesion. Make regular attempts to reevaluate and/or reassess what is happening and to understand how people feel about the progress they or making or the difficulties they face. When the need is identified, make course corrections.

Focus on Engagement

Most leadership and management scholars agree that the kind of engagement we have discussed with LMX is important. In a 2012 (Stillman) study, research findings revealed great disagreement in the way employees and leaders view engagement. The study asked employees, CEOs, and human resources professionals the same questions about how people view their organization and their answers differed widely.

More than 60 percent of the employees surveyed said they preferred immediate feedback, but less than 25 percent said received it. However, more than half of the CEOs said that spontaneous feedback happened frequently in their organizations. Only 11 percent of human resources professionals believed employees were receiving immediate feedback. Bosses were overly optimistic about the frequency with which their employees were being recognized for their contributions. When asked about the frequency of recognition, human resources professionals were pessimistic about its occurrence and employees seemed to be divided about how often it happened (Stillman, 2012).

Stillman's 2012 results demonstrate that leaders need to engage with team members to make sure there is a shared understanding about work tasks, recognition, and other issues. Collect feedback; do not be too busy or distracted to be in touch with the everyday experiences of your team members. That makes it challenging to get a real view of daily operations, thoughts, and stressors. Leaders must ensure communication up and down the chain of command whether people are onsite or remote. Take the time to ask people what they are doing and why. Ensure that there is time for one-on-one engagements to allow for the best two-way communication in real time.

Be patient when managing leadership style because changes probably will not come fast or easy. Persistence and cooperation should bring long-lasting trust and communication that will make any organization more effective and fun to be a part of.

Leaders have a great opportunity to inspire people by being calm when there is chaos, by being deliberate when there is doubt, and by caring when there is trouble. They can make sure every person enjoys the journey by donating their kindness to others every day and by connecting with those who do the same.

Leadership Roles

Leaders must be effective in managing, in supervising, and in making critical decisions that affect the majority of the workforce. To be effective, supervisors must revitalize leadership skills at every opportunity. Yes, leaders have experience, but that only means they have done these tasks before. It says nothing about the ability to be good at it today or to be better at it tomorrow.

As your people watch you in action, what do they see? Is your leadership style obvious? Is there a consistency in your decision-making actions that enables your team to anticipate what you are looking for? Does your enthusiasm (or lack thereof) for the work and the organization shine through? Do you make sure you are sending positive messages as much as possible? Do many of your decisions follow the plan and the goals of your organization with a consistency that is reliable?

Answer these important questions as you continue to address challenges you face in the workplace. For instance, when you upgrade to new technologies, do not just send your members to be trained. You need the training too so that you obtain new skills as well. If you simply cannot get away for the training, take a "train the trainer" approach: deputize one of your team members to receive the training and have him or her come back and train you. Having one of your team members train you can be a great incentive and motivating for a subordinate because it allows someone get personal time to bring the boss up to speed.

Leaders often do the right thing and look to refresh or reinvent the organization. Self-improvement is important, so leadership and management courses and refresher sessions can assist in developing improved or innovative approaches to building your team and making it effective and productive. Practice what you preach instead of simply asking employees to improve themselves. Set the standards and show them that you are dedicated to lifelong learning through personal example—take a vested interest in their development. This is a great way to build trustworthiness and an opportunity to connect with individual employees, which is especially critical to any adopted leadership style if the entire team is teleworking.

Brainstorm ways to exert your leadership will on your organization. List and explain personal and organizational challenges for the current year and for the next five years, then discuss them with your staff. By getting employee input you will always have the benefit of new approaches to feedback, support to members, and recognition. You may not pursue these things, but your team will appreciate the opportunity to discuss them.

One approach could be to bring your team in for an improvement session. If your team is larger than four or five people, be sure to form an effective group for this process. Group size has a profound effect on how a group finds cohesiveness and their ability to reach succinct group decisions. Care must be taken because dysfunctional conflicts can arise. For instance, disagreements in groups of two, or dyads, will most likely lead to one winner and one loser. A dyad relies on a negotiated resolution to the issue, so they tend to be characterized by tension and anxiety.

Another effective approach is triads. Triads are groups of three people, in which each actor must observe and evaluate the behavior of the other two people, making it tougher for actors to coordinate their behaviors. Triads that end in successful exchanges are considered very significant due to the level of interaction (Lawler, Thye, & Yoon, 2000, p. 625). Triads can be positive interactions when two disagree and a third can reach consensus or when two agree and convince or out-vote the third.

Careful management of group size is essential to reaching consensus. One study established a "Rule of Seven" in which the authors found that seven is the magic number of people to involve in decision making (Blenko, Mankins, & Rogers, 2010). According to the results, adding more people than seven to the effort will result in a 10 percent drop in effectiveness. Even-numbered groups are less capable than odd-numbered ones in making decisions because votes can end in a tie. For instance, one study explained that a group of four will only make a decision 25 percent of the time because of the probability of ties (NCHS, 2001). The majority available in odd-numbered groups improves the group dynamic and in turn the decision process.

As we consider the size of the group for decision success, the Rule of Seven seems sound. However, a National Center for Health Statistics study argues that five is the optimum number for group decision-making. The research supporting this view demonstrated that five people will have a 99 percent chance of successful decision making, even if only one group member has the right answer (NCHS, 2001). Because group dynamics can influence members' passivity, the more assertive members become more aggressive and drown out the voices of more passive group members; thus, limiting the numbers should assist the group leader in making sure every voice is heard.

Another study supported groups with five members as the most effective in achieving consensus in the largest number of situations (Rawlins, 1992, pp. 155-156). The study suggested that when consensus is desired in a conflict situation, groups with three to five members and no formal leader will be the most effective for solving the conflict. The research also determined that when a particularly complex problem must be solved, seven to 12 group members, each of whom has different information and biases, will result in the best quality decision. This finding is especially true when there is a formal leader participating in the group. Just keep in mind the precautions about even-numbered groups and ties in decision making.

Once you have formed the correct size group for decision-making, you can attack the list of needed improvements or action. List and discuss elements of creating and maintaining an effective team, then narrow the list to three items. Take your findings and apply them to the organization to promote continuous improvement. In this way you should already have buy-in because everyone participated in crafting the list.

Most importantly, apply sound leadership techniques. One way that good leaders can make life better for their team is by assessing the comfort levels of their staff. Are they happy? Are they content? Do they want to be here? All answers should be yes, or you should reengage with the group and make the necessary adjustments or agreements.

Another way to ensure group success is for the leader to look in the mirror and find commitment. The leader must always be committed to setting an agenda that matches the required outcome and to performing regular checks and balances of operations. Leaders must set an agenda that lets everyone know what is expected. The agenda should address, at a minimum, training tasks and goals, effective communications, and team rules.

Telework programs require training to be effective. Ensure that training tasks can be effective remotely and are linked to mission requirements, vision, and even short-term and long-term plans. Use effective communication techniques to let everyone know the training schedule as well as the progress of the program. Is the training working? Have we seen improvements in the areas where we have concentrated our training? Share the news with your team, even if progress is slow or nonexistent. By being honest about problem areas, leaders will find that team members are often more than willing to help find ways to energize productivity.

Team rules include holding members accountable for their actions and maintaining standards and discipline. Everyone must understand the rules and how they apply to all situations. More importantly, leaders need to apply the rules consistently because when this does not happen, problems arise in a hurry and morale normally takes a nosedive.

Once you have assessed your capabilities in training, communicating, and setting and applying rules consistently, take another look at the agenda. It should be logically ordered and should make sense to everyone who is required to follow it. You can come up with an agenda on your own but find ways to get input on what it should contain. Make sure you ask managers what they are working on and where they think the organization needs to improve. Get in touch with workers and let them tell you about things that make their job harder and about things that make their job easier. Emphasize the good and fix the bad through your agenda.

Next, improving leaders need to perform maintenance (Table 2). Maintenance requires applying a balanced management approach, allowing creativity, making regular level checks, and evaluating effectively. It is important to step back from the action and observe the group at work. Getting a wider view can reveal some considerations that would not otherwise come to light.

Table 2. Perform Maintenance

Maintenance Steps
Apply Balanced Management Approach
Allow Creativity
Perform Level Checks
Evaluate Effectively

Applying a balanced management approach is simply a way of striving for consistency of action and of letting everyone know what to expect. Take control of all situations and manage and monitor personal actions. Try to avoid extreme highs and lows when acting on or reacting to issues or situations. Anyone in charge needs to stay focused on the goal by controlling emotions and avoid confusing the issues by keeping parent and friend roles distinct and separate.

What are parent and friend roles? These are roles in which all leaders and managers find themselves at one time or another. The parent role involves an aggressive stance on getting things done, encouraging, establishing rules, applying discipline, and providing rewards. The parent role is one of setting standards, maintaining accountability, and ensuring productivity. Be careful not to give the impression that you think you are better than the members of your team, and make sure you do not talk down to them like parents sometimes do with their children.

The friend role is more cooperative and flexible, offering companionship, sympathy, empathy, and advice. Getting too friendly or sympathizing too intensely can lead to problems when it is time to discipline someone or pass them over for promotion. Maintain a healthy professional distance by being more of a collaborative partner than a buddy.

Performing maintenance also requires allowing team members to be creative. Give them a project they can own and give them room to succeed, but do not give them enough room to fail completely. Little stumbles are okay here, but do not let it get too far out of hand. It can be difficult to be sure you have assessed their talents and abilities correctly, but it is often worth the risk to find out. Let them pursue their ideas while you give them continuous feedback. This two-way communication allows you to keep track of what successes and failures. Set the standard, watch their efforts, and be ready to make course corrections if necessary.

Maintenance means making regular level checks to see if people are being recognized in a fair and equitable way and if there are ample opportunities for career advancement. Recognize individuals and the team. Watch for burnout, which occurs when people just cannot give any more. Burnout is characterized by people feeling that their hearts and minds are no longer willing because they have been pushed too hard, stretched too thin, or they just feel bored by doing the same thing over and over, year in and year out. Fight burnout by rotating jobs when possible, especially when some members' responsibilities require them to work longer hours than their teammates.

For instance, how many times do you see the same person or group of people working overtime when the rest of the work force has gone home? There may not be a problem, but it can be a sign of trouble. Is the tasking too large to be completed in the time available? Do the task owners understand what needs to be done? Is the overall workload of the organization misaligned, with one section handling more than anyone else? Is production falling off in the affected section, causing them to fall behind and, ultimately, requiring you to direct other parts of your force to bail them out?

Finding out why overtime is necessary can go a long way toward identifying a potential sign of burnout. If the problem is not burnout, you may find that the information you have gathered by examining operations can help your productivity by heading off a problem that would not have surfaced for some time.

Leadership maintenance efforts are not complete without effective evaluation. Set clear goals and expectations, ensure team members understand what needs to be done, and then move out of the way and let them work. Do not fall victim to people with "potential" because the only thing that really matters is each person's performance each day, not what they may be capable of doing in the future. Potential means giving credit for something they have never done. Potential means they should be able to do great things, but they may not have done anything up to this point.

In addition, evaluate people fairly based on their overall performance. Treat isolated instances of poor or substandard performance with care by asking whether it identified with a pattern of behavior and whether it continued for an extended period. If the answer to either or both is no, you might want to give the person a second chance. If you do give that second chance, monitor the situation closely for a period to make sure you can identify any unwanted reoccurrence. Always evaluate without emotion. If you are incredibly happy or very sad, put the evaluation off until you return to a "normal" frame of mind.

Performing maintenance will help, but the most important thing a leader must do is establish their ability to be someone others will follow. Address the leadership challenges of vision, reality, ethics and courage specified in P. Koestenbaum's Leadership Diamond Model© (Koestenbaum, 1991, pp. 40-42).

In the diamond, the leadership mind tends to embrace vision, courage, reality, and ethics to achieve greatness (Koestenbaum, 1991, pp., p. 40-42). These attributes are sometimes conflicting professional, social, psychological, and philosophical levels. Job skill is at the professional level while the social level is about networking skills. Childhood remembrances and "affairs of the heart" are represented by the psychological level, and the philosophical level represents the challenges of being a human in this world.

Vision, then, is about thinking great thoughts, striving for improvement, and thinking on a larger scale than you currently think. Reality is about being in touch with the world around you and understanding how others might perceive you. Ethics, more than the traditional definition of acting in a moral way, is about respecting feelings and relationships and about seeing someone else's point of view. Courage is about dedicating oneself to professionalism and initiative to achieve long-lasting results. Courage lends itself to the use of power, which should be applied to help others and not to advance the personal benefit of the leader. Correctly applied, power can be perfectly integrated with teamwork for success.

Table 3 gives an overview.

Table 3. Based on P. Koestenbaum's Leadership Diamond Model

<table>
<tr><th colspan="4">Leadership Diamond Model©</th></tr>
<tr><td><u>Professional:</u>
Job Competence</td><td><u>Social:</u>
Networking</td><td><u>Psychological:</u>
Personal Growth</td><td><u>Philosophical:</u>
The Human Condition</td></tr>
<tr><td colspan="4"><u>Vision:</u> See the larger perspective. Dreamers think big to find a better way.</td></tr>
<tr><td colspan="4"><u>Reality:</u> Respond to the facts and reject illusions about what the situation really is, what the person really meant, and what actions are really necessary. See clearly.</td></tr>
<tr><td colspan="4"><u>Ethics:</u> Be sensitive to people and provide a service of caring for their needs.</td></tr>
<tr><td colspan="4"><u>Courage:</u> Step up to the daily challenge and claim the power to initiate, act, and risk. Maintain a sustained initiative to do what it takes for you to improve and to empower your team members.</td></tr>
</table>

© (Koestenbaum, 1991).

Table 4. Important Challenges for Managers

Manager Challenges
Set high goals
Overcome stereotypes
Plan for success
Recognize the uniqueness of time
Persevere
Believe in something beyond yourself

Using the table, make sure that you set effective agendas, practice sound maintenance principles, and then strive for leadership greatness. These tools will help you gain the support and loyalty of your team.

Accept the challenge of leadership and practice effective management techniques. A strong leader with five people committed to a common goal has more impact than a good manager with 50 people who merely report to him or her. There are some simple steps you can take to get ready for your leadership opportunity, illustrated in Table 4.

Motivate yourself and others by setting extremely high goals. This is important because small goals do not excite us or make it worth our while to make a really dedicated effort.

Overcome stereotyped pictures of yourself because they limit you. We can only achieve if we believe in ourselves, so try to imagine all the wonderful things you can accomplish despite what people say. Do not be held back because you see yourself in a small role today. Think big!

Become a better planner because success lies not in hard work but smart work. A few moments of planning spares hours of execution. A plan requires that you assess what needs to be done and whether you have the resources and the time to get it done. If you are driving across country, your plan would include checking your vehicle to ensure it is in good working order, making a budget to determine what the trip will cost, and planning where you can stop for the night when you are tired.

Table 5. RAMP to Success

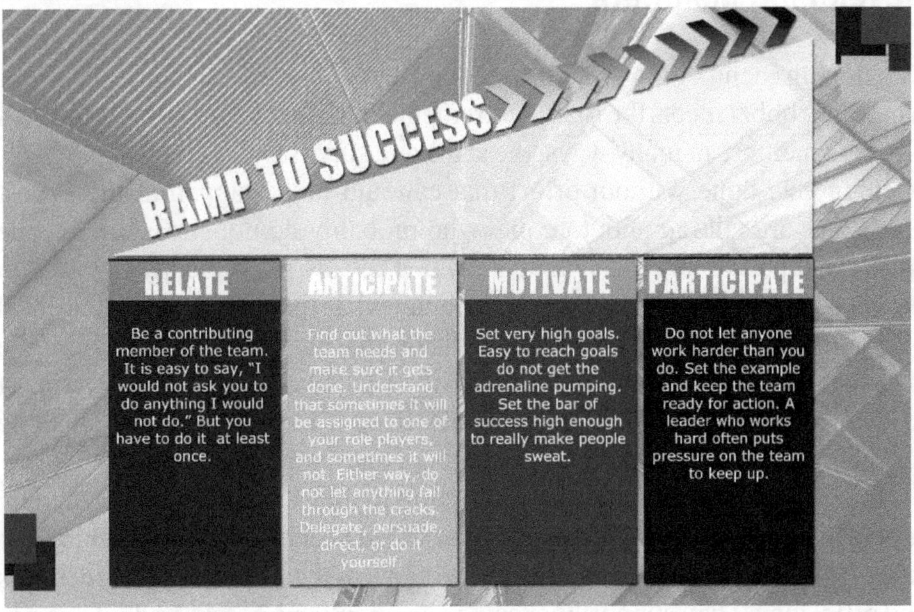

Recognize the uniqueness of time. We have 86,400 seconds daily and we cannot ever use them again. We all have the same amount of time; some just use it better.

Learn to persevere in your daily trials and tribulations and overcome adversity. We all suffer disappointments, defeats, and setbacks, but leaders keep trying until they succeed. Abraham Lincoln lost seven times running for political office before being elected president twice, proving that the person who keeps trying improves their chances of winning.

Finally, believe in something beyond yourself, because there are occasions when you must be able to reach out and draw upon an external reservoir of strength, whether it comes from religion, family, or friends. Believe there is more out there for you than you can see today, and that once you reach that plateau, there will be another pot of gold at the end of another rainbow. Effective managers believe in themselves without limits and have a redeeming belief in the good of people. They believe that investing in people brings rewards in the form of productivity, potential, and pride.

That is a general list, and as you prepare a step-by-step approach is helpful. Table 5 is a RAMP system I designed that leaders can use to pave the road to success.

Developing Members

Developing members is crucial to team success because this person works where the rubber meets the road. Just remember that a leader with no followers is a team member in many ways, the same as a supervisor with no employees. Nothing gets done without effort that can and must happen at the lowest levels. We are talking about people who probably do not supervise anyone and are not part of any management team. They are not typically involved in decision making, but what they contribute, what they think, and their level of commitment are crucial to any decision that is made. They address the daily challenges of performing at a good level, finding and giving support to keep the operation going, accepting the need to be personally accountable for their actions, and contributing to team cohesiveness.

Team members are adept at committing to goals and objectives, thereby supporting the unit. They understand the stated agenda and work within their roles. They take responsibility for their actions as they strive for effectiveness and efficiency. They support the team in accomplishing tasks and pitching in to help coworkers when their own work is done. Done well, all these activities and commitments lead to great personal and team performance.

Members understand that they can best support the organization by improving themselves and doing everything they can to help the bottom line. This personal accountability is invaluable to effective teams. Donna A. Lopiano, Ph.D., former executive director of the Women's Sports Foundation, provides a great characterization of outstanding team members in "Glory: Photographs of Athletes (Corman, 1999, p. 75)."

"Great players are not dependent on the adulation of others," Dr. Lopiano said. "They give rather than take. Even in the midst of defeat or failure, they look inward to see what they could have done differently to prevent a loss or an error. They never blame someone else on their team or look for excuses. Great players separate their performance from their self-worth, and thus they are capable of objectively analyzing their deficiencies, supporting others, and encouraging their teammates."

In addition to pushing themselves, members use evaluation and feedback from leaders to optimize their strengths and minimize their weaknesses. They are in tune with the team's stage of development, and they work every day to become experts at their craft.

Even the most loyal, dedicated, and motivated members need the team's support and commitment to succeed. Loeb and Kindel say teams create benefits for their members. When the responsibilities that go along with being part of a team are accepted, members gain certain very important rights (Loeb & Kindel, 1999, pp., p 257-260).

Team members seek ownership of their work. Ownership can be literal – you and your team are the sole beneficiaries of the output of your work – or it can be figurative, in that you wind up taking great pride in your accomplishments, even though the larger organization benefits. Ownership is another way of describing acceptance of responsibility, and with it comes both the benefits of success and the penalties of failure. When you own your work as a team member, you are, by definition, becoming a leader even if nobody gives you the title.

Great team members seek accountability and take pride when they know they are personally responsible for the outcome. This chance to step into the spotlight can really get the adrenaline flowing and promote increased attention to detail.

Team members seek permission. In a teamwork organization, a good portion of the decisions flow from members upward to the leader, who has ultimate authority. So, the leader grants permission instead of giving orders. This is where a leader who is a good listener is an asset because often people are not asking for straightforward permission but rather for encouragement. A good leader will be able to understand the difference.

Team members seek acceptance, becoming a part of a larger whole. There is always a warm feeling when people are accepted as part of a team. Everyone gets to share in the successes of the organization, and everyone feels responsible for avoiding failures.

Team members seek forgiveness. There is nothing more destructive to team management than the human desire to blame someone when things go wrong. Great leaders resist that desire at all costs! Members feel free to work hard, stretch the envelope, and occasionally make a mistake without losing their job.

Ownership, accountability, permission, acceptance, and forgiveness all contribute to team cohesiveness. Manage them with care.

Team cohesiveness is a crucial ingredient to organizational success. Team members should work with leaders and managers to answer a variety of questions or issues. Employees may wonder how their work counts towards the bottom line or how it makes a difference in moving the organization ahead. This is a good subject to follow when recognizing members for their work.

In addition, team members often wonder why they come to work, what is their value when they get there, and what rights do they have. The members who understand these issues, whether because they figured it out or because their leadership explained it, do very well on most days. The members who struggle are the ones still searching for answers and belonging. Everyone wants their job to enrich their life. They want to work at a place where they would be proud to bring their family for special events or days. They want to trust the people they work for and work beside. They want to know they can use their skill or influence to help everyone.

Leaders who partner with members to sort through these issues will help everyone decide how they can work together to create – or improve – the work atmosphere. One of the questions to help spark conversation might be to ask team members, "If you could change something here, what would it be?" The answer might be surprising, even valuable. These types of tactics allow everyone in the organization to get involved in communicating about improving the workplace, teamwork, trust, motivation, and other important topics. That interaction can create a situation that is conducive to healthy teams.

Defining roles and responsibilities and ensuring that everyone is accountable for what they are charged to do can only help the team. Once you have taken care of the roles, turn your attention to making sure you have created a quality environment in which the team can grow and prosper.

People naturally want to belong to something. That's what Maslow's Hierarchy of Needs is all about (Maslow, 1970). Providing a clear and enduring purpose satisfies a person's belonging needs.

As the group gathers to pursue one purpose, success is enhanced by mutual support. Members trust each other and make sacrifices, big or small, to ensure goal achievement and ease of working together. Many times, the team will find its own way to solving challenges and creating new ideas and efficiencies. This is a form of social capital. Social capital can be defined as the value and cooperation that is created by social networks and other human relationships. Woolcock and Narayan (2000) discussed the evolution of social capital research that identified synergy view as one of four distinct approaches. Work with groups should focus on the synergy view because it emphasizes incorporating different levels and dimensions of interactions as well as different environments. It also recognizes the positive and negative outcomes that social capital can generate.

The organization benefits from dedicated contributions when the team sets about building social capital in support of each other. Many leadership and management experts may talk about how important it is that each member contributes equally, but contributions from each member just need to add up to the organizational achievement. While I agree that they should add up, they do not have to match. Dedicated contributions mean that each member gives all that they can give within the confines of their ability. Some will give more, and some will give less, but trust throughout the organization will allow the parts to become a whole.

This approach sparks collaboration. Effective groups help the leader determine the strengths and weaknesses of each person, and a fair and honest effort to contribute follows. Do not misunderstand; the effort should be equal among all members. It is the outcome of that effort that may differ based on skills and abilities.

FUTURE RESEARCH DIRECTIONS

Researchers can help the telework operation by examining the leader-member relationship, roles and responsibilities, and an environment that facilitates effective operations. This examination must consider the hybrid nature of today's telework where organizations might be engaging in hybrid operations where they must manage onsite and remote workers simultaneously. If the organization is open to flexible schedules, they will also deal with resistance to change conflicts. Some workers will embrace onsite or remote work, but some may not be comfortable with either. These are considerations that must be explored.

More important, what relationships are actual or perceived in terms of telework and acceptance or rejection of it? This interplay between leaders and members is not new, but the pandemic has exposed the world to different versions of old conversations. This is where researchers should be doing their work.

CONCLUSION

At this point, we have covered key considerations in leadership from the leader's responsibility to the member's participation. We have discussed the focus on leader engagement and covered the ways leadership roles are developed, maintained, and improved. We have also discussed all of the ways members can and should focus on their own performance and accountability to support the leader in particular and the organization in general. Throughout the discussion, the emphasis has been on LMX and how those relationships are crucial to team success. Good leaders guide and accompany their teams through good and bad times, adjusting their approach to get the most out of each member. The path to success is helped when leaders find ways to stay connected to members. Some ways to do this are to remember the fine details of a member's performance, find ways to spend time with your members when there is no deadline pending, praise them in public, encourage their growth, and listen when they speak.

REFERENCES

Bhargavi, S., & Yaseen, A. (2016). Leadership styles and organizational performance. *Strategic Management Quarterly*, *4*(1), 87–117.

Blenko, M. W., Mankins, M. C., & Rogers, P. (2010). *Decide & deliver: 5 steps to breakthrough performance in your organization*. Harvard Business Press.

Corman, R. (1999). *Glory: photographs of athletes*. Morrow.

Koestenbaum, P. (1991). *Leadership: The inner side of greatness: a philosophy for leaders*. Jossey-Bass.

Lawler, E. J., Thye, S. R., & Yoon, J. (2000). Emotion and Group Cohesion in Productive Exchange 1. *American Journal of Sociology*, *106*(3), 616–657. doi:10.1086/318965

Loeb, M., & Kindel, S. (1999). *Leadership for Dummies*. IDG Books Worldwide, Inc.

Maslow, A. H. (1970). *Motivation and personality*. Harper & Row.

NCHS. (2001). *First marriage dissolution, divorce, and remarriage*.

Rawlins, C. (1992). *Introduction to management*. HarperCollins Publishers.

Stillman, J. (2012). *Do Bosses and Employees See Eye to Eye on Anything?* Retrieved from https://www.inc.com/jessica-stillman/do-bosses-and-employee-see-eye-to-eye-on-anything.html

Woolcock, M., & Narayan, D. (2000). Social Capital: Implications for Development Theory, Research, and Policy. *The World Bank Research Observer*, *15*(2), 225–249. doi:10.1093/wbro/15.2.225

Chapter 7 Motivation

ABSTRACT

This chapter explores a management framework created primarily by Gary P. Latham's Work Motivation: History, Theory, Research, and Practice (2012). Several other important works are examined to enhance the value of the analysis. One benefit of teleworking consistently expressed by teleworkers is increased employee happiness, so the authors explore the reasonable connection to motivation. The chapter examines the history and background in the field to trace the development of workplace motivation theories and offers a framework that provides insights for the analyses in this book. They study motivation before they move on to issues of productivity in the next chapter. The framework presented sheds light on the human elements of motivation and leads to reference points necessary to develop effective trustworthiness and improved performance studied throughout the book. Through a detailed examination of the role of motivation in the management framework presented, leaders will understand that many theorists argue that current theories of motivation focus on different aspects of the process.

BACKGROUND

Leader-member relationships can achieve motivational goals through mutual understanding. This understanding is important to building a cohesive unit that not only understands each other, but that has found a way to manage the tough times. The management framework provided in this chapter allows leaders the flexibility of having a wide range of resources in terms of management

DOI: 10.4018/978-1-7998-8950-2.ch007

approaches that can be used to motivate workers whether they are onsite or remote. Motivation and leadership development should be team activities that, done well, create great relationships.

A focus on relationships is important in this context because it would be wrong to analyze performance and leader resistance without also taking an in-depth look at employee motivation. This chapter will trace the development of workplace motivation theories by providing history and background in the field. We will trace the development and then offer a comprehensive framework that ties together some important theories of work motivation. This should be helpful to leaders if they understand that many motivation theorists argue that current theories of work motivation focus on different aspects of the motivation process. This work will show they are in fact complementary in many ways. The analysis can be effective for leader and team development.

The framework for this analysis is taken from Gary P. Latham's *Work Motivation: History, Theory, Research, and Practice (2012).* The framework also includes the works of Conor Vibert, *Theories of Macro Organizational Behavior (2004)*, and John Miner, *Essential Theories of Motivation and Leadership (2005)*, for background, information, and reflection. While these works are important, this chapter's emphasis is based on Latham's work. The reason for the dependence on Latham is the power of his assertions on the past, the present, and the future and how they help today's leader.

Latham's organization fit well with the framework developed herein. It allows the acceptance of the best available leadership and management theory that can be used by leaders, members, and organizations, separately or together, to foster communication and effective use of all the theoretical tools available in this and in the referenced works.

The motivation process is situational, and the task seems always to come down to whose interests have the most weight, and who has the telling "voice" in the decision-making effort (Roberts & O'Reilly III, 1973). Voice is that part of the deliberations that carries the most weight in when the final decisions are made. The theoretical framework herein can help in that effort.

This analysis makes several assumptions. The first assumption is that the work does not omit a theorist whose work is critical to the current effort. The second assumption is that the review is thorough enough to do justice to the theoretical comparisons and linkages in the way they are presented. The next assumption is that others will see the value of Latham's approach with the same enthusiasm and support given in this work. The final assumption is that this work takes for granted that there will be challenges, disagreements, and varying viewpoints that support or criticize the assumptions made here. Despite the assumptions, the ability to debate the pros and cons is important to any learning endeavor.

Also, despite the assumptions, my point of view is clear: I see this effort from where I sit. I have held numerous leader and member positions, and the framework I have created would have served me well at any of the critical learning and growing times in my life and career. There are certainly other points of view to consider, and you should explore alternative methods and viewpoints on the matter extensively, even beyond those presented here. The potential academic and real-world exchange is an exciting proposition.

History and Background

Latham (2012) asserts that there are three pillars that define motivation in the workplace: choice, effort, and persistence. Further, he shows motivation as an integral aspect of training and as a core competency of leadership. He offers the importance of galvanizing and inspiring people to exert effort as key requirements for effective leadership. He relates this to committing to and persisting in the pursuit of an organization's values or goals.

Let us use Latham's framing of history to trace the development of workplace motivation theories. He sets 25-year periods in the 20th century for the examination and begins an analysis of the 21st century.

1900-1925

Key theorists of the period include Sigmund Freud, William James, John B. Watson, E. Thorndike, Frank and Lilian Gilbreth, and Frederick Taylor.

In looking to the early 1900s, Sigmund Freud (1856-1939) was the first to advance the notion of a focus on the unconscious in pursuit of a healthier mental attitude. Freud's assertions developed an understanding of the life of groups, organizations, and societies. In Freud's work, patients work together with their therapists to use certain clues to recover and discuss a portion of the patient's life history that has formerly been concealed. In this way, group psychology discussed the "unconscious life of the group."

Freud advanced the scientific myth of the primal horde, where groups form to control a part of the natural or social world around them. During this "forming" the groups inevitably do damage to that world, and they assume a certain amount of guilt because of the damage they have done. Freud argued that human relationships are ambivalent because of *Eros-Thanatos*, the main point of his theory. *Eros* concerns the biological need to develop bonds with others and *Thanatos* concerns the need to dominate others.

The needs addressed by Freud play a large role in how people exist in civilization, which implies constraint. In civilization, there is a requirement that people give up a part of their autonomy and submit to the restrictions of the group, and that requirement creates tension in *Eros-Thanatos*. This tension hints at Freud's argument that friendships are affected by implicit if not explicit resentment as well as competition.

Latham asserted that unlike Freud, William James was more interested in hypothetical constructs of unconsciousness (i.e., id, superego, and ego) and the use of dreams as a methodology for studying behavior. James was the author of *Principles of Psychology* (1892, 2007), which was important in the field as one of the earliest textbooks on psychology.

James' notion of psychology focused on four methods: analysis, introspection, experiments, and comparisons. Analysis concerns precursor and contemporary views of the mind. Introspection is the psychologist's examination of one's own states of mind. Experiments are examinations of people and their environment, e.g., in hypnosis or neurology. Comparisons are when psychologists distinguish norms from anomalies using statistics.

James asserted that the individual sense of self is a "duplex" of objective and subjective selves. *Principles* differentiates the self as *I*, or the knower, and as *me*, or the known. The author asserted that the self is not separate but is distinctly two discriminated aspects. James was also one of the first writers to use the term self-esteem, describing it as a self-feeling that depends on what a person decides to be or accomplish.

Moving beyond the sense of self, behavior came to the forefront of the field with American psychologist John B. Watson's *Behaviorism* (2017), though it was not embraced by the field until the 1970s. He advanced the notion that psychology is not concerned with human consciousness or the mind. It is only concerned with behavior, with the notion that men could be studied objectively, like rats and apes.

Watson based his work on the experiments of Ivan Pavlov, who studied animal responses to conditioning. Watson agreed with Pavlov's assertions that humans react to stimuli in the same way as did the dogs that he studied.

During this time in history, behaviorists were studying rats and pigeons, for instance, for reasons of cost and convenience. The behaviorists, according to Latham, attached no importance to the reasoning capacity of human beings.

Leading experimental psychologist E. Thorndike found that by presenting a reward immediately after an experimenter-targeted behavior occurred resulted in an increased frequency of the behavior. This is Thorndike's law of effect, which states that responses to a situation which are followed by a rewarding state of affairs will be strengthened and become habitual responses to that situation.

Latham also points to the value of Thorndike's 1917 empirical study on satisfaction (1917), published in the first volume of the *Journal of Applied Psychology*. That study examined adults who filled out compositions over two days, analyzing speed, quality of work, and satisfaction. Latham asserts:

> *The results indicated that the quality and quantity of work remained the same during the 2-hour period, but 'satisfyingness' decreased steadily. Thorndike concluded that lack of rest affected a person's interest, willingness, or tolerance rather than the quality and quantity of the product produced. The seeds were now planted for what was to become a major controversy throughout the 20th century, namely, the relationship between job satisfaction and performance (2012, p. 12).*

In the 19th and early 20th centuries, there was a shift from small, independent, family-run businesses to large industrial organizations. Frank and Lillian Gilbreth addressed efficiency and effectiveness occurring during this shift by focusing on method, identifying the most basic motions in work and analyzing the way these motions are combined to form methods of operation, and the basic time each motion took (1917). They filmed individual physical labor movements, believing that it is possible to design work methods whose times could be estimated in advance, rather than relying upon observation-based time studies.

The Gilbreths argued that there could be one best way to perform a particular function or task. The theorists employed motion studies and time studies and argued that the one best way could be replaced when a better way was discovered. They defined the motion study as dividing work into the most fundamental elements possible and studying those elements separately and in relation to one another. Then, taking the time required for these studied elements, building methods of least waste. They defined time study as an in-depth scientific analysis of methods and equipment used or planned in doing a piece of work, logical determination of the details of the best way of doing it, and determination of the time required.

Taylor believed there was one best way to perform a task, and in 1911 he developed scientific management. His scientific management was intended to assist private-sector management in adapting production practices to the needs of an emerging industrial economy in the early 1900s (Taylor, 2004).

Scientific management rested on four underlying values which formed the framework within which the remainder of Taylor's theory could be worked out.

1. Efficiency in production – obtaining the maximum possible from a given investment of resources.
2. Rationality in work procedures – the arrangement of work in the most direct relationship to objectives sought.
3. Productivity – maintaining the highest levels possible.
4. Profit – the ultimate objective of everyone within the organization.

Taylor assumed that management and labor would share the same objectives and that there would be no conflict over organizing to achieve them. He did not allow for the effects of supply and demand in this assumption, and that would be problematic for his theory when American industry tried to put scientific management into practice. Nonetheless, he did push organization theory toward a different direction, and his arguments showed how productivity could be increased.

The first 25-year period, according to Latham, was highlighted by Thorndike's law of effect and the importance that engineers placed on tying rewards or money to performance. Latham argued that the next 25-year period featured three events that had significant impact on Industrial and Organizational (I/O) Psychology.

1925-1950

Latham's significant events included the crash of world's economy, embracement of I/O psychology by departments of psychology, and the duration of World War II. With the Great Depression, for instance, the focus shifted from selection of workers to the plight of human beings and the attendant humanization of the workplace.

Latham advanced Morris Viteles' notion that disagreed with the use of financial incentive programs advocated by Taylor, using an instinct hypothesis that focused on worker feelings and experiences. Focusing on curiosity, acquisition, anger, etc., his hypothesis was tied to Freud's concepts of repression, rationalization, and sublimation.

Viteles is considered the founder of the industrial psychology field because he published *Industrial Psychology* in 1932 at age 34 (1932). Viteles, however, credited Hugo Münsterberg with that honor (1915). Due to the length of the work, Viteles planned to update it after World War II. He began by revising the original 15 pages on "*Motivation in Industry*," one of his chapters, and ended up with a new 500-page work called *Motivation and Morale in Industry* (1953). This edition was also extremely popular in the field.

Vitele's work, according to Latham, pushed I/O psychologists to change their emphasis to finding ways of measuring attitudes of employees to identify sources of motivation in the workplace. Attitude was at the forefront of the field's attention, and Louis Leon Thurstone's law of comparative judgment was a pioneering development in the approach to measurement in factor analysis (1927, 1931). Considered the father of attitude scaling, he advanced a methodology to measure attitude. It involved defining and identifying the feelings and experiences of workers, then making a pool of opinion statements; some positive, some negative, and some neutral.
Thurstone developed three scales for measuring attitude:

1. Paired Comparisons – attitude comparisons should be paired in every possible combination.
2. Equal-appearing intervals – judges sort statements one at a time on a range of extremely favorable to extremely unfavorable.
3. Successive intervals – this method tries to statistically place items on a continuum instead of relying on subjective answers given by judges. It uses the number of times different judges rate a statement to develop the rank order for the scales.

There are some similarities between Thurstone's methodology and that of Rensis Likert (1961). Likert advanced the notion that it is easier to measure for tangible objects than for abstract objects. His method argues that if we want to measure abstract objects, we must define them clearly so the researcher and the subject will have the same object in mind.

Likert argued for constructing multiple scales, or for narrowly defining scales so other dimensions would not be included. He generated an item pool which included statements about beliefs for the object in question. Each item was clearly positive or negative. He did not use neutral statements; most surveys using this methodology use five scales ranging from strongly agree to strongly disagree.

Latham discusses the value of laboratory experiments like those conducted in 1935 by C.A. Mace (1935) in Great Britain and field experiments like the ones conducted by S. Wyatt, J.A. Fraser, and F.G.L. Stock (1929) and by S.

Wyatt, L. Frost, and F.G.L. Stock (1934). Mace's laboratory experiments found that a set standard only affected a person's performance when the person's skill had developed to the point where the individual had a reasonable expectation that the standard could be reached.

Wyatt, Fraser, and Stock conducted a field experiment on job fatigue in Great Britain, finding that piece-rate pay resulted in fewer symptoms of boredom than hourly pay, supporting Taylor's 1911 conclusions. Wyatt, Frost, and Stock conducted field research on goal setting. In that work, factory workers reduced their boredom by creating "definite aims" to complete a certain number of units in a given period of time.

Elton Mayo, partially in response to the increased difficulties between employees and labor management due to the application of scientific management in the 1920s, made some observations and concluded that problems were caused by the monotony of the work. He and his colleagues were asked to study employee productivity. The Hawthorne Studies, conducted between 1927 and 1933, are significant because they demonstrated the influence of human factors on worker productivity (Mayo, Follett, & McGregor, 1949).

The studies, which provided details about worker attitudes, had four major phases: the illumination experiments, the relay assembly group experiments, the interviewing program, and the bank writing group studies. The studies concluded that there was no cause-and-effect relationship between working conditions and productivity. The Hawthorne Studies showed worker attitude to be important, and 21,000 employee interviews were conducted to determine employee attitudes toward the company and their jobs. The major outcome for Mayo and his colleagues was to show supervisors that an employee's complaint frequently is a symptom of some underlying problem on the job, at home, or in the person's past. The reaction to the findings led to the coining of the term, "the Hawthorne effect."

Latham asserts that in response to the findings of the Hawthorne studies, employee participation in the decision-making process was an implicit if not explicit hypothesis on the part of I/O psychologists and some union leaders. He covers several seminal works. In 1946, N.R.F. Maier concluded that the most undeveloped aspect of industrial progress is management of labor power (1949). According to Latham, Maier cited an unpublished field experiment by Alex Bavelas (Maier, 1949) as an example of how to motivate workers. Authors E. E. Ghiselli and C.W. Brown argued that the new emphasis of industrial psychology should be to maximize productivity consistent with the abilities, energies, interests, and motives of the worker (1948). Also, L.

Coch and J.R.P. French (1948) showed that employee participation in decision making can overcome resistance to change.

R. Stagner (1956) stated that the problem of industrial harmony would not be solved until there is a realization that both executives and workers want democratic self-assertion. Meanwhile, J. Tiffin (1948) disputed that workers were simply "hired hands." He argued that four factors affect a worker's morale: how the person feels about the job, how the boss regards the employee, social factors, and working conditions. These factors are similar to those found in the Hawthorne studies.

It is interesting here to note the possible influence of Lewin. Researchers mentioned earlier, Bavelas, Ghiselli, Brown, and French, were his former students. Lewin (1942) proposed a general model of change consisting of three phases, "unfreezing, change, refreezing," in his Field Theory in Social Science. This model would become the conceptual frame for organization development. Clearly, the emphasis on workers and their behavior and needs relates well to Lewin's arguments in terms of identifying what exists, making changes, and instituting new policies.

These are examples of the work at the end of the 20th century's second quarter and beginning of the third quarter. This was a time when scientific management was heavily criticized, and theorists were advancing the notion that effort does not remain constant throughout comparisons of different work methods. This was a challenge to the time and motion study methodologies. It was also a time when researchers were finding that people do not want a superior who commands, they want one who guides and directs. Latham argues that the theoretical environment in I/O psychology research was about to change because of a 1943 essay written by Abraham Maslow (1943).

1950-1975

Before looking to Maslow's research, it is important to understand what was going on in I/O psychology at the beginning of this period. As Latham sets the period in his book, he explains that behaviorism was very popular in experimental psychology with B.F. Skinner (1950) as its articulate champion. Animal research had shown the importance of antecedent stimuli and external consequences on behavior.

T.A. Ryan and P.C. Smith (1954) argued for new paradigms of experimental and clinical psychology. They argued that it was useless and misleading to try to translate worker goals into the 1925 argument of Watson concerning stimuli and responses. The difficulty, they argued, was that Watson's assertion implies that the laws that govern these stimuli and responses in experimental laboratory paradigms are the same as those that hold for all other stimuli and responses in everyday situations. They argued, instead, for a focus on the wants, wishes, desires, and experiences of the individual.

Much research was directed to job satisfaction and job performance during this period. In 1953, Viteles was equating motivation with employee performance and morale. Employee morale or satisfaction was of great interest to I/O psychologists because of attitude survey inferences in the field and the Hawthorne studies. Those beliefs, however, were challenged through the work of A.H. Brayfield and W.H. Crockett, who showed that there was little or no relationship between those two variables (1955). Victor Vroom's 1964 quantitative review is relevant here, and I will examine his contribution of Expectancy Theory later in this chronological journey (1964).

Latham asserts, however, that regardless of the utility of the work of Brayfield, Crockett, and Vroom, employee performance and morale would remain interdependent for the foreseeable future. That brings one to the works of Maslow.

Maslow wrote *A Theory of Human Motivation* for *Psychological Review (1943)*. This essay contained the most familiar and influential feature of Maslow's theory of motivation, the notion of a hierarchy of human need ordered according to their prepotency. Prepotency refers to the urgency of the satisfaction of a particular need. Maslow argued that a "lower" or more primitive need must be satisfied before a higher need becomes relevant to the person as a source of motivation. The argument continues that a satisfied need is no longer a motivator.

Maslow had five levels in his need hierarchy.

1. Physiological – chiefly food and shelter.
2. Safety – freedom from physical harm and deprivation.
3. Love – the desire for affectionate and supportive relationships with family, friends, and associates.
4. Esteem – the recognition by others of one's competence, achievements, and overall personal worth.
5. Self-actualization (or self-realization) – the need to realize one's inherent potential, one's creative abilities, "to be everything one is capable of becoming."

So, Maslow argues that as one need is fulfilled, its strength is diminished and the strength of the next need in the hierarchy is increased. Maslow's theory had a tremendous influence on Douglas McGregor's Theory X and Theory Y (1960).

McGregor viewed himself as a behavioral scientist and advanced the notion in 1957 that it was time to apply the social sciences to make human organizations truly effective. McGregor based his argument on assumptions about motivation. McGregor made assumptions about human motivation that leads to two approaches.

Theory X: People inherently dislike work, they must be coerced or controlled to do work to achieve objectives, and they prefer to be directed.

Theory Y: People will exercise self-direction and self-control towards achieving objectives they are committed to, and people will learn to accept and seek responsibility.

He argued that the conventional view of employees, or Theory X, is that without active intervention by management, people will not actively support or pursue organizational needs.

The Theory X assumption, then, is that people McGregor believed that Theory X is not accurate. His Theory Y advances that notion, placing exclusive reliance not on external control of behavior but instead on self-control and self-direction.

The criticisms of Maslow's and McGregor's theories focused on the lack of available supporting data. Lyman Porter was the first to conduct theory-driven empirical research in support of these theorists.

Porter conducted five studies, largely using Maslow's theory as a framework (1961). Latham explains Porter's proficiency scale as requiring people to rate the importance of characteristics present in their job as well as how much of each characteristic they would prefer to have in the job. In 1961, Porter conducted a study of foremen and mid-level managers of three different companies. He found that the highest order need, self-actualization, is the most critical of those studied in terms of both perceived deficiency in fulfillment and perceived importance to the individual.

Porter's second study in 1962 replicated the first study, showing that the needs for autonomy and self-actualization were reported as the least fulfilled for a nationwide survey of managers. A third study in 1963 concluded with findings that higher level managers placed more emphasis on self-actualization and autonomy needs than did lower-level managers. The same year, Porter's fourth study analyzed horizontal rather than vertical differences in responses of managers. In this study, fulfillment of needs for esteem and self-actualization were the largest differences. Porter's fifth and final study, also in 1963, supported his hypothesis that at the lower levels of management, managers in smaller companies reported greater fulfillment and satisfaction of their needs than their counterparts in large companies.

Porter's work, however, did not lead to greater support for Maslow and McGregor. In fact, Latham asserts that hierarchy theory was largely abandoned. In the 1960s, Clayton Alderfer argued that three related needs – existence, relatedness, and growth – can affect a person simultaneously. Existence refers to one's concern with basic material existence motivators (1969). Relatedness refers to the motivation a person has for maintaining interpersonal relationships. Growth refers to an intrinsic desire for personal development.

Alderfer's ERG Theory was a reformulation of Maslow's work and was intended to align the Hierarchy of Needs Theory more closely with empirical research of the time. Latham argued that Alderfer's work yielded mixed results, even in the view of Alderfer.

Job characteristics were another important focus of the period, and Frederick Herzberg developed a theory with several names. Herzberg's work is called the Two Factor Theory, Motivation-Hygiene Theory, or Job Enrichment (1966). Herzberg's theory states that there are certain factors in the workplace that cause job satisfaction, while a separate set of factors cause dissatisfaction. The theory was based around interviews with 203 American accountants and engineers, chosen because of their professions' growing importance in the business world. The subjects were asked to relate times when they felt exceptionally good or bad about their present job or any previous job, and to provide reasons. The subjects were also asked to give a description of the sequence of events giving rise to that positive or negative feeling.

Motivation-Hygiene Theory distinguishes between motivators and hygiene factors. Motivators like challenging work, recognition, and responsibility give positive satisfaction. Hygiene factors like status, job security, salary and fringe benefits do not give positive satisfaction, although dissatisfaction results from their absence. Essentially, motivation factors are needed to motivate an employee to higher performance. Hygiene factors are needed to ensure an employee is not dissatisfied. Herzberg also further classified our actions and how and why we do them, for example, if you perform a work-related action because you *have* to, then that is considered to be movement, but if you perform a work-related action because you *want* to, then that is considered to be motivation.

Herzberg's work was criticized by Vroom because his results could only be replicated when the critical incident technique was used. The criticism centered on the fact that the same events caused both satisfaction and dissatisfaction, but different agents were perceived by employees as responsible – the self for satisfying events, and variables other than the self for dissatisfying events. Herzberg, according to Latham, was unable to overcome this attack.

Latham advances the notion that in Herzberg's theory, money, or the lack of it, can be a major source of dissatisfaction, but little is said about what the person will do because of this dissatisfaction. Latham argues that Equity Theory, developed by J. "Stacey" Adams (1963; 2010), filled the void.

Equity Theory deals primarily with money, focusing on a person's perceptions of fairness with respect to a relationship. It is built on the belief that employees become de-motivated, both in relation to their job and their employer, if they feel as though their inputs are greater than the outputs. Employees can be expected to respond to this in different ways, including de-motivation, reduced effort, becoming disgruntled, or, in more extreme cases, perhaps even becoming disruptive. This theory was later attacked for lack of precision.

As we analyze Latham's book, it now turns to Vroom. Rather than focus on factors in a job that energize and sustain behavior, Vroom used motivation to refer to processes governing choices made among alternative forms of activity.

Vroom's Expectancy Theory (1964) examines motivation from the perspective of why people would choose to follow a particular course of action. The theory is that an individual will act in a certain way based on the expectation that the act will be followed by a given outcome and on the attractiveness of that outcome to the individual.

The theory introduces three variables which are valence, expectancy, and instrumentality. Valence is the importance that the individual places upon the expected outcome of a situation. Expectancy is the belief that output from the individual and the success of the situation are linked. Finally, instrumentality is the belief that the success of the situation is linked to the expected outcome of the situation.

Vroom's theory suggests that although individuals may have different sets of goals, they can be motivated if they believe several things:

- There is a positive correlation between efforts and performance
- Favorable performance will result in a desirable reward
- The reward will satisfy an important need

- The desire to satisfy the need is strong enough to make the effort worthwhile

Following Vroom's research, I/O psychologists began to examine the applicability of behaviorism in the workplace, despite the concerns voiced decades earlier by Ryan and Smith. Skinner's 1974 advocacy of environmental determinism led him to develop behaviorism, or the theory of operant conditioning (1966). This was the idea that we behave the way we do because this kind of behavior has had certain consequences in the past.

Skinner asserted that changes in behavior are the result of an individual's response to events (stimuli) that occur in the environment. A response produces a consequence such as defining a word, hitting a ball, or solving a math problem. Skinner analyzed Stimulus-Response (S-R) patterns, arguing that when a particular S-R pattern is reinforced (rewarded), the individual is conditioned to respond. Reinforcement is the key, and a reinforcer is anything that strengthens the desired response.

The culmination of Locke's experiments led to three propositions that would subsequently lead to the development of goal setting theory in 1990: (1) Specific high goals lead to higher performance than no goals or even an abstract goal such as "do your best"; (2) given goal commitment, the higher the goal the higher the performance, and (3) variables such as monetary incentives, participation in decision making, feedback, or knowledge of results affect performance only to the extent that they lead to the setting of and commitment to specific high goals. In short, goals have the effect of directing attention and action (choice), mobilizing energy expenditure or effort, prolonging effort over time (persistence), and motivating the individual to develop relevant strategies (cognition) for goal attainment. Given goal commitment, job performance improves because the goal provides a regulatory mechanism that allows the employee to observe, monitor, subjectively evaluate, and adjust job behavior to attain the goal. Goal setting taps a fundamental attribute of human behavior, namely, goal directedness (Latham, 2012, pp. 53-54).

Edwin Locke was an ardent critic of behaviorism, and his 1964 doctoral dissertation was based on experiments testing Ryan's hypothesis regarding the effect of intentions. Latham recounts the results (1965a).

Locke's Goal Setting Theory (Locke, 1968, 1991) states that individuals make calculated decisions about their desired goals. Once individuals determine the goals they intend to achieve, these goals and intentions direct and motivate efforts to attain them. Thus, setting goals affects behavior of the individuals and their job-related performance.

Latham asserts that the decline of behaviorism in I/O psychology opened the path for a new theory, goal setting, to dominate the literature on motivation for the remainder of the 20th century. He and Locke met at the 1974 annual meeting of the American Psychological Association and began what he called a career-long collaboration on goal-setting theory.

1975-2000

Latham advances the notion that dust bowl empiricism, the "if it works, use it" way of thinking, was dead by the final quarter of the 20th century. He mentions two significant literature reviews that began to address the significant number of empirical studies on goal setting.

In a review of organizational behavior theories, John B. Miner found that goal setting was one of only four theories that were both valid and practical (1984). C.C. Pinder's work was also highly supportive of goal setting theory (1984), concluding that it provided more scientific validity than any other theory or approach to work at that time.

Subsequently, Latham discovered Locke's laboratory experiments in *Psychological Abstracts (1965b)*. His follow-up study to replicate Locke's work examined logging crews; one group that had a high goal and the other group that was urged to do their best. The study showed that, within a week, the productivity of the subject logging crews in the goal-setting condition as well as their job attendance was significantly higher than that of crews who were in a "do best" condition. Latham asserts that the change in the two dependent variables occurred so soon because goal setting had instilled a sense of purpose, challenge, and meaning into what had been previously perceived by the crews as a tedious and physically exhausting task.

Latham asserts that Social Cognitive Theory is another theorist's emphasis on goal setting's importance to motivation. A. Bandura's *Social Foundations of Thought and Action: A Social Cognitive Theory (1986)* advanced the notion of human functioning that accords a central role to cognitive, vicarious, self-regulatory, and self-reflective processes in human adaptation and change.

People are viewed as self-organizing, proactive, self-reflecting and self-regulating rather than as reactive organisms shaped and shepherded by environmental forces or driven by concealed inner impulses. From this perspective, human functioning is viewed as the product of a dynamic interplay of personal, behavioral, and environmental influences. Bandura's concept of *reciprocal determinism* is the view that (a) personal factors in the form of cognition, affect, and biological events, (b) behavior, and (c) environmental influences create interactions that result in a *triadic reciprocality* (Bandura's terms are in italics).

Bandura renamed his theory from social learning to social "cognitive" both to distance it from prevalent social learning theories of the day and to emphasize that cognition plays a critical role in people's capability to construct reality, self-regulate, encode information, and perform behaviors. Latham draws similarities and differences between goal-setting theory and social cognitive theory. Latham asserts that both emphasize the importance of conscious goals for predicting, explaining, and regulating performance as well as the importance of feedback as a moderator of the goal-performance relationship. Also, both offer a framework for self-management.

They differ, Latham argues, primarily in their relative emphasis on the variables that constitute them. Goal-setting's emphasis is on the core properties of an effective goal, namely specificity and difficulty levels, as well as the mediators, namely direction, effort, persistence, and strategy, and the moderators, namely ability, commitment, feedback, and situational constraints. Latham asserts that social cognitive theory and the research that underlies it emphasize the importance of self-efficacy (relates to a person's perception of their ability to reach a goal) as well as outcome expectancy. These are two different motivational systems that enhance goal commitment and persistence in the face of environmental difficulties.

Latham goes on to discuss his work with Colette Frayne in self-regulation, which involves processes that through modulation of thought, affect, and behavior enable people to guide their goal-directed activities over time (1987). Latham and Frayne advanced the notion that training in self-regulation teaches people skills in self-observation, to compare their behavior with the goals they set, and to administer reinforcers and punishers to bring about and sustain goal commitment (Frayne & Latham, 1987).

Greg Oldham, J. Hackman, and J. Pearce developed the Job Characteristics Model (1976). The theoretical basis asserts that there are five characteristics that can lead to job satisfaction, performance, and motivation. They are:

1. Skill variety refers to the need to use several different abilities and skills to accomplish a task.
2. Task identity refers to the ability of workers to see their task as a whole and complete action with an end product instead of just one small piece.
3. Task significance refers to the way the task influences, or is useful to, the other people in the company or organization.
4. Autonomy is the feeling of freedom within one's job, and the ability to make one's own choices about things such as workspace, schedule, dress, etc. It is also linked to feelings of independence and responsibility.

5. Feedback is the extent to which an employee is given information about the quality of individual performance, either by management, co-workers, or the job itself.

The theory holds that one can determine the satisfaction of the employee by averaging the first three characteristics and then multiplying by the other two core characteristics. The resulting number is designated as the Motivation Potential Score (MPS). In examining the Job Characteristics Model, Latham asserts that its importance was incorporated into the High-Performance Cycle, a framework that he and Locke developed at the end of the 20th century for predicting, explaining, and influencing a person's work motivation.

Latham closes his examination of the century with a look to principles of organizational justice. He asserts that C.A. O'Reilly (1991) found that the majority of organizational behavior studies focus on the dominant theories of goal setting and equity. Latham advances the notion that organizational justice principles are as much about leadership as they are about employee motivation. There are two considerations: (1) Distributive justice focuses on what was distributed, who it was distributed to, and who received what distribution; and (2) Procedural justice is concerned with whether there are procedures, processes, or systems in place for determining what was distributed to whom.

Latham lists two key factors that affect feelings of procedural justice, which are a priori criteria for making decisions and "voice." If the a priori criteria are applied consistently, bias is suppressed, and actions are based on accurate information, as well as other logical considerations. So, Latham argues that people are likely to accept and understand the basis for an organizational decision even when they do not necessarily agree with it. Voice refers to the concept of participation in decision making. To the extent that people feel that their voice is heard, Latham argues, they are likely to support decisions that are not congruent with their earlier viewpoint.

The widespread applicability of principles of organizational justice to the workplace is a clear reason for the attention it has received from scientist-practitioners. At the end of the 20th century, Latham argues, feelings of trust and fairness in the workplace were being studied within the framework of organizational justice principles.

Latham lists four controversies that have dominated research and theory throughout the 20th century. They are money as a motivator, the distinction between intrinsic and extrinsic motivators, the causal relationship between job satisfaction and job performance or the converse, and the importance of participation in decision making as a motivational technique.

2000-2005

Latham next looks at what he calls "The Starting Point for Motivation," the first years of the new century in his view. The highlights of that look follow.

Conscious motivation had been seriously examined by human resource management, I/O psychologists, and organizational behavior scholars at the end of the 20th century. Latham believed that the new century would see an integration of personality and affective processes. The comments of Bandura and of Miner are insightful.

In 2003, Bandura believed that consciousness is the very substance of mental life. He asserted that a functional consciousness involves intentional accessing and deliberative use of semantic and programmatic information to manage life events. That same year, Miner advanced the notion that motivation continues to hold a prominent place with scholars in the present century. "If one wishes to create a highly valid theory, which is also constructed with the purpose of enhanced usefulness in practice in mind, it would be best to look to motivation theories…for an appropriate model," Miner said (2015).

There was also a resurgence of interest in Maslow's Need Hierarchy Theory because, Latham argues, needs affect a person's survival and wellbeing and thus are the starting points of motivation. F.W. Wicker, G. Brown, J.A. Wiehe, A.S. Hagen, and J.L. Reed (1993) argued that Maslow's theory can better predict a relationship between a person's intentions and behavior than is examining a person's ratings of "importance." Maslow is also important because many scholars assert that a person's needs dictate the way motivation processes operate.

As researchers examined needs and goal setting, Latham argued for a different focus on needs. Robert and Joyce Hogan developed Socioanalytic Theory (2001). The theory asserts that people are constantly in need of either getting along or getting ahead. They are pursuing getting along when they pursue acceptance, approval, and popularity. Getting ahead involves the need for power, control, and status. Interpersonal relationships are inherently problematic because of the dichotomy of actions. One can solve the problem of getting along by simply acting in a way that would avoid disapproval. However, to get ahead one may need to adopt more active and manipulative forms of self-presentation.

Latham asserts that a resurgence of interest in individual differences must go together with continuing examination of and attention to needs.

A Framework for Motivation Processes

Clearly, there are issues that go beyond Latham's assertions that the field still contends with to this day. I agree with the view that current theories of work motivation focus on different aspects of the motivation process. The key question for our examination of telework, trustworthiness, and performance is a simple one: What framework can be developed to capitalize on the salient points of organizational and behavioral theory to assist leaders and members navigate today's telework challenges?

First, I believe it is necessary to organize the epistemology of the 20th century (and beyond) in an order that allows leaders and researchers to focus on the development of the field and the linkages that exist in the relevant theories. For leaders, Table 1 offers ways to identify and define leadership styles. By examining theories based on individual versus organizational considerations, it is possible to understand the needs and considerations of the individual as they relate to the needs and considerations of the organization.

Table 1 organizes the theories from the preceding discussion based on who is served or, better, who is the object of primary consideration. Of note, Tables 1 and 11 were not developed with LMX Theory in mind because I was not aware of this theory until I completed my research for this book. I have listed the theory ***<u>with special emphasis</u>*** in each table to show where it fits in the notion of motivation. LMX Theory appeared in 1975 with a seminal article from Fred Dansereau and others (Dansereau, Graen, & Haga, 1975) evolving the theory from vertical dyad linkage. Because the theory is used extensively throughout the book, the coverage of it in this chapter is extremely limited despite that fact that it is used extensively as a foundation for the discovery in this book.

The analysis in Table 10 remains within Latham's time segments because it provides an excellent way to move through construction of a theoretical framework that will help individuals and organizations. This Framework for Motivation ties relevant theories together and searches for an integrative, overarching conceptual framework that serves an analysis of workplace motivation.

The rationale for this framework is that there have always been relationship tensions, both good and bad, in human interactions with each other and with

Table 1. Individual and Organizational Considerations: A Framework for Motivation

1900-1925	
Individual Considerations • Eros-Thanatos (Freud) o Seek to bond with others o Seek to dominate others • Self-esteem (James) o Seek sense of self	Organizational Considerations • Examine unconsciousness or unexplained behavior through dreams (James) • Reward display of targeted behavior (Thorndike) • Behaviorism and response to stimuli (Watson) • Focus on method through time and motion studies (R. and J. Gilbreth) • One best way (Taylor)
1925-1950	
Individual Considerations • Personal loss/crisis due to the Great Depression and WW II (Latham) • Display feelings and experiences (Viteles) • Emotion (Freud and Viteles) • Morale (Tiffin) • Humanizing the workforce (Latham)	Organizational Considerations • Humanize the workplace (Latham) • Measurement methodologies – attitude surveys, laboratory, and field experiments – (Thurstone, Likert, Porter) • Observation through Hawthorne studies (Mayo) • "Unfreezing, changing, refreezing" (Lewin)
1950-1975	
Individual Considerations • Display worker wants, wishes, desires and experiences (Ryan and Smith) • Seek job satisfaction and improve job performance (I/O psychologists per Latham) • Seek satisfaction of expectations in terms of inputs versus outputs (Vroom) • Seek reward in money/equity (Adams)	Organizational Considerations • Theory Y instead of Theory X (McGregor) • Need for supporting data (Porter) • Hygiene factors (Herzberg)
1975-2000	
Individual Considerations • **Stress importance of dyadic interaction (Dansereau)** • Reward for stimulus response – behaviorism (Skinner) • Offer employee participation and commitment (Locke) • Seek employee "voice" (O'Reilly) • Seek trust and fairness in the workplace (Latham)	Organizational Considerations • ***Each member is unique individual (Dansereau)*** • "New" behaviorism with attention to human factors (Skinner) • Reward appropriate stimulus response pattern – behaviorism (Skinner) • Promote workplace trust and fairness (Latham)
2000-Present	
Individual Considerations • Goal setting (Locke and Latham) • Self-observation, comparison, and adjustments for goal commitment (Latham and Frayne; can be connected back to James' notion of self-esteem) • Motivation through organizational justice (O'Reilly) • Needs fulfillment (F. and L. Hogan) o Getting along – seeking acceptance, approval, or popularity o Getting ahead – seeking power, control, or status	Organizational Considerations • Self-regulation training (Latham and Frayne) • Leading and motivating through organizational justice (O'Reilly)

their environment. This has been true for ages, and certainly true since the first notion advanced in this chapter, that of Sigmund Freud's discussion of the "primal horde" in the early 1900s. *Eros-Thanatos* still applies today:

people need to bond, but they also need some form of domination to either get ahead or to differentiate themselves from others.

Table 2. Theoretical Background

Individual Focus	Organizational Focus
Needs and sense of self ◆ 1890, William James, *Principles of Psychology* ◆ 1913, Sigmund Freud, Primal Horde ◆ 1932, Morris Viteles, *Industrial Psychology* ◆ 1943, Abraham Maslow, Hierarchy of Needs ◆ 1952, J. Tiffin, worker morale ◆ 1954, T.A. Ryan & P.C. Smith, focus on wants, needs, desires, & experiences of the individual ◆ 1974, B.F. Skinner, Theory of operant conditioning (behaviorism)	**Observation/interaction with individual** ◆ 1911, Frederick Taylor, scientific management ◆ 1917, E. Thorndike, law of effect (rewards) ◆ 1923, Frank & Lilian Gilbreth, time & motion studies ◆ 1927, Elton Mayo, Hawthorne Studies ◆ 1951, Kurt Lewin, Change Theory ◆ 1963, J. Stacy Adams, Equity Theory ◆ 1964, Victor Vroom, Expectancy Theory ◆ ***1975, Fred Dansereau, LMX Theory*** ◆ 1989, Gary P. Latham & Colette Frayne, self-regulation training ◆ 1991, C.A. O'Reilly, principles of organizational justice
Measurement Methodology	
Individual & Organizational Foundations ◆ 1929, Louis Leon Thurstone, law of comparative judgment (attitude scaling) ◆ 1932, Rensis Likert, attitude scaling ◆ 1961, Lyman Porter, proficiency scale	

The framework is most useful when employed with a theoretical background that traces the development of an individual versus organizational focus. Table 2 is offered in support of that framework.

It is important to examine linkages of theories because nothing in the I/O psychology field is new. The 1890 *Principles of Psychology* (James, 2007) provided a methodology that is useful for studying behavior, that of examining the unconsciousness and the use of dreams. James' work connects well to the Socioanalytic Theory (Hogan & Hogan, 2001), in part because the examination of the unconsciousness may offer explanations about behavior that is otherwise unexplained.

James's considerations for researchers – analysis, introspection, experiment, and comparison – complement Taylor's scientific management because each is evident in Taylor's finding that "one best way," distinguishing norms from anomalies through observation. Like Taylor's work, the Gilbreths brought to light the importance of observing and interacting with workers to get a sense of methods, motivations, and responses to stimuli. Of course, Taylor's scientific management was more popular and far-reaching. Two assumptions, however, limit the scientific method.

First, Taylor assumed that management and labor would share the same objectives and that there would be no conflict over organizing to achieve them. Second, he did not allow for the effects of supply and demand in this assumption. There are other theories that make up for the limits of these assumptions. For instance, emphasis on tying rewards or money to performance was highlighted by Thorndike in the 1900s (1917), and is a primary consideration in present day debates.

Latham argues that the first 25-year period was highlighted by Thorndike's law of effect and the importance that engineers placed on tying rewards or money to performance. However, his belief is that the stock market crash, the Great Depression, and World War II pushed the plight of human beings and the concern with humanizing the workplace to the forefront in the second quarter of the 20th century.

In the 1930s, Viteles argued for a focus on worker feelings and experiences, connecting the field once again with emotional considerations that are tied to Freud's concepts of repression, rationalization, and sublimation. In the same period, measurement efforts for organizations increased in importance. The works of Thurstone and Likert provided approaches to measurement in factor analysis that had the potential to enhance both quantitative and qualitative analysis. For instance, Likert argued that if we want to measure abstract objects, we must define them clearly so the researcher and the subject will have the same object in mind.

The ground-breaking measurement methods started a period of more rigorous methods, with attitude surveys, laboratory experiments, and field experiments increasing in number and scope. The Hawthorne studies of Mayo and his colleagues provided methodology and findings that are still valuable for qualitative studies that are focused on human factors as they relate to intrinsic and extrinsic motivation and work environment.

The third quarter of the century was characterized by a stronger focus on motivation processes and morale. Tiffin's four factors affecting a worker's morale are important to relationships between person and environment (1948). The factors are (1) how the person feels about the job, (2) how the boss regards the employee, (3) social factors, and (4) working conditions. Tiffin's factors do not directly address needs, which are also important when considering the human condition in the motivation environment.

In a form of response, Ryan and Smith successfully argued for a departure from Watson's argument for translating worker goals into stimuli and responses. They attempted to move the field's focus to the wants, wishes, desires, and experiences of the individual. That change in focus was well timed because much research was directed to job satisfaction and job performance during this period.

Employee performance and morale would remain interdependent, despite objections, until the work of Maslow. Maslow's needs theory has survived temporal challenges, in part because of the field's continued emphasis on the human condition, and in part because of the development of goal setting theory. There is even some correlation between hierarchy of needs theory and Socioanalytic Theory. I also believe the reason that Maslow's theory is still considered relevant today is that organizations and their leaders have found time and again that addressing and solving employee needs is the key to many variables: trustworthiness, motivation, performance, loyalty, job satisfaction, productivity, and burnout, to name a few.

Organizations have come to realize that the way to be effective is to take McGregor's Theory Y approach to motivating employees. It is doubtful that anyone would argue long that there are some employees who, like in the Theory X position, want to be directed. However, those individuals may also want direction that frees them to be productive and creative on their own. They may even flourish given that kind of opportunity. In essence, they want verification that the "bus" they are about to get on will take them to their home, but they do not want managers who will ride home with them. Now, on the bus by themselves, Theory Y self-control and self-direction takes over. There is a substantial and relevant difference between the two positions.

Next, Herzberg's work on job characteristics was necessary to sharpen the focus on motivation processes. His hygiene factors presented possibilities for motivating an employee to higher performance. Motivation-Hygiene Theory is crucial to organizational issues because it has implications for increasing awareness of the underlying reasons for an employee's action, or lack thereof.

Perhaps most important about Herzberg's theory was his further classification of our actions and how and why we take them, discussing the difference between movement (what we must do) and motivation (what we want to do). According to Latham, Herzberg's theory is linked to Adams' Equity Theory. Herzberg asserted that money or the lack of it can be a major source of dissatisfaction but offers little about what the person will do because of this dissatisfaction. Latham advances the notion that Equity Theory fills the void, dealing primarily with money and focusing on a person's perceptions of fairness with respect to a relationship.

In Equity Theory, the individual seeks rewards in money or equity for their contribution. It fits well with the Vroom's Expectancy Theory, which uses motivation to refer to processes governing choices made by people or lower organisms among alternative forms of activity. Vroom argues that an individual will act in a certain way based on the expectation that the act will be followed by a given outcome and on the attractiveness of that outcome to the individual.

Vroom's research led I/O psychologists back to the potential applicability of behaviorism in the workplace. Regardless of the criticisms of behaviorism, it can be beneficial to allow the notion from that theory that people behave the way they do because this kind of behavior has had certain consequences in the past. If this thinking is correct, organizations can model past successes to foster future successes. Basically, Skinner argued that once a Stimulus-Response (S-R) pattern is rewarded, the individual is conditioned to respond. Logically, organizations that reward or reinforce successful behaviors should have an expectation that other successes will follow as subsequent S-R patterns are rewarded.

This kind of "rebirth" of behaviorism was followed by, or possibly led to, Locke's experiments leading to three propositions that would lead to goal setting theory in 1990. In short, high goals lead to higher performance than no goals or recommendations to "do your best"; the higher the goal the higher the performance; and certain variables, monetary incentives to name one, only affect performance to the extent that they lead to setting and committing to high goals.

In fact, through the framework offered herein one could easily address the seven variables Latham listed for predicting, explaining, and influencing employee motivation in the 21st century.

1. Needs for physical and psychological wellbeing.
2. Personal traits that drive needs.
3. Values which one considers good or beneficial and acts to gain or keep.
4. Context affects the extent to which needs are met and values are fulfilled.
    a. Societal culture
    b. Job design characteristics
    c. Person-context fit must be examined
5. Cognition, particularly goals, the situationally specific form of values, the specific object or aim of an action.
6. Affect or emotion does not depend on cognition, but the two are usually reciprocally related.
7. An employee's motivation is affected by rewards or incentives. These incentives, however, affect effort and persistence only to the extent that they satisfy one or more values of an employee.

Numerous controversies in motivation literature are constantly in debate and discovery. They involve money as a motivator, as well as the ability to identify causal relationships, in either direction, between job satisfaction or job performance. There is also a recurring need to differentiate between intrinsic and extrinsic motivators. Finally, the importance of participatory decision making continues to be important as a motivational technique.

Whether one is addressing Latham's seven variables or the relevant controversy of the day, this chapter offers help. This examination of Latham's work and viewpoints suggests five theories that, taken together, are relevant for individuals and organizations in support of motivational processes. They are Needs Theory, Goal Setting Theory, Principles of Organizational Justice, Self-Regulation principles, and Socioanalytic Theory.

Certainly, any of these processes can be helpful alone or together. What the framework in this chapter offers is the use of those theories and more in an interconnected way. The learning process of leading and managing can be helped with this framework.

The motivation process is situational and the challenge for leaders and members to understand the dynamics of the human interaction to make sound judgments. The key to doing that is to determine whose interests have the most weight at the time and who has the telling "voice" in the decision-making effort.

Clearly, needs affect a person's survival and wellbeing and dictate the way motivation processes operate. There is a constant requirement for individuals and organizations to understand their environment, understand how they interrelate, and make sense of the motivational effort. Hopefully, this framework will prove useful in those endeavors.

FUTURE RESEARCH DIRECTIONS

Researchers should be engaged in determining how to motivate in telework situations. This involves examining relationships that are beneficial or harmful to successful operations. In situations where telework is not an option, researchers should examine how the organization can leverage employee relationships to find suitable solutions for everyone involved. Any study of motivation requires evaluating the basic needs of all involved parties to ensure everyone's survival and wellbeing.

CONCLUSION

Latham's concluding comments in chapter 6 of *Work Motivation: History, Theory, Research, and Practice* are helpful (Latham, 2012). His comments clearly illustrate the requirement for a holistic approach to addressing the relationship between the person and the environment. He says, "Although need-based theories explain why a person must act, they do not explain why specific actions are chosen in specific situations to obtain specific outcomes." Latham's point, which is well taken, is that the ever-evolving interest in individual differences must go hand-in-hand with continuing examination of and attention to individual and organizational needs.

This chapter is intended to help leaders with motivating members in telework and other organizational situations.

REFERENCES

Adams, J. S. (1963). *Equity Theory on job motivation.* Academic Press.

Adams, J. S. (2010). *Equity Theory.* Academic Press.

Alderfer, C. P. (1969). An empirical test of a new theory of human needs. *Organizational Behavior and Human Performance*, *4*(2), 142–175. doi:10.1016/0030-5073(69)90004-X

Bandura, A. (1986). Social foundations of thought and action. Academic Press.

Brayfield, A. H., & Crockett, W. H. (1955). Employee attitudes and employee performance. *Psychological Bulletin*, *52*(5), 396–424. doi:10.1037/h0045899 PMID:13266929

Coch, L., & French, J. R. P. Jr. (1948). Overcoming resistance to change. *Human Relations*, *1*(4), 512–532. doi:10.1177/001872674800100408

Dansereau, F. Jr, Graen, G., & Haga, W. J. (1975). A vertical dyad linkage approach to leadership within formal organizations: A longitudinal investigation of the role making process. *Organizational Behavior and Human Performance*, *13*(1), 46–78. doi:10.1016/0030-5073(75)90005-7

Frayne, C. A., & Latham, G. P. (1987). Application of social learning theory to employee self-management of attendance. *The Journal of Applied Psychology*, *72*(3), 387–392. doi:10.1037/0021-9010.72.3.387

Ghiselli, E. E., & Brown, C. W. (1948). *Personnel and industrial psychology*. Academic Press.

Gilbreth, F. B., & Gilbreth, L. M. (1917). *Applied motion study: A collection of papers on the efficient method to industrial preparedness*. Sturgis & Walton Company.

Herzberg, F. (1966). *Work and the nature of man*. World Pub. Co.

Hogan, R., & Hogan, J. (2001). Assessing leadership: A view from the dark side. *International Journal of Selection and Assessment*, *9*(1-2), 40–51. doi:10.1111/1468-2389.00162

James, W. (1892). *Psychology. Academic Press.*

James, W. (2007). *The principles of psychology* (Vol. 1). Cosimo, Inc.

Latham, G. P. (2012). Work motivation: History, theory, research, and practice. *Sage (Atlanta, Ga.)*. Advance online publication. doi:10.4135/9781506335520

Lewin, K. (1942). *Field theory and learning*. Academic Press.

Likert, R. (1961). *New patterns of management*. Academic Press.

Locke, E. A. (1965a). Interaction of ability and motivation in performance. *Perceptual and Motor Skills*, *21*(3), 719–725. doi:10.2466/pms.1965.21.3.719 PMID:5855908

Locke, E. A. (1965b). The relationship of task success to task liking and satisfaction. *The Journal of Applied Psychology*, *49*(5), 379–385. doi:10.1037/h0022520 PMID:5828990

Locke, E. A. (1968). Toward a theory of task motivation and incentives. *Organizational Behavior and Human Performance*, *3*(2), 157–189. doi:10.1016/0030-5073(68)90004-4

Locke, E. A. (1991). The motivation sequence, the motivation hub, and the motivation core. *Organizational Behavior and Human Decision Processes*, *50*(2), 288–299. doi:10.1016/0749-5978(91)90023-M

Mace, C. A. (1935). Incentives. Some Experimental Studies. *Incentives. Some Experimental Studies,* (72).

Maier, N. R. F. (1949). *Frustration: the study of behavior without a goal*. McGraw-Hill.

Maslow, A. H. (1943). A theory of human motivation. *Psychological Review*, *50*(4), 370–396. doi:10.1037/h0054346

Mayo, E., Follett, M. P., & McGregor, D. (1949). *Organization theory*. Penguine Education.

McGregor, D. (1960). Theory X and theory Y. *Organization Theory, 358*(1), 374.

Miner, J. (2005). Essential theories of motivation and leadership. *Organizational Behavior*, 1-25.

Miner, J. B. (1984). The validity and usefulness of theories in an emerging organizational science. *Academy of Management Review*, *9*(2), 296–306. doi:10.5465/amr.1984.4277659

Miner, J. B. (2015). *Organizational behavior 3*. Routledge.

Münsterberg, H. (1915). Psychology, general and applied. D. Appleton. doi:10.1037/11627-000

O'Reilly, C. A. III. (1991). Organizational behavior: Where we've been, where we're going. *Annual Review of Psychology*, *42*(1), 427–458. doi:10.1146/annurev.ps.42.020191.002235 PMID:19090761

Oldham, G. R., Hackman, J. R., & Pearce, J. L. (1976). Conditions under which employees respond positively to enriched work. *The Journal of Applied Psychology*, *61*(4), 395–403. doi:10.1037/0021-9010.61.4.395

Pinder, C. C. (1984). *Work motivation: Theory, issues, and applications*. Scott Foresman & Company.

Porter, L. W. (1961). A study of perceived need satisfactions in bottom and middle management jobs. *The Journal of Applied Psychology*, *45*(1), 1–10. doi:10.1037/h0043121

Roberts, K. H., & O'Reilly, C. A. III. (1973). *Some problems in measuring organizational communication*. Academic Press.

Ryan, T. A., & Smith, P. C. (1954). *Principles of industrial psychology*. Academic Press.

Skinner, B. F. (1950). Are theories of learning necessary? *Psychological Review*, *57*(4), 193–216. doi:10.1037/h0054367 PMID:15440996

Skinner, B. F. (1966). What is the experimental analysis of behavior? *Journal of the Experimental Analysis of Behavior, 9*(3), 213–218. doi:10.1901/jeab.1966.9-213 PMID:16811287

Stagner, R. (1956). *Psychology of industrial conflict.* Academic Press.

Taylor, F. W. (2004). *Scientific management.* Routledge. doi:10.4324/9780203498569

Thorndike, E. L. (1917). The curve of work and the curve of satisfyingness. *The Journal of Applied Psychology, 1*(3), 265–267. doi:10.1037/h0074929

Thurstone, L. L. (1927). Three psychophysical laws. *Psychological Review, 34*(6), 424–432. doi:10.1037/h0073028

Thurstone, L. L. (1931). The measurement of social attitudes. *Journal of Abnormal and Social Psychology, 26*(3), 249–269. doi:10.1037/h0070363

Tiffin, J. (1948). Industrial noise and hearing. *The Journal of Applied Psychology, 32*(5), 476–489. doi:10.1037/h0061762 PMID:18889449

Vibert, C. (2004). *Theories of macro organizational behavior: A handbook of ideas and explanations.* ME Sharpe.

Viteles, M. S. (1953). *Motivation and morale in industry.* Academic Press.

Viteles, M. S., & Brief, A. (1932). *Industrial psychology.* WW Norton.

Vroom, V. H. (1964). *Work and motivation.* Academic Press.

Watson, J. B. (2017). *Behaviorism.* Routledge. doi:10.4324/9781351314329

Wicker, F. W., Brown, G., Wiehe, J. A., Hagen, A. S., & Reed, J. L. (1993). On reconsidering Maslow: An examination of the deprivation/domination proposition. *Journal of Research in Personality, 27*(2), 118–133. doi:10.1006/jrpe.1993.1008

Wyatt, S., Fraser, J., & Stock, F. (1929). *The effects of monotony in work.* Industrial Fatigue Research Board.

Wyatt, S., Frost, L., & Stock, F. (1934). Incentives in repetitive work. Industrial Health Research Board (Great Britain) Report (69).

Chapter 8
Productivity

ABSTRACT

As we continue to examine and work to achieve trustworthiness and improved performance, our focus must remain on analyzing telework benefits gained and risks involved. The success factors involved in helping organizations are productivity, employee risk, achievement, and accountability. Combining productivity and improved performance in an analytical undertaking can lead to a complete picture of success or failure. Success relies on achieving the best possible outcome with a minimum of input, and productivity is related in that it is a concentration on the output, or what is produced. Productivity is often activity based to understand the value of inputs, outputs, and return on investments. The authors also examine factors that reduce the stress of performing every day: social distancing, flexibility, enhanced work-life balance, and worker independence. These factors can continue to be employed to lessen the impact of COVID-19-related challenges (or the next crisis) so people can focus on health and safety. Managing these stressors reduces the physical and mental input required to perform.

BACKGROUND

Analyzing telework benefits that are gained and the risks involved to achieve trustworthiness and performance is not actually complete at this point. As mentioned in the introduction, there is a need to compare success factors that work with these two constructs to help leaders and members. We must look at productivity in terms of employee risk, achievement, and accountability.

DOI: 10.4018/978-1-7998-8950-2.ch008

The evaluation of performance in the last chapter must be compared with productivity to get a complete picture of success or failure. Productivity is a concentration on the output, or what is produced, and it is usually activity based. The key to success is achieving the best possible outcome with a minimum of input.

Productivity can be analyzed in terms of the output of an employee or group as a measure of efficiency. Why is productivity important if people are performing well? Productivity can take the organization to the next level. In Good to Great, Jim Collins says "Good is the enemy of great. … Few people attain great lives, in large part because it is just so easy to settle for a good life. The vast majority of companies never become great, precisely because the vast majority become quite good… (Collins, 2009, p. 1)." His point is that organizations have no motivation to achieve great if they are content with being just good.

By promoting good work-life balance, an organization's human resources stance improves when it can better utilize the contributions of happy and healthy employees. These benefits can translate into good customer service and great community relationships. The resulting increase in productivity can enrich organizational culture and improve morale leading to an improved work environment. The whole organization can feel an increase in productivity because it results in opportunities to grow personally and professionally.

Productivity is enhanced when there are defined roles that everyone understands. When COVID-19 forced almost everyone into telework or unemployment, it became important for leaders who were trying to keep their teams together as cohesive units to find the best solution for personal and family health while paying attention to the needs of the organization. This is a delicate balancing act and many organizations had to determine the best way to handle it.

Organizations have gone through a prolonged period of making decisions for effective telework. Hopefully, those decisions were based on a consideration of the work and personal needs of the workforce. Working to keep people safe, implementing telework plans, and addressing productivity should have included the full participation of the workforce.

Productivity can also be enhanced when leaders exhibit caring and collaborative behaviors. Empathetic behaviors and flexibility are keys to helping employees adjust to the telework plan and focus on personal productivity. This takes pressure off employees which enables them to better focus on the tasks they are assigned.

On the other hand, team members should focus on what I call leading from behind. Understand the leader and the manager and anticipate how they will view your work or your ideas. Team members should try to answer questions and solve problems before submitting the finished work. Employees are now leaders in their own right, asking tough questions of themselves and striving for the best product or service they can provide.

The roles are important because individual and team success are inextricably tied to one another. Each person, regardless of role, should work toward the stated goal or end state. Every person on the team can be productive when they deliver consistency of effort and flexibility when challenges arise. Scheduling in-person and/or online training sessions on team dynamics may reveal some approaches or techniques that are best for the mix of mission and people. An in-depth look at the situation coupled with acceptance of team inputs will help achieve maximum effectiveness. Determine relevant guidance, set an agenda that everyone understands, and seek buy-in from above and below. Feedback and recognition are ways to keep everyone motivated and productive.

Productivity requires that members of the team accept the importance of performance, support, personal accountability, and team cohesiveness. Each person has the responsibility to determine how to be successful without causing the team to lose time, money, or momentum.

Now, let us look at productivity and stress. Social distance, flexibility, enhanced work-life balance, and worker independence are factors that reduce the stress of performing each day. These are intended to lessen the impact of COVID-19, or the current crisis, so people can focus on personal and family health and safety. Consider that reducing the stressors of these items lessens the physical and mental input required of members to perform. When that happens, they can increase their production given the freedom to manage their environment to the best of their ability. The stress relief comes from fewer work breaks, sick days, reduced or eliminated commute time, and a quiet or controlled work environment, all considered productivity-enhancing mechanisms (Choudhury, Foroughi, & Larson, 2020).

One example of the reduced stress leading to productivity is a study of 128 information technology (IT) workers. The study demonstrated that people who benefited from reduced time communicating with co-workers, adequate work from home resources, and ability to address health care needs while working from home reported higher productivity (Nakrošienė, Bučiūnienė, & Goštautaitė, 2019).

The science and health communities demonstrated that social distancing was highly beneficial in fighting the spread of COVID-19. Telework improved on social distancing by allowing people to avoid gatherings that were called "super spreaders" due to the lack of social distancing, limited mask use, and unknown exposure to infection. This approach also allows people to operate in what was called the "bubble," spending most of their time with people who are known to them and in many cases are relatives.

Employee Risk

Organizations must deal with risks that employees experience. Many employees want to be given the opportunity to telework when possible, and they want the opportunity to be available to all equally based on set standards. Teleworkers want to understand organization rules and goals. Teleworkers want organizational support in terms of professional development and access to necessary resources.

A December 2020 report illustrates how organizations are forced to deal with different categories of workers who are teleworking, or not, and seeking the COVID-19 vaccine. The Advisory Committee on Immunization Practices (ACIP) reported the following categories.

Figure 1. Advisory Committee on Immunization Practices (ACIP) report, December 1, 2020
(https://www.cdc.gov/vaccines/acip/meetings/downloads/slides-2020-12/COVID-19-02-Dooling.pdf)

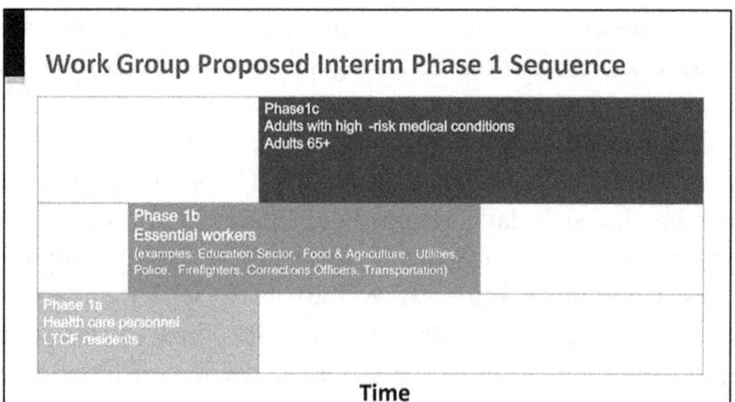

Organizations should be willing to examine ethical, legal, or other issues that employees may view as high-risk issues. Some of these are privacy and confidentiality issues, security (passwords, encryption, and network firewalls), wage and hour issues, liability in the event of injury, discriminatory practices, and Americans with Disabilities Act (ADA) implications. The leader must understand the organization's policy on all these issues and must be able to articulate that policy to employees.

For instance, the telecommuting arrangement should be in a written, specific plan that both sides agree to in advance. The organization should have clear rules on who is eligible to telework and how they get the specific permission. Many organizations have undertaken a full review of all positions to determine which are eligible for telework.

Regular telework allows performance of work at an approved alternate worksite during any regular, paid hours for the organization. The alternate worksite can be the home or a telework center, for instance. Situational telework should be approved on a case-by-case basis. These hours worked are not part of a previously approved, ongoing, and regular telework arrangement. This type of telework is often referred to as unscheduled, intermittent, ad-hoc, or episodic. It is often used in response to emerging crises such as a pandemic or during inclement weather.

Everyone in the organization should understand that teleworking can blur the lines between working and nonworking hours and be ready to address any issues that arise with open, honest communication. Everyone must also pay strict attention to the rules for possession and handling of confidential or classified information. There should be training to solidify that everyone understands how the process works whether they are in regular or situational telework arrangements.

Achievement

Workers are almost always concerned about recognition and promotion. The lack of daily, face-to-face interactions between supervisor and employee deprives both of contextual, personal, job-related information that is crucial to building relationships. People want their supervisor to see them working and to appreciate the effort and results. Teleworking robs both of what can be defining moments in the work relationship. That is not to say that these moments do not happen, or that they cannot be captured. The point is that there can be a disconnect in the work relationship at times that are important and concerning accomplishments that are crucial to recognition and promotion. This is called "distance."

The "distance" created through telework programs may work against success in these areas. There are reasons for thinking this could be the case. The literature review for this project provides a consistent theme of organization or leader resistance to the process, regardless of the reasons. Manager resistance was the number one response in a survey of federal executives who were asked about obstacles to telework (Analytics, 2013, p. 36). Recognition and promotion require that employees show positive results over a specified period, and they rely on support from leaders and the organization. Manager resistance and other nonproductive indicators listed below can detract from the likelihood that recognition or promotion is on the way to the employee (Analytics, 2013, pp. 36-39).

- Lack of company commitment
- Company culture against remote work
- Idea that teamwork requires everyone in the same place
- Belief that people will not be as productive working remotely
- Communication or interaction is difficult with teleworkers
- Leaders are not fully supportive of telework
- Teleworkers may be unavailable when needed
- Some leaders believe it is difficult to evaluate teleworkers they cannot see
- The organization sees telework as a misuse of tax dollars (for government agencies)

Employee perceptions that any of the beliefs mentioned above becomes reality, can create employee stress, and can lead to organizational conflict. As mentioned throughout this evaluation of teleworking, trustworthiness, and performance, organizations need to make a full commitment to the process. That means involving everyone, communicating vigorously up and down the hierarchy, making LMX the foundation of the telework policy, creating and maintaining an education program, and measuring and refining on a recurring schedule. Survey participants (2013, p. 42) rated the following categories as necessary for the education program:

- How to manage teleworkers
- Culture change
- Managing by results
- Using technology
- Being an effective teleworker

- Security protocols
- New office concepts
- Non-teleworker training

Accountability

Leaders often complain that telework is risky or ineffective because it is hard to verify that people are working or that things are getting done. Some leaders may be hesitant to challenge their workers because it may seem like an accusation and cause tension. However, doing nothing to verify progress or productivity is not the answer. These issues can be helped through accountability. Worker accountability requires that they commit to accept responsibility for their own actions.

Leaders can address accountability by stressing how important it is to their team. By setting clear expectations for the conduct of at-home or remote location work. It requires specificity, like creating SMART objectives. A SMART objective is Specific, Measurable, Achievable, Relevant, and Time-bound (see Figure 2). Leaders who set clear expectations should be able to avoid micromanaging and concentrate on communicating about the progress of specific tasks, demonstrating trust in their team members. Team members can then trust that their leaders are resourceful, inclusive, compassionate, and readily accessible to partner with them as they deal with work-life balance. An intentional meeting schedule that combines continuity with acceptable periods of freedom is invaluable to managing the team.

For instance, an emergency in the County of Santa Clara in 2020 required accountability and the workforce responded.

> *On March 16, 2020, Health Officer Dr. Sara H. Cody of the County of Santa Clara issued a shelter-in-place (SIP) order in an effort to slow the spread of Coronavirus Disease 2019 (COVID-19), a global pandemic that has interrupted every aspect of normalcy throughout our communities (Mendoza, p. 187).*

Those charged with addressing the SIP order were aware that increased teleworking was needed and that its success depended on flexibility and self-discipline, accountability, to ensure tasks were completed and work responsibilities were met. "Something specific that worked remarkably well to create principles around trust and accountability within the office was to have explicit written telework expectations for all supervisors and staff

(Mendoza, p. 189)." This is another example of how leaders can set the tone for accountability, taking the pressure off their workforce.

Figure 2. SMART Objectives.

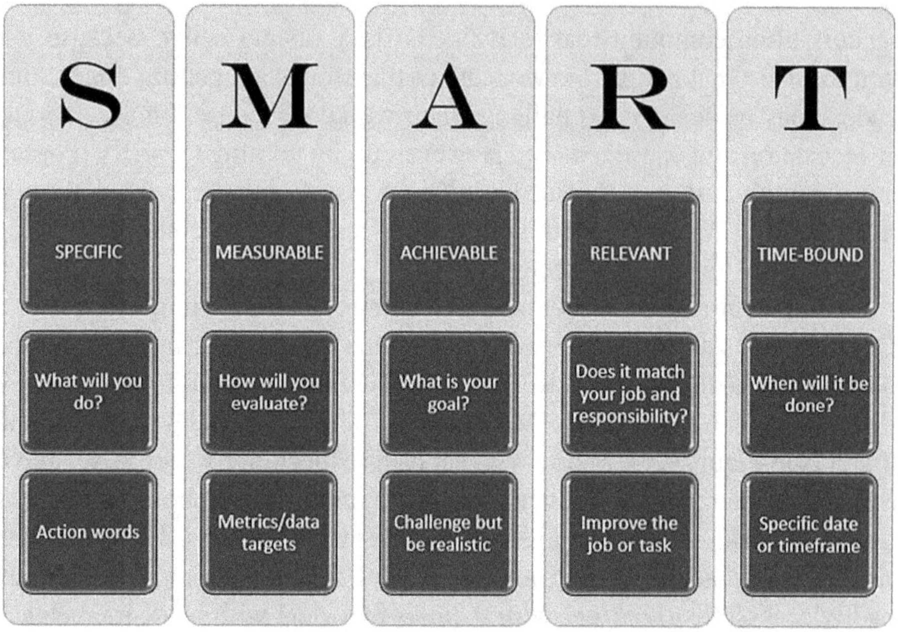

Leaders who set expectations that are specific empower their employees for success. When you hold people accountable you give them freedom to work the activities they are charged with. This approach gives the leader a structured way to provide support when there are issues. It also gives the leader chances to offer praise and encouragement when employees are doing the right things right. Accountability is not easy, but it can be done if leaders and members work together to achieve the desired behaviors that contribute to it. It takes commitment by all parties to use the SMART objectives to achieve a common goal.

Accountability is as much a requirement for the member as it is for the leader. People who hold themselves accountable typically refuse to see themselves as victims of circumstance. They take ownership of the assigned task and for the consequences of their actions. They make sure that the work they do daily directly contributes to goal achievement. They do the work themselves and while they may collaborate, they do not let others do what they should be doing.

Members who hold themselves accountable are self-driven. Effective accountability postures make people feel good and allows them to celebrate accomplishment. They feel that they can work without boundaries, create great results, and trust themselves to get it right.

Leaders and members must embrace accountability together. A good practice is asking the right questions. First, when you have a problem with a big or small issue, can you admit fault? Second, if you admit fault, do you make an excuse or do you address the problem and the solution? Can you say, "I don't know?" The answers to these questions say a lot about your accountability.

Everyone can improve their accountability by taking full responsibility, supporting the organization culture and goals, committing to a collaborative environment, communicating openly, and being honest with themselves. When people are accountable for their actions, they value their work. Good accountability can reduce the time and effort spent on behavior that is unproductive and activities that are distracting.

Employee risk, achievement, and accountability are vital to good productivity. The bottom line in using LMX to improve productivity is that there must be a collaborative relationship. Working together avoids resentment and builds trust and respect.

FUTURE RESEARCH DIRECTIONS

The future direction is simple. What outcomes do organizations and leaders need to achieve to see the benefit of telework? Did organizations and employers evaluate productivity, and performance, during and after the height of the pandemic to see trends? If not, have they tried to do an analysis of operations using 2019, 2020, and 2021 metrics? If any of the answers are no, now is the time for that research.

CONCLUSION

Productivity brings benefits such as making the company more competitive, increasing engagement, optimizing resources, improving customer service, reducing employee burnout, and improving morale. It can also lower operating costs, increase profitability, help the business grow, reduce waste, and improve organizational culture. These benefits are available when productivity delivers increased production at a lower cost, thus providing increased profit because overhead costs can be maintained at current levels. If these benefits can be sustained over time, they can lead to higher wages and bonuses and better standards of living for workers.

Teleworking can be one of the ways organizations can leverage the benefits gained from higher productivity. For instance, discussions of employee engagement in Chapter 2 referenced an article by an Upwork chief economist assessing the future of telework (Ozimek, 2020). The article recounted a study of 1,500 hiring officials - executives, vice presidents, and managers – who gave their thoughts on remote work (Ozimek, 2020, p. 2)." The research suggested opportunities to convince leadership to accept and support remote work. In fact, many leaders were presently surprised at the improvements in productivity they found when comparing pre- and post-COVID-19 results. Survey respondents indicated optimism that productivity has increased. Thirty-two percent of hiring managers reported an increase in productivity as opposed to 22 percent who reported a decrease.

REFERENCES

Analytics, G. W. (2013). *The Bottom Line on Telework.* Academic Press.

Choudhury, P., Foroughi, C., & Larson, B. Z. (2020). Work-from-Anywhere: The Productivity Effects of Geographic Flexibility. Academy of Management Proceedings, 2020(1), 21199. doi:10.5465/AMBPP.2020.225

Collins, J. C. (2009). *Good to great: why some companies make the leap ... and others don't.* Collins.

Mendoza, M. (n.d.). *During the COVID-19 Pandemic: Reflections from Santa Clara County Eligibility Benefits.* Academic Press.

Nakrošienė, A., Bučiūnienė, I., & Goštautaitė, B. (2019). Working from home: Characteristics and outcomes of telework. *International Journal of Manpower, 40*(1), 87–101. doi:10.1108/IJM-07-2017-0172

OzimekA. (2020). The future of remote work. Available at SSRN 3638597.

Chapter 9
Emotional Intelligence (EI)

ABSTRACT

This chapter evaluates EI research, introduces the concept of engaged interaction, and explains how leaders can use EI for self-improvement. Goleman describes EI as a manager's ability to recognize the emotions in self and others. The manager then uses this information to make improvements in self-management and relationships with others. EI leads people to gain awareness by recognizing personal emotions and the emotions of others. This creates an emotional state of consciousness where people use the information skillfully and intelligently in deliberate, purposeful decision-making activities. The concept of engaged interaction is achieved when all parties participate in flexible, full-range communication, making sure to listen, hear, and understand. This open and flexible communication must continue until interaction and shared understanding are achieved. Leaders can combine EI, engaged interaction, and strategic flexibility to improve operations and team building.

BACKGROUND

Much of the teleworking research to date deals with emotional impacts from teleworking. Some of the discovery points to negative impacts of teleworking. For instance, Sandi Mann and Lynn Holdsworth (2003) found evidence of negative emotions in teleworking operations. They specifically cited worry, guilt, irritability, and loneliness. This view of teleworking points to the need to cultivate relationships and to ensure ongoing, effective communication to

DOI: 10.4018/978-1-7998-8950-2.ch009

ensure all workers feel a part of the organization whether they are onsite or remote.

The research also points to the need to use EI to embrace emotions and help teleworkers feel connected through innovative opportunities for interaction. This is important because EI is an effective theory to help LMX in your organization. This chapter evaluates EI research, introduces the concept of Engaged Interaction, and explains how leaders can use EI for self-improvement. This chapter shows how emotions play a critical role in leadership activities and decisions.

A meta-analysis conducted in 2016 is helpful in understanding how leaders' EI relates to members' job satisfaction (Miao, Humphrey, & Qian). The study findings demonstrate that EI leads to job satisfaction when savvy leaders cultivate an emotionally intelligent organizational culture. In this environment, members tend to overcome negative feelings and enter nurturing interactions. Effective personnel development through training helps achieve these outcomes.

Another relevant study analyzed data from 373 managers in the Australian Defense industry (Rezvani et al., 2016). The presence of EI was shown to have positive impacts on project success, job satisfaction, and trust. The intended result in this situation is that leaders learn to control their emotions and create productive outcomes for everyone. This helps with dealing with negative emotions and stress in the workplace. Teleworkers who do not have good communications with the office may feel isolation that creates stress (Mann & Holdsworth, 2003, pp. 208-210).

Leaders can benefit from a strategic focus based on controlled emotions. The strategic focus builds trust while anxiety levels decrease, and the leader's self-interest is balanced with that of team members. Focusing on solutions instead of placing blame ensures the team can communicate and enjoy their work while producing at a high level.

Most scholars define EI as a multifaceted concept that involves a broad range of skills and behaviors. Goleman (1995) describes EI as a manager's ability to recognize the emotions in self and others and to use this information to make improvements in self-management and relationships with others. EI leads people to gain awareness by recognizing personal emotions and the emotions of others. This creates an emotional state of consciousness where people use the information skillfully and intelligently in deliberate, purposeful decision-making activities. Typically, EI skills and behaviors involve the domains of self-awareness, self-management, social awareness, and relationship management (Berman & West, 2008; Cherniss, 2001; Druskat, 2001; Hood, 2004). Workplace settings can be improved using EI principles.

EI starts with self-awareness and the ability to recognize your own emotions and to have a strong sense of your own tendencies and abilities. Effective telework requires developing people skills that include active listening, acknowledging others, and mindful speaking (Goleman, 2006, 2001). If leaders can connect with their own feelings, they can benefit from a source of feedback that tends to help people focus on their strengths, weaknesses, and values. This kind of focus often results in increased self-confidence (Gowing, 2001; Jacobs, 2001; Macaleer, 2002). Another concept, self-management, is defined as "the ability to accomplish objectives while working through one's emotions and perceptions as they arise and to maintain one's values (such as integrity) and standards in the process (Berman & West, 2008)." Self-management includes keeping disruptive emotions in check, thinking clearly under difficult or stressful conditions, having flexibility and adaptability to avoid being rigid in responding to others, and taking tough or unpopular positions on issues (Caudron, 1999; Dearborn, 2002; Smigla, 2000).

EI is the ability to sense, understand, and effectively apply the power and acumen of emotions as a source of human energy, information, trust, creativity and influence (Cooper, 1997). Paying attention to emotions can save the leader time by directing energies more effectively, allowing the leader to expand opportunities. Research shows that EI far outweighs IQ and raw brain power as the primary success factor in decision making, creating dynamic organizations, and achieving lifestyle satisfaction and success (Cooper, 1997).

The core capacities of EI are drawn together and put into action in the workplace through the framework of the Four Cornerstone Model of Emotional Intelligence, first envisioned by Ayman Sawaf of Advance Intelligence Technologies (Cooper, 1997). The four cornerstones are emotional literacy, emotional fitness, emotional depth, and emotional alchemy. Emotional literacy requires developing a clear and useful vocabulary for emotional literacy and recognizing, respecting, and valuing the inherent wisdom of feelings. Emotional fitness involves trust, authenticity, resilience, renewal, and constructive discontent.

Emotional depth calls forth the person's core character, identifying and advancing the unique potential and purpose that define destiny. Emotional depth manifests commitment, drive, initiative, conscience, and accountability. Emotional depth also applies integrity and increases a person's influence beyond authority, rank, and title. Emotional alchemy blends the forces that enable us to discover creative opportunities and transform lesser ideas into greater ones.

Another construct called verbal literacy is defined as the basic building blocks for reading and writing in the same way that emotional literacy is the basis for perceiving and communicating emotions. Becoming emotionally literate is just like learning the alphabet, grammar, and vocabulary of our emotional lives.

The ability to read others – to be aware of their needs and feelings – and to anticipate and address the needs of others, is part of social awareness. It also includes verbalizing emotions experienced by others, acknowledging sensitivity to and consideration for the perspectives of others, and staying in touch with others' feelings. The concept of social awareness is basic to creating environments where diverse people can thrive. A related concept is relationship management, which is the ability to build bonds of alignment, appreciation, and support. Effective relationship management requires communication, teamwork, conflict management skills, and the ability to help people work toward common objectives (Macaleer, 2002).

Self-awareness, social awareness, and relationship management are key management skills, highlighting various behaviors and skills that relevant literature mentions and uses for assessment and measurement. Berman and West (2008) argue that EI acknowledges that although emotions are non-cognitive in nature, people can learn to recognize what they feel. People can develop courses of action that consider a rational dialogue about their own feelings and those of others.

Improving EI and using it to the manager's advantage is also a consideration of change. If negative emotions present significant problems and indicate the need for adaptability or change, leaders may have to deal with radical change and other important dynamics as they manage their team and grow their members.

Enthusiasm and commitment may increase when managers create an atmosphere of understanding and acceptance (Goldsmith, 2004; Light, 2005; Sosik, 1999), and that atmosphere must extend beyond the office to include teleworkers. Managers should go beyond focusing on just "people skills," instead fully understanding what these skills are and what they mean in terms of emotional considerations. It is obvious that work practices, policies, and the workplace environment create emotions. A manager's understanding of emotions allows workplace success in terms of norming and shaping motivational interactions with employees, especially when working human resource (HR) management issues or agendas. Berman and West (2008) argued that "acknowledging the place of emotional content in administrative scholarship and practice is not new, but its significance has often been relegated to secondary status, if not ignored."

An EI framework for workplace relationships between leaders and their teams is important. The focus in this work is on examining how organizational policies and practices affect leader emotional skills in public organizations. Berman and West (2008) addressed managing EI in U.S. cities, studying the social skills of public managers and the need for better integration of emotions in management theory. The researchers examined the range and salience of organizational efforts.

Berman and West assessed local governments' perceptions of managerial emotional intelligence, and practices and policies that affect it. They surveyed city managers and chief administrative officers (CAOs) in all 662 U.S. cities with populations over 50,000 (ICMA 2005). They argued that "though few cities offer training programs for managers that are called 'emotional intelligence,' many cities engage in activities that target or address EI skills." These findings are insightful because they help us examine the potential for leaders to improve communication in a variety of areas, such as knowing their own strengths and weaknesses, being more capable of handling negative emotions, increasing their adaptability, and finding ways to improve relationship and communication skills.

All the information presented here leads us to understand that adjusted or learned EI skills can help people and organizations adopt strategies and policies that promote efficiency and can enhance telework operations. Organizations have always tried to ensure the emotional skill of managers, but the vehicles have been employee selection, appraisal systems, and formal or informal feedback mechanisms. Improvements in managerial EI will not eliminate the need for those avenues of improvement; however, it can provide a mainstream way to transform and improve current practices and enhance existing knowledge.

The features of EI fit well with the concept of Engaged Interaction.

Engaged Interaction

I formed the listen, hear, understand principle of Engaged Interaction as illustrated in the graphic below (Brown, 2017, pp., p. 148). Engaged Interaction is achieved when all parties participate in flexible, full-range communication, making sure to listen, hear, and understand. This open and flexible communication must continue until interaction and shared understanding are achieved.

Figure 1. Engaged interaction.

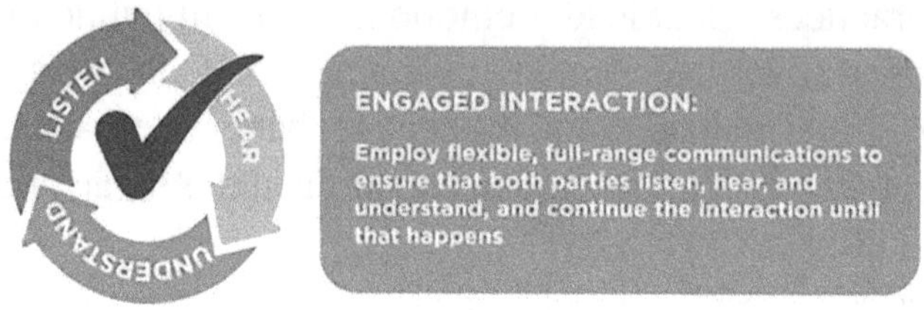

Engaged Interaction is especially important when dealing with telework communications to ensure that there is two-way exchange and feedback that leads to a shared understanding. Leader training often covers listening skills but does not teach "hearing." Emphasis on "hearing" is about synthesizing what the person really says. Hearing is improved when leaders create a learning environment conducive to open and honest communication and feedback. The learning environment can be improved when distractions are minimized in terms of the use of jargon, physical barriers, and differences in language or culture. Hearing is improved when all parties make eye contact, avoid multitasking, and ask for clarification where necessary. The key is to pay attention to feedback and ask questions if you are not getting feedback during the communication.

Engaged interaction has similarities with EI because it relies on empathy. Leaders need to see what others see, allowing them to understand what others think about what they see. There are three aspects of Engaged Interaction: knowing yourself, knowing others, and knowing the goal.

1. Know Yourself: Engage in open and honest interactions by accepting your feelings.
2. Know Others: Strive to understand their thoughts, feelings, and their commitment to the communication activity.
3. Know the Goal: Once you understand yourself and others, you can tailor the communication to best suit everyone's needs.

Combining EI, Engaged Interaction, and strategic flexibility offers more opportunities to improve your abilities to lead. Strategic flexibility is defined as acting in response to external environmental changes or driving intentional changes and adapting to environmental changes. It is about changing the message in response to external and internal influences to increase the likelihood that the message will achieve the desired result. This concept involves several steps (Brown, 2017, pp., p. 154):

1. Assess the situation
2. Evaluate the communication environment
3. Use various skills (tone of voice, gestures, expressions, body language, etc.)
4. Be creative
5. Do not be afraid to adapt or change
6. Reassess and reevaluate

These actions allow the leader to use their style to influence and motivate a member or group to achieve a goal or goals. Leaders must supervise and motivate the team, directing a reasonable process to move the organization toward goal achievement.

Leader self-improvement efforts should result in an understanding of how organizations work. Gaining a foundation of understanding personal leadership style offers the chance to be successful in any organization and paves the way for effective productivity and togetherness in a work environment. Self-improvement also helps with answers to some of the questions every leader encounters. For instance, how do you bring a group together that is completely at odds? How much do success and productivity depend on members making a commitment to vision, analysis, and training? What tools does a leader have available to make the job easier? How meaningful are a leader's qualities and abilities like commitment to vision, analysis, and training in the eyes of his or her followers? Can role definition make or break an organization? Asking and answering these questions can make the leader and the organization better.

FUTURE RESEARCH DIRECTIONS

What is needed now is EI research that measures the range of emotions qualitatively and quantitatively as they relate to teleworking. This teleworking analysis requires understanding the effects of a person's emotions whether those emotions are positive or negative. Mitigation strategies must be studied to increased understanding of how emotions related to work stress, quality of life, and health issues.

CONCLUSION

The EI philosophy in this chapter is beneficial to the success of teleworking. More important, it is beneficial to considering the positive and negative emotions of workers whether they are onsite or remote. Leadership is an individual's state of mind that makes her or him do the right things: things that motivate people to take the actions that are conducive to desired behaviors. Taking care of people first ensures that the organization is healthy and can be effective. Leadership is the talent to believe in yourself and others and to have the conviction in your heart to do what is right.

Great leaders recognize the importance of seeing and following a path to the goal. Great leaders know the importance of everyone understanding the journey so that members can give 100 percent of their being to goal achievement. Goal, journey, and achievement determine success or failure and wins and losses. Sometimes organizations and teams make it by talent, sometimes by pure luck, but there are always avenues to improve the chances that one can determine the outcome by using these tools to create a formula for success.

REFERENCES

Berman, E. M., & West, J. P. (2008). Managing Emotional Intelligence in U.S. Cities: A Study of Social Skills among Public Managers. *Public Administration Review*, *68*(4), 742–758. doi:10.1111/j.1540-6210.2008.00912.x

Brown, M. A. Sr. (2017). *Solutions for High-Touch Communications in a High-Tech World*. IGI Global. doi:10.4018/978-1-5225-1897-6

Caudron, S. (1999). The Hard Case for Soft Skills. *Workforce*, *78*(7), 60–66.

Cherniss, C., & Goleman, D. (2001). *The Emotionally Intelligence Workplace: How to Select for, Measure, and Improve Emotional Intelligence in Individuals, Groups, and Organizations*. San Francisco: Jossey-Bass.

Cooper, R. K. (1997). Applying Emotional Intelligence in the Workplace. *Training & Development*, *51*(12), 31–38.

Dearborn, K. (2002). Studies in Emotional Intelligence Redefine Our Approach to Leadership Development. *Public Personnel Management, 31*(4), 523–530. doi:10.1177/009102600203100408

Druskat, U., & Wolff, S. (2001). Building the Emotional Intelligence of Groups. *Harvard Business Review, 79*(3), 81–90. PMID:11246926

Evan, M., & Berman, J. P. W. (2008). Managing Emotional Intelligence in U.S. Cities: A Study of Social Skills among Public Managers. *Public Administration Review, 68*(4), 742–758. doi:10.1111/j.1540-6210.2008.00912.x

Goldsmith, S., & Eggers, W. D. (2004). *Governing by Network: The New Shape of the Public Sector*. Washington, DC: Brookings Institute Press.

Goleman, D. (1995). *Emotional Intelligence*. Bantam.

Goleman, D. (Ed.). (2001). *The Emotionally Intelligent Workplace* (Vols. 27-44). Jossey-Bass.

Goleman, D. (2006). *Social Intelligence*. Bantam.

Gowing, M. K. (Ed.). (2001). *The Emotionally Intelligent Workplace*. Jossey-Bass.

Hood, C., & Lodge, M. (2004). Competency, Bureaucracy, and Public Management Reform: A Competency Analysis. *Governance: An International Journal of Policy, Administration and Institutions, 17*(3), 313–333. doi:10.1111/j.0952-1895.2004.00248.x

Jacobs, R. L. (Ed.). (2001). *The Emotionally Intelligent Workplace*. Jossey-Bass.

Light, P. C. (2005). *The Four Pillars of High Performance: How Robust Organizations Achieve Extraordinary Results*. McGraw-Hill.

Macaleer, W. D., & Shannon, J. B. (2002). Emotional Intelligence: How Does it Affect Leadership? *Employment Relations Today, 29*(3), 9–19. doi:10.1002/ert.10047

Mann, S., & Holdsworth, L. (2003). The psychological impact of teleworking: Stress, emotions and health. *New Technology, Work and Employment, 18*(3), 196–211. doi:10.1111/1468-005X.00121

Miao, C., Humphrey, R. H., & Qian, S. (2016). Leader emotional intelligence and subordinate job satisfaction: A meta-analysis of main, mediator, and moderator effects. *Personality and Individual Differences*, *102*, 13–24. doi:10.1016/j.paid.2016.06.056

Rezvani, A., Chang, A., Wiewiora, A., Ashkanasy, N. M., Jordan, P. J., & Zolin, R. (2016). Manager emotional intelligence and project success: The mediating role of job satisfaction and trust. *International Journal of Project Management*, *34*(7), 1112–1122. doi:10.1016/j.ijproman.2016.05.012

Smigla, J. E., & Pastoria, G. (2000). Emotional Intelligence: Some Have It, Others Can Learn. *The CPA Journal*, *70*(6), 60–61.

Sosik, J. J., & Megerian, L. E. (1999). Understanding Leader Emotional Intelligence and Performance. *Group & Organization Management*, *24*(3), 367–390. doi:10.1177/1059601199243006

Chapter 10
Radical Change

ABSTRACT

As we examine teleworking rules and best practices, we see people deal every day with the requirement to account for their time, performance, and efficiency. This can be emotionally charged due to a lack of clarity in the ways telework is managed, and that is why the authors examine radical change. Radical change involves behavioral indicators that can prove invaluable to starting or improving teleworking. The effect of emotion on radical change dynamics can be best understood by looking at the change process as separate components. There are three critical steps required to achieve radical change: receptivity, mobilization, and learning. At any fixed point in time, a person can accept the need for the proposed change if there is an interpretive, attitudinal state on the cognitive and emotional level. These steps are used to adjust to the cognitive and emotional levels of people involved in change operations.

BACKGROUND

COVID-19 forced changes in the way businesses operate. These changes range from where people work, to how tasks are accomplished, how we communicate internally, and how organizations deal with the public. This breadth of change is startling, especially when one realizes that it might take years for an organization to deal with these issues. The pandemic forced adjustments in all these areas in a compressed time frame. For more than a year, the world was sent home to heal or stay safe as the disease ravaged us.

DOI: 10.4018/978-1-7998-8950-2.ch010

Just as the world started to seemingly recover from the pandemic and vaccines became available, the world was faced with the Delta variant and the Mu variant. This change is even more dynamic. At the time of this writing, the U.S. is stuck between mask or no masks, vaccines or no vaccines, mandates, or no mandates. This is change at an astronomical level.

Employer-employee resistance is sometimes an issue in change situations, but the pandemic was so pervasive that challenges may have been avoided by the sudden necessity to find work alternatives. In terms of the current or future pandemic or crisis, the management of change requires organizations to rethink future work in light of what we have experienced (Van Looy, 2021, pp. 7-8). Organizations must understand the tensions that may occur based on "…being open to or fighting against telework, or between having primarily social contacts in real-life versus being digitally connected (Van Looy, 2021, p. 8)."

As we deal with the myriad of changes driven by the pandemic, it is important to find ways to adjust to change with strategic decisions on collaborations, appropriate policies and programs, information sharing, and committed organization members (Agba, Agba, & Chukwurah, 2021). These issues are important to getting or managing the behavior modification that may occur in change situations.

we must understand how change affects people and organizations to be successful in telework operations. What seems to be clear is that whether they want to or not, organizations must deal with some level of telework. Even organizations that choose not to deal with telework would do well to have some sort of plan for future crisis situations. Having a plan can help people deal with change in the event of a future crisis.

This chapter presents radical change and dynamic change and strategies for dealing with each. In radical change, examining several separate components helps in understanding the effect of emotion on radical change dynamics. Receptivity, mobilization, and learning are critical steps needed to achieve radical change (Huy, 1999). Receptivity is a person's willingness to consider change. It is a state and a process that consider that at any fixed point in time, a person can accept the need for the proposed change on the cognitive and emotional level.

The concrete action a person takes in the direction of change is mobilization. This is the process of rallying and propelling different segments of the organization to undertake joint action and to realize common change goals (Huy, 1999).

Learning comes from receptivity and mobilization. People learn by thinking and then acting, using the outcome of action to revise their belief systems (Kim, 1993). Receptivity is an observed change, where individuals exhibit various stages of willingness to accept the proposed change, from resigned, passive acceptance to enthusiastic endorsement (Huy, 1999).

Huy's (1999) characterization of the radical change process maintains that when receptivity leads to motivation, individuals and organizations also can learn from the outcomes of the changes they enact, and learning provides a feedback loop from the outcomes of behavioral change back to receptivity. The learning process is a beginning leading back to sustained receptivity at the desired level. Sustained receptivity at the correct level leads to continued mobilization and so forth. The key issue, then, is how the radical change process begins and continues.

Conversations and academic literature about teleworking rules or best practices is increasing every day. The requirement to account for one's time, performance, and efficiency can be emotionally charged due to a lack of clarity. For this reason, we should examine radical change. Radical change involves behavioral indicators that can prove invaluable to starting or improving teleworking.

Chapter 9 introduced EI which is important in radical change evaluation as well. Leaders should understand that effectively using EI can acknowledge and value feelings in leaders and in others and can respond to those feelings in an effective way. Paying attention to emotions can save the leader time by directing energies more effectively and expanding opportunities. Since radical change can be emotional or even confrontational, using EI principles makes sense.

Teleworking can represent radical change for both leaders and members, and this radical change can be positive or negative. Stress can be created when the leader sees the change as negative and the member sees it as positive, and the reverse situation can also cause stress. The effect of emotion on radical change dynamics can be best understood by looking at the change process as separate components. Paying attention to issues of receptivity, mobilization, and learning is important to the continued success of the leader.

Defining Dynamic Change

Radical, or dynamic, change is an important construct. We are using this adjusted term, dynamic change, because we are only focusing on the receptivity and mobilization characteristics from radical change theory. What we are changing is the degree of change, not necessarily the way to make it happen.

Several theories relate to motivation in terms of making behavioral adjustments based on individual decisions that hopefully will support team goals. What you need to know as a leader is what factors hinder your ability to motivate and what tools you have at your disposal.

Research in the areas of leadership, motivation, change management, team building, and other similar fields provides great insight into understanding teams and your people. Discussions about leadership and management sometimes blur the lines between the team and its people. Somehow, leaders must keep the focus on members because they are the team, and you cannot have a team without at least one other person.

Dynamic change was never more at work in organizations than is has been during the COVID-19 pandemic. Dynamic change is defined as drastic or extreme change from accepted or traditional forms or processes. Figure 1 describes it as a continuous and productive departure from accepted or traditional courses of action.

Mass scale teleworking across America is our example of dynamic change. When COVID-19 forced many companies to adopt and allow expanded telework practices, the resulting dynamic forced an activity that was in some ways different than the way we have experienced the world of work in the past. As mentioned, several times in this book, some organizations changed their telework approach, some organizations discovered a telework approach, and some organizations found grand innovations in their telework approach.

Figure 1. Defining Dynamic Change.

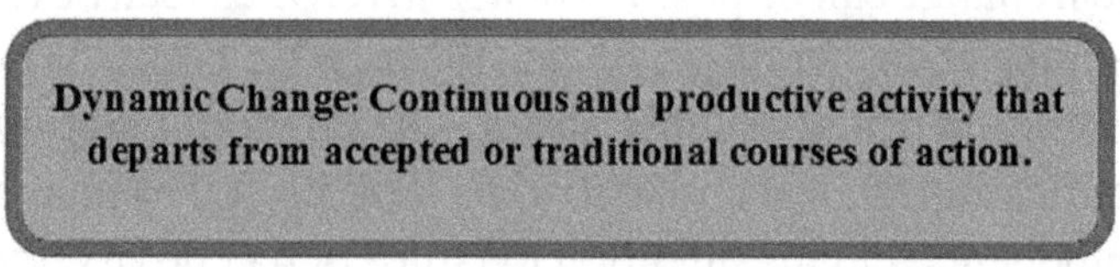

If leaders and managers understand receptivity and mobilization, they can be more effective in achieving dynamic change. The basis for our pursuit of dynamic change comes from several sources. Kurt Lewin's Force Field Analysis Theory of the change process states that preceding a change, the force field is in equilibrium between forces favorable to change and forces resisting it. Lewin called this a quasi-stationary social equilibrium. This equilibrium must be disturbed, either by adding forces favoring the desired change or by diminishing opposing forces (Lewin, 1951; Miner, 2005). For instance, if an organization wants to improve their training program, they should analyze driving forces (supportive leaders, continuing requests for instruction, teachers using the process) versus restraining forces (teachers reluctant to have analysts in their class, reluctance to give up the time to gather data). The next step would be to strengthen contributions of driving forces and mitigate challenges presented by restraining forces.

McClelland's (1961) Achievement Motivation Theory relates to the acquisition of motives. His theory asserts that human motivation comprises three dominant needs: the need for achievement (N-Ach), the need for power (N-Pow), and the need for affiliation (N-Affil). Success in dynamic change relies on satisfying achievement, power, and affiliation needs of those who are charged to make the change.

Victor Vroom contributed to the field with his Expectancy Theory of motivation and management. The theory assumes that behavior results in the conscious choices people make when measuring alternatives in order to maximize pleasure and pain (Muchinsky, 1977; Vroom, 1964). It maintains that there are different sets of goals and that individuals can be motivated if they believe that:

1. There is a positive correlation between efforts and performance
2. Favorable performance will result in a desirable reward
3. The reward will satisfy an important need
4. The desire to satisfy the need is strong enough to make the effort worthwhile

You can start with the construct of opportunism, or opportunistic behavior, if your team lacks drive or initiative. Several researchers (Chen, Peng, & Saparito, 2002) have examined the effects of opportunism as they relate to inter-group and intra-group settings. Opportunism is focused on taking an action that is counter to the mission or direction of the group and that is intended to create personal gain or recognition. Opportunistic behavior is not always desirable. But when drive or initiative is the issue, having someone to follow can be the spark that individuals need. Opportunism can cause team problems, but sometimes it is more important to get moving on an initiative, any initiative, to avoid being stuck without activity. The departure may even suggest a better way to arrive at the desired course of action. Leaders just need to be able to recognize this behavior and work to control or channel it when necessary.

These theories are about motivation, and they can deliver great benefits when dealing with dynamic change. That is because motivation, when viewed as an effort to induce a person or a group to take an action that they would not take without the treatment, becomes dynamic change!

Dynamic change can be successfully managed in another way. We can apply the notion from Chapter 7 that leaders benefit by observing members and interacting with them to get a sense of their methods, motivations, and responses to stimuli (Gilbreth & Gilbreth, 1917; James, 1892). This research focused on avoiding the assumption that management and labor would share the same objectives and that there would be no conflicts between the parties in terms of goal achievement and the methods used. It also focused on ensuring that issues of supply and demand are part of the LMX interaction.

Dynamic change can also be addressed using four factors shown to affect member morale and the important relationships between person and environment (Tiffin, 1948). The factors address the member's feelings about the job, how the boss regards and interacts with the member, how the social situation affects work relationships, and the work conditions themselves.

Also, as we analyzed EI in Chapter 9, we briefly discussed relationship management. Effective relationship management requires communication, teamwork, conflict management skills, and the ability to help people work toward common objectives (Macaleer, 2002). This relates to radical and dynamic change in that they create changes in behavior that can be positive or negative. The relationships between leaders and members require an understanding that changes are taking place and a willingness to address the changes in an open, honest communication environment.

FUTURE RESEARCH DIRECTIONS

Future research should address telework in terms of change management activities. One approach should be an analysis of how to protect organizational culture and build balance in the environment while dealing with radical or dynamic change. Researchers should also turn their attention to issues of health, absenteeism, and other factors to truly understand the effects of change in a pandemic or other crisis.

CONCLUSION

Whether we call it radical change or dynamic change, it involves behavioral indicators that can prove invaluable to the use of telework in organizations. Leaders should take advantage of any combination of theory-based skills that work in their specific situation. That could include opportunism, scientific theory, Tiffin's four factors of production, or relationship management. LMX is the way to apply whatever theory fits and to create effective relationships to manage any change that causes challenges for the organization.

REFERENCES

Agba, M. S., Agba, A. O., & Chukwurah, D. C. J. (2021). COVID-19 Pandemic and Workplace Adjustments/Decentralization: A Focus on Teleworking in the New Normal. *BRAIN. Broad Research in Artificial Intelligence and Neuroscience*, *11*(4), 185–200. doi:10.18662/brain/11.4/148

Chen, C. C., Peng, M. W., & Saparito, P. A. (2002). Individualism, Collectivism, and Opportunism: A Cultural Perspective on Transaction Cost Economics. *Journal of Management*, *28*(4), 567–583. doi:10.1177/014920630202800405

Gilbreth, F. B., & Gilbreth, L. M. (1917). *Applied motion study: A collection of papers on the efficient method to industrial preparedness*. Sturgis & Walton Company.

Huy, Q. N. (1999). Emotional Capability, Emotional Intelligence, and Radical Change. *Academy of Management Review*, *24*(2), 325–345. doi:10.5465/amr.1999.1893939

James, W. (1892). *Psychology. Academic Press.*

Kim, D. H. (1993). The link between individual learning and organizational learning. *Sloan Management Review*, *35*(Fall), 379–500.

Lewin, K. (1951). *Field Theory in Social Science*. Harper and Row.

Macaleer, W. D., & Shannon, J. B. (2002). Emotional Intelligence: How Does it Affect Leadership? *Employment Relations Today*, *29*(3), 9–19. doi:10.1002/ert.10047

McClelland, D. C. (1961). *The Achieving Society*. Van Nostrand. doi:10.1037/14359-000

Miner, J. B. (2005). *Organizational Behavior 1: Essential Theories of Motivation and Leadership*. M.E. Sharpe.

Muchinsky, P. M. (1977). A Comparison of within- and Across-Subjects Analyses of the Expectancy-Valence Model for Predicting Effort. *Academy of Management Journal*, *20*(1), 154–158.

Tiffin, J. (1948). Industrial noise and hearing. *The Journal of Applied Psychology*, *32*(5), 476–489. doi:10.1037/h0061762 PMID:18889449

Van Looy, A. (2021). How the COVID-19 pandemic can stimulate more radical business process improvements: Using the metaphor of a tree. *Knowledge and Process Management*, *28*(2), 107–116. doi:10.1002/kpm.1659

Vroom, V. H. (1964). *Work and Motivation*. Wiley.

Section 3

Analyzing the Data to Facilitate Fact-Based Decisions

Chapter 11
Teleworking Research

ABSTRACT

A March 2021 survey is used to consider three hypotheses relating to working adults. Hypothesis 1 is that teleworking perceptions of leaders and employees are related in terms of promoting increased trust and improved performance. Hypothesis 2 is that a structured plan with associated resources to sustain long-term telework situations will be positively associated with program effectiveness. Hypothesis 3 is that a structured plan with associated resources to sustain long-term telework situations will be positively associated with improved performance. Presidents/CEOs (67%), upper managers (80%), and mid-level managers (75%) believe there is daily telework accountability, but the level of belief is different for those who are subordinate to them. Just 55% and 29% of supervisors and employees, respectively, share that belief. These differing viewpoints can make it difficult to manage the kind of work environment and work relationship issues that are crucial in addressing a pandemic or other crisis. In the search for shared understanding, one path to success is rules-based trust.

BACKGROUND

A survey conducted by professors at Florida Institute of Technology in March 2021 focused on working adults by considering three hypotheses as listed below. The survey was designed by starting with brainstorming to think about potential telework questions. The researchers looked at several relevant issues, such as how online applications revised their approach to provide

DOI: 10.4018/978-1-7998-8950-2.ch011

online meeting capabilities. These capabilities were focused on providing more technology than was available before. For instance, one major company created a semi-secure application that was employed by the military. That initiative led the Navy to start working on its own application so that it could maintain security when dealing with non-military affiliated customers.

That meant the conversation also included how to maintain and improve cybersecurity. Whenever you discuss cybersecurity, you must discuss trustworthiness, so that was naturally a part of the conversations as the researchers weighed the appropriateness of including each question. The researchers next discussed real-world, current situations that could provide insight as the survey was finalized. Several informal interviews were conducted to measure individual perceptions related to telework, trustworthiness, and performance. An overview of some of the information from those informal interviews is below. This kind of discovery was central to how the survey was completed.

Several interviewees mentioned a perceived organizational lack of trust in employees who are working remotely. The employee must do the time-consuming task of document all work done from home when the workload is already excessive. This is part of a problem of organizational culture that requires an understanding of how best to manage remote workers. While people may agree that work outcome is important and should be measured, some said leadership should invest time into getting real information about how people are being managed in the remote work environment.

Hypothesis 1: Teleworking perceptions of leaders and employees are related in terms of promoting increased trust and improved performance.

Presidents/CEOs (67%), upper managers (80%), and mid-level managers (75%) believe there is daily telework accountability, but the level of belief is different for those who are subordinate to them. Just 55% and 29% of supervisors and employees, respectively, share that belief. This presents challenges to the organization in terms of shared understanding.

The need for shared understanding is clear. One way to achieve it is to focus on rules-based trust, where leaders and members accept and adhere to a system of rules that establish the standards of appropriate behavior (Kramer, 1999, pp. 575-579; Lewicki & Bunker, 1995, p. 142; McAllister, Lewicki, & Chaturvedi, 2006). This type of trust helps everyone commit to the same standards and appropriate behavior throughout the organization.

Shared understanding is also a cornerstone of LMX where engagement is crucial. Disparities of perceptions about telework are consistent with conclusions drawn from relevant research." (Stillman, 2012). Like this referenced study, our examination focuses on getting everyone on the same page in terms of understanding the strengths and weaknesses of teleworking. In other words, we are getting a great understanding of the importance of leaders engaging to achieve shared understanding about work tasks, recognition, trustworthiness, and related issues.

Hypothesis 2: A structured plan with associated resources to sustain long-term telework situations will be positively associated with program effectiveness.

Survey respondents shared many issues related to creating effective telework situations, suggesting the need for a structured approach by organizations and leaders. The issues included changes in childcare needs, reduced internet or technical capabilities that are often left to the employee to solve, time management, length of workday, and lack of connection to other members of the team.

Hypothesis 3: A structured plan with associated resources to sustain long-term telework situations will be positively associated with improved performance.

The respondents also discussed employee-centered concerns like work life balance, space constraints, lack of a quiet space to work, distractions, self-motivation, childcare issues, lack of belonging, lack of an end time for the workday, and difficult communications.

The structured plan suggested by hypothesis 2 and 3 requires a teleworking system that can be energized at a moment's notice and that can be maintained over an extended period of time (Preno, 2020). There must be a capability to transition in and out of telework situations. Success in this area requires knowledge of external, environmental emergency conditions to match resources to need and ensure the effectiveness of internal working conditions (Preno, 2020, p. 31).

The 10-question survey was announced in March 2021 on LinkedIn by Dr. Denise Siegfeldt and on LinkedIn and Twitter by Dr. Michael A. Brown, Sr. Siegfeldt and Brown are professors at Florida Institute of Technology. Additionally, Tracy Wemett, president, and co-founder of BroadPR, Inc., announced the survey on LinkedIn and Twitter. The survey received 135 responses before it was closed. The first question asked respondents to consent to participate, a requirement of the Florida Institute of Technology Institutional Review Board (IRB) considering that Siegfeldt and Brown teach there. Those consent forms are on file with Dr. Siegfeldt. Of those 135 responses, 133 people consented to participate; however, all respondents completed all or most of the survey questions.

The survey used a convenience sample to identify subjects who were readily available. This non-probability sampling is useful when, as was the case for the researchers involved in this survey, there is no specific population from which to access participants. The first available data source, in this case people who are available via social media platforms, provided a convenient, usable sample that required no inclusion criteria to be identified prior to selection of participants.

There are of course advantages and disadvantages in using this type of sampling. The first disadvantage is that the selected audience is highly vulnerable to selection bias and to influences beyond the ability of the researcher to control. The second is that the sampling error tends to be exceedingly high. These disadvantages lead to the third one, and that is the lack of credibility associated with the sample.

The first advantage is that there is an ease of doing the research and the sampling approach is simple. The second advantage is that convenience sampling is a great approach for hypothesis generation and pilot studies. The third advantage is that the researcher can quickly get data collected. The fourth advantage is that it tends to be the cheapest of the alternative sampling methods.

Convenience sampling is very appropriate for the telework, trustworthiness, and performance survey that was conducted in 2021 because of its usefulness in hypothesis generation and pilot studies. While there were several new studies in the same areas as those involved here, this survey focused on specific areas of interest as they relate to COVID-19's influence on increased telework across the nation.

The researchers determined that the advantages outweighed the disadvantages. While the results cannot be generalized to the entire population, it allowed the researchers to choose a sample from a large population. While many academics frown on this method, it is helpful when the researcher's time, workforce, or resources are limited. The method was useful in this case to generate and analyze results that can be later used to create entire population generalizations. Convenience sampling has also been used to recruit generalizable samples for future research, but that was not the case for this survey. This was a first attempt by the researchers in an area of inquiry, and it is hoped that there will be more studies like it in the future.

Again, the researchers decided to move forward with this methodology to capture the COVID-19 environment in real time. Subsequent studies will almost certainly take different approaches than what is done here.

Table 1. Convenience Sampling Primer

Convenience Sampling Characteristics	
• Collect Data Quickly	• Fewer Rules to Follow
• Inexpensive to Create Samples	• Vulnerable to Selection Bias
• Easy to do Research	• High Sampling Error
• Low Cost	• Lack of Credibility
• Readily Available Sample	

Survey Findings

A review of the survey demographics shows, among other things, a total of 113 respondents provided information about their gender, with 62 (55%) identifying as female and 51 (45%) identifying as male. Twenty-one respondents made no specification by skipping the question.

Question 8 was skipped by 10 participants, the most of any question. The question was: What are some challenges the supervisor/boss should understand? The next most skipped question was number 6, with three people not answering: Do you think your supervisor/boss believes that you are working a full day? The other questions skipped were:

- One person skipped Question 5; How strongly do you believe in your organization's support for teleworking?
- One person skipped Question 7; Do you believe your supervisor/boss understands the challenge of working from home?
- One person skipped Question 9; Do you believe your supervisor/boss cares about the challenge of working from home?
- No survey respondent skipped Question 10.
- Questions 1, 2, 3, 4, and 10 were not skipped.

For those respondents who were required to account for daily activities, 76% reported a requirement to verify an online presence. The accountability for performance or productivity while commuting was low in these instances. For those who did not have to account for daily activities, 46% reported a requirement to verify an online presence, and 54% were accountable for performance or productivity while commuting. In other words, accountability for performance or productivity increased when there was no requirement to verify online presence.

The survey respondents were virtually split on whether their organization used an automated system for daily online accountability and work performance. Fifty percent had no systems and 45% had some system.

The survey was inconclusive in determining whether people believe that employees are working a full 8 hours while teleworking. Twenty-nine percent of respondents answered that they believe that employees are working less than 8 hours per day. Twenty-five percent answered that they believe that employees are working 8 hours a day. Twenty-seven percent answered that they believe employees are working more than 8 hours a day.

The survey results also showed a great deal of support for teleworking in the survey population. While this cannot be generalized to any larger population, the numbers are still impressive. Organizational support for teleworking ranged from "moderate" to "a great deal" for 115 of 133 respondents. The breakdown of responses to this question was 50% for "a great deal," 20% for "a lot," and 17% for "a moderate amount."

Ninety-eight, or 74%, of respondents said their supervisor or boss believe they are putting in a full day while teleworking. The respondents were also highly positive about supervisor or boss understanding of the challenge of working from home. There were 104 people, or 78%, who said their leadership was supportive.

Question 8 was skipped by 10 respondents, but 131 provided details on challenges the supervisor or boss should understand. The word cloud in Figure 1 gives an overview of those comments.

FUTURE RESEARCH DIRECTIONS

The use of a convenience sample in this survey has advantages and disadvantages. The sample was simple to obtain and allowed hypothesis generation that led to quick data collection. However, the disadvantages include possible selection bias, sampling error, and lack of credibility of the sample. The researchers decided that the advantages outweighed disadvantages. However, future research with a targeted sample and a different sampling method is advised.

Figure 1. Telework Challenges

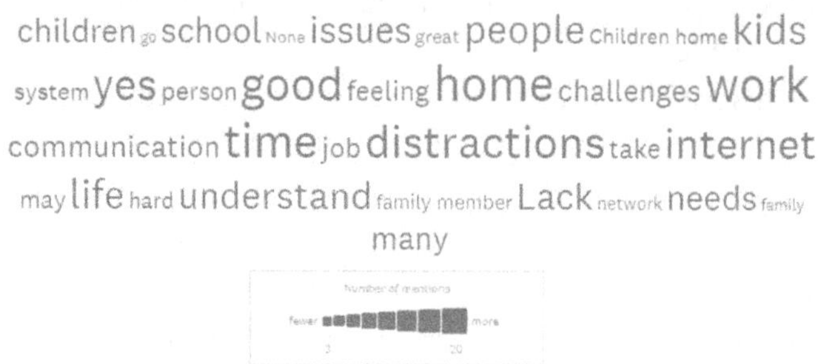

The focus of this research was to quickly gather data while the pandemic was at or near its peak and draw inferences relative to telework, trustworthiness, and performance. There is ample opportunity for future research to address these issues from practical and theoretical viewpoints. This study was intended to be an important first step that could lead to future examinations.

CONCLUSION

Some of the responses included the fact that teleworking is harder or more challenging when you have children. There was mention of the challenge of downtime for internet or technical difficulties, the need for current technology, and the possibility that there is less capability at home since people do not have an "enterprise level system." Some respondents talked about bosses needing to understand the issues of finishing work on time, time management, length of the workday, lack of connection to other members of the team, and people having to pay for their own work expenses while at home. There were comments about the merging of home and work life and the daily struggles associated with that. There were also comments that were more about employee-centered concerns like work life balance, space constraints, lack of a quiet space to work, distractions, self-motivation, childcare issues, lack of belonging, lack of an end time for the workday, and difficult communications.

These are all pressing issues, and 104 of 132 survey respondents reported that their supervisor or boss cares about the challenge of working from home. The survey participants were well spread over the roles in the organization. There were 77 of 132 respondents who were in some type of leadership position: president/CEO/etc., upper management, mid-level management, and supervisor.

All questions and breakdowns of responses are in the Appendix.

REFERENCES

Kramer, R. M. (1999). Trust and distrust in organizations: Emerging perspectives, enduring questions. *Annual Review of Psychology*, *50*(1), 569–598. doi:10.1146/annurev.psych.50.1.569 PMID:15012464

Lewicki, R. J., & Bunker, B. B. (1995). Trust in relationships. *Administrative Science Quarterly*, *5*(1), 583–601.

McAllister, D. J., Lewicki, R. J., & Chaturvedi, S. (2006). Trust in developing relationships: from theory to measurement. *Academy of Management Proceedings*. 10.5465/ambpp.2006.22897235

Preno, G. (2020). *Long-term effects of teleworking during Covid-19 quarantine*. California State University.

Stillman, J. (2012). *Do Bosses and Employees See Eye to Eye on Anything?* Retrieved from https://www.inc.com/jessica-stillman/do-bosses-and-employee-see-eye-to-eye-on-anything.html

APPENDIX: SURVEY RESPONSE OVERVIEW

Question 1 (Agreement). Answered 133, Skipped 0. There were 135 total responses, but 2 people disagreed to the terms of question 1 and were deleted from the database.

I have read the survey procedure described above. I voluntarily agree to participate in the survey, and I have received a copy of this description.

Please feel free to print a copy of the consent form for your records. Electronic Consent: Please choose your response below by either clicking on the "Agree" button or the "Disagree" button.

Question 2. Answered 133, Skipped 0.

Are you required to account for daily activities while teleworking and/or commuting?

Question 3. Answered 133, Skipped 0.

Does your organization use an automated system for daily online accountability and work performance?

Question 4. Answered 133, Skipped 0.

Do you believe your employees are working (number of hours)?

Question 5. Answered 132, Skipped 1.

How strongly do you believe in your organization's support for teleworking?

Question 6. Answered 130, Skipped 3.

Do you think your supervisor/boss believes that you are working a full day?

Question 7. Answered 132, Skipped 1.

Do you believe your supervisor/boss understands the challenge of working from home?

Question 8. Answered 123, Skipped 10.

What are some challenges the supervisor/boss should understand?

Question 9. Answered 132, Skipped 1.

Do you believe your supervisor/boss cares about the challenge of working from home?

Table 2.

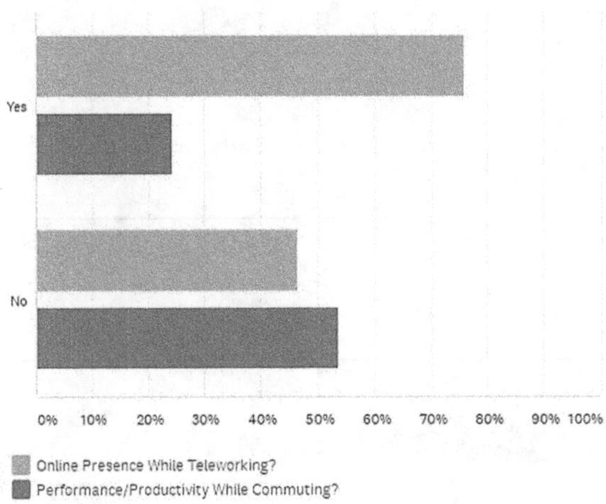

	ONLINE PRESENCE WHILE TELEWORKING?	PERFORMANCE/PRODUCTIVITY WHILE COMMUTING?	TOTAL	WEIGHTED AVERAGE
Yes	75.76% 75	24.24% 24	99	1.24
No	46.34% 38	53.66% 44	82	1.54

Question 10. Answered 133, Skipped 0.

What is your position?

See the tables below for survey respondent location, age, and type of device used to answer the survey.

Table 3.

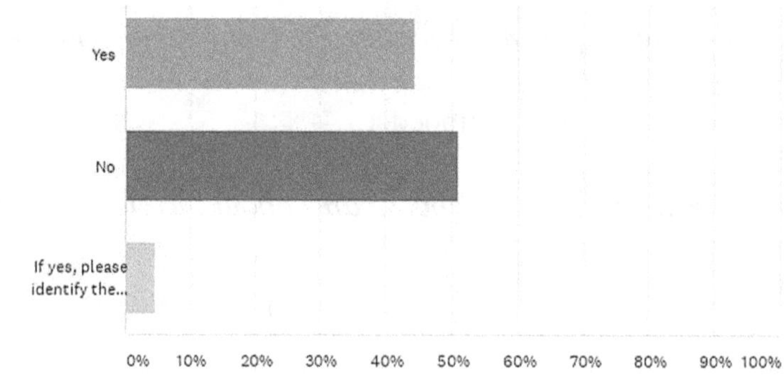

ANSWER CHOICES	RESPONSES	
Yes	44.36%	59
No	51.13%	68
If yes, please identify the system (or systems) that is used by your employer.	4.51%	6
TOTAL		133

Table 4.

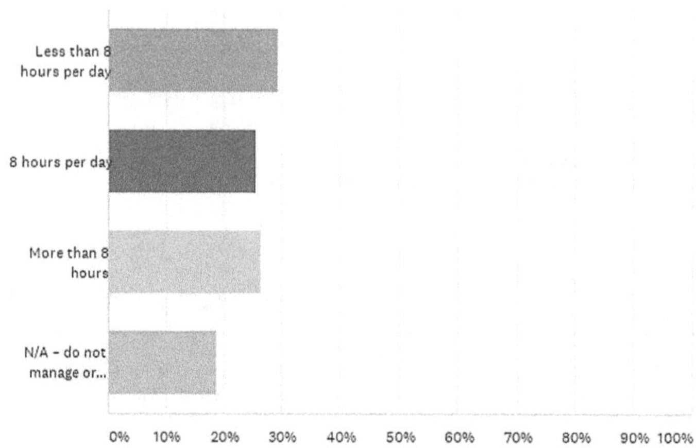

ANSWER CHOICES	RESPONSES	
Less than 8 hours per day	29.32%	39
8 hours per day	25.56%	34
More than 8 hours	26.32%	35
N/A – do not manage or supervise others	18.80%	25
TOTAL		133

Question 11. *Gender* – Answered 111, Skipped 22.

Sixty of the survey participants reported their annual income between $25,000 and $99,999. See below for the breakdowns.

Question 12. *Household Income* – Answered 111, Skipped 22.

Question 13. *Region* – Answered 111, Skipped 22.

Question 14. *Age* – Answered 111, Skipped 22.

Question 15. *Device Type* – Answered 111, Skipped 22.

That completes all the survey data.

Table 5.

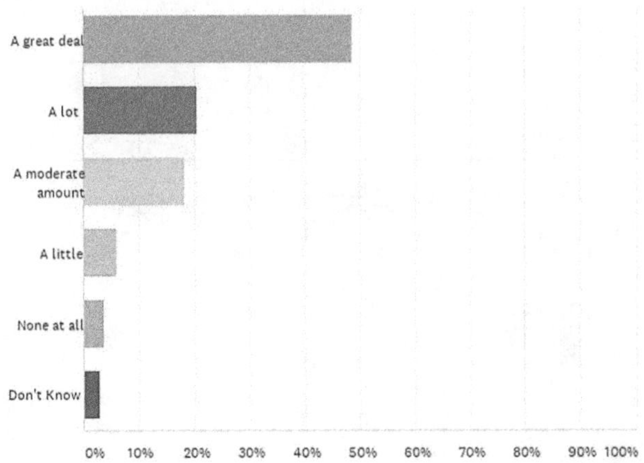

ANSWER CHOICES	RESPONSES	
A great deal	48.48%	64
A lot	20.45%	27
A moderate amount	18.18%	24
A little	6.06%	8
None at all	3.79%	5
Don't Know	3.03%	4
TOTAL		132

Table 6.

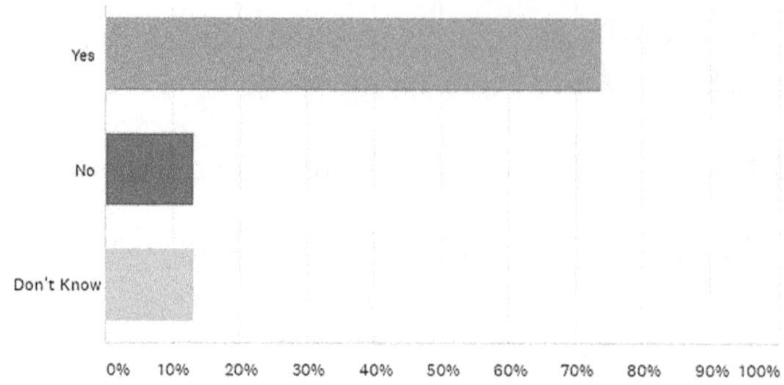

ANSWER CHOICES	RESPONSES	
Yes	73.85%	96
No	13.08%	17
Don't Know	13.08%	17
TOTAL		130

Table 7.

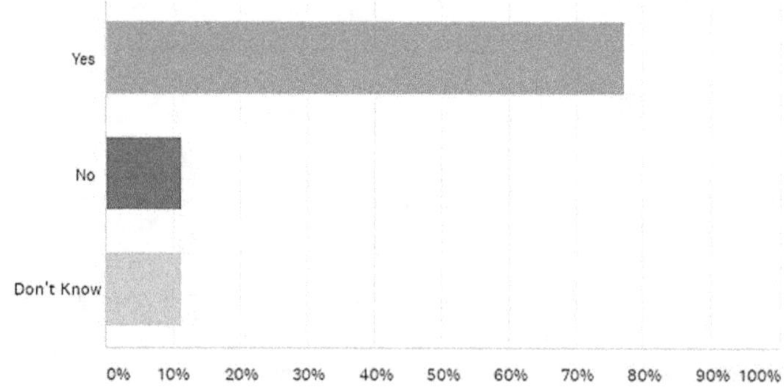

ANSWER CHOICES	RESPONSES	
Yes	77.27%	102
No	11.36%	15
Don't Know	11.36%	15
TOTAL		132

Table 8.

Improve or create a formal or organizationally sanctioned program
LMX that addresses the pros and cons to motivate the target audience of team members
Continuation of a culture of self-motivation and/or enforcement to ensure success (it is hoped that this culture already exists in the organization)
Development of buy in throughout the organization

Table 9.

Idea	Action
Reinforce	Get in touch with what we know about our current experience.
Discover	Understand the issues that leaders and members face and start the conversation.
Identify	Find new and better ways to be productive.

Table 10.

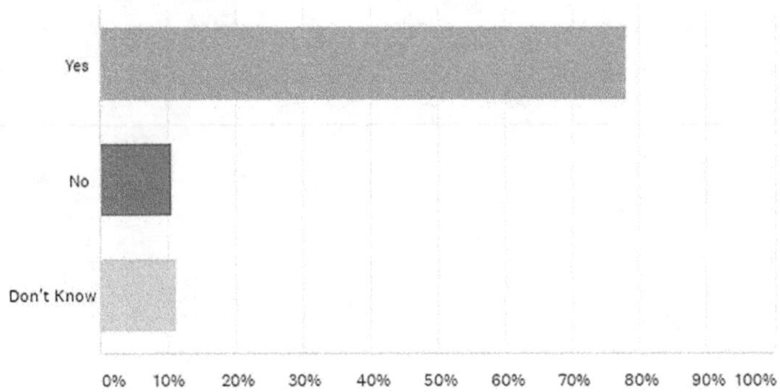

ANSWER CHOICES	RESPONSES	
Yes	78.03%	103
No	10.61%	14
Don't Know	11.36%	15
TOTAL		132

Table 11.

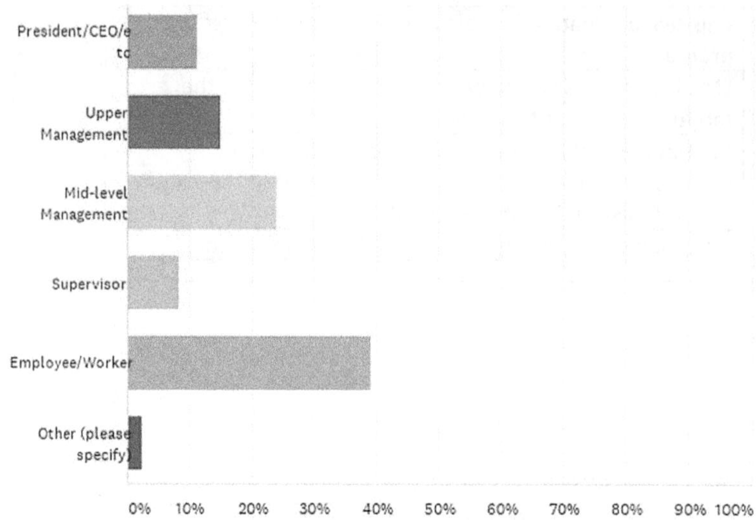

ANSWER CHOICES	RESPONSES	
President/CEO/etc	11.28%	15
Upper Management	15.04%	20
Mid-level Management	24.06%	32
Supervisor	8.27%	11
Employee/Worker	39.10%	52
Other (please specify)	2.26%	3
TOTAL		133

Table 12.

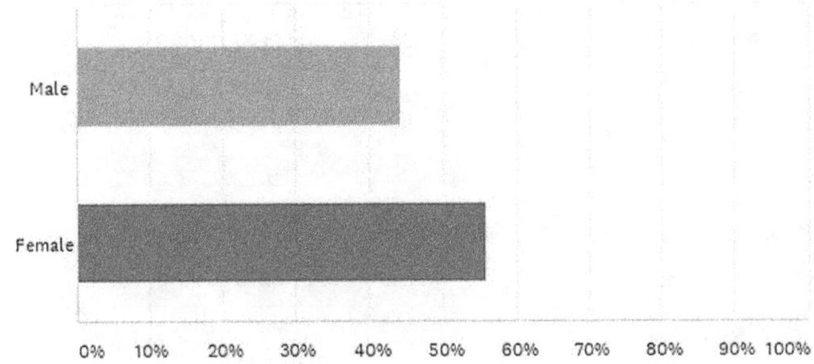

ANSWER CHOICES	RESPONSES	
Male	44.14%	49
Female	55.86%	62
TOTAL		111

Table 13.

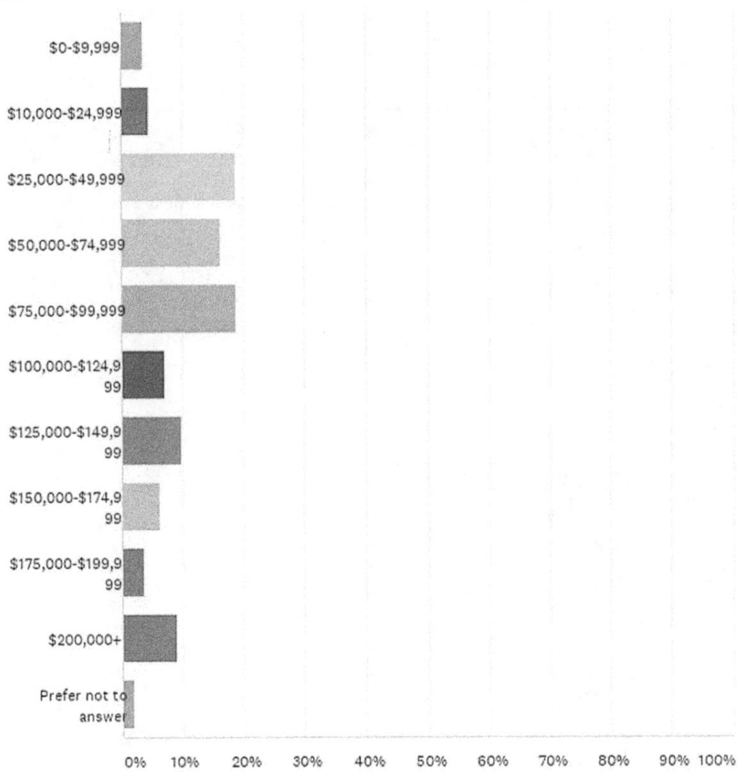

Table 14.

ANSWER CHOICES	RESPONSES	
$0-$9,999	3.60%	4
$10,000-$24,999	4.50%	5
$25,000-$49,999	18.92%	21
$50,000-$74,999	16.22%	18
$75,000-$99,999	18.92%	21
$100,000-$124,999	7.21%	8
$125,000-$149,999	9.91%	11
$150,000-$174,999	6.31%	7
$175,000-$199,999	3.60%	4
$200,000+	9.01%	10
Prefer not to answer	1.80%	2
TOTAL		111

Table 15.

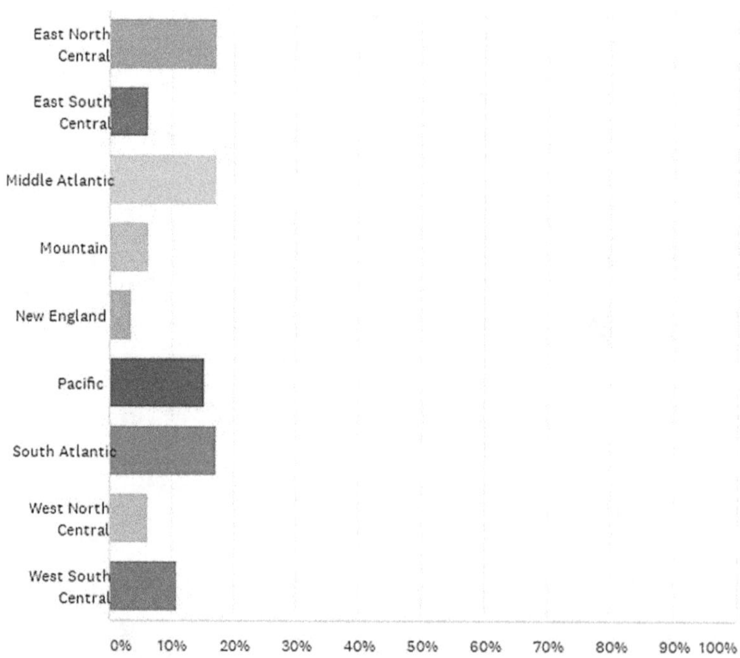

Table 16.

ANSWER CHOICES	RESPONSES	
East North Central	17.12%	19
East South Central	6.31%	7
Middle Atlantic	17.12%	19
Mountain	6.31%	7
New England	3.60%	4
Pacific	15.32%	17
South Atlantic	17.12%	19
West North Central	6.31%	7
West South Central	10.81%	12
TOTAL		111

Chapter 12
Recommended Approaches

ABSTRACT

This chapter looks at several approaches to improving teleworking through increased trustworthiness and performance. Any combination of these methods should be beneficial. Some of the methods deal with analyzing LMX and improving its use. One of the ways to do that is to mitigate "distance" in LMX. "Distance" is a disconnect in the work relationship at times that are important. It concerns accomplishments that are crucial to recognition and promotion. Organizations need collective agreements that guide teams and foster shared understanding, collaboration, and innovation. Another valuable approach is an asynchronous one with work characterized by flexibility. Asynchronized working creates a situation where employees work a schedule without fixed hours. This is said to promote constant feedback and deep-thinking by freeing employees to manage necessary contacts with managers and other employees while self-managing their work-life balance in the process. The need for meetings is minimized and, when meetings are necessary, they may be more effective if they allow participant flexibility.

BACKGROUND

This chapter looks back at all the discussion and discovery in the preceding pages to suggest beneficial approaches. We examine several approaches that can make teleworking a viable solution for any organization. The previous chapters have attempted to cover a full range of possible alternatives for organizations. We examined ways to employ teleworking to its best advantage

DOI: 10.4018/978-1-7998-8950-2.ch012

based on the way our world is changing due to COVID-19. We analyzed trustworthiness, performance, leadership development, employee motivation, and productivity under the lens of telework.

Starting with Chapter 7, we made sure that we had a sound theoretical foundation by focusing on motivation, productivity, EI, and radical change and then using that knowledge as we examined a research project created to help with discovery and solutions. The March 2021 survey considered three hypotheses dealing with teleworking, trustworthiness, and performance. The findings led to the various approaches we will discuss in this chapter.

To get the best results from this multi-faceted analysis that combines personal interviews, survey results, and the results of an online LinkedIn survey, I used triangulation to arrive at my conclusions. Certainly, other surveys were used and there are other methods for arriving at conclusions, but triangulation works just fine. Triangulation was rooted in mathematics in the 1970s but then researchers and other scholars began to use it as a sociological method. A leader of that movement was Norman Denzin, who identified four types of triangulation in 1978 (Denzin, 2012).

1. Data triangulation uses various data sources in a single study.
2. Investigator triangulation uses multiple researchers or investigators to study some phenomenon.
3. Theory triangulation interprets the results of a study using multiple theoretical perspectives.
4. Methodological triangulation uses multiple methods to conduct an analysis.

I am using data triangulation to arrive at conclusions here. The use is intended to enhance validity of the research effort, find different ways to understand these complex issues, and create a broader picture of the research problems and the subsequent findings. While I may have ended up with more a multi-method approach than triangulation, my ends justify my means in this case.

Understanding the process by which the volumes of data and discovery were analyzed is important. Now we are free to examine several approaches to teleworking success suggested by our learning journey. They include the use of LMX theory, the need to create or improve the telework process, the use of an asynchronous approach, a focus on key telework plan features, ways to show full telework commitment, and the importance of managing leadership controversies. What follows is an in-depth look at each of the suggested approaches.

LMX Applications

What are the best ways to use LMX? How do organizations incorporate it into daily operations?

Figure 1. LMX

LMX helps leaders examine their leadership style in terms of individual relationships instead of dealing with entire groups as if every person were the same. This is consistent with what we know about emotional intelligence. The resulting relationships can help leaders impact efficient and productive work situations. Through LMX, leaders can understand that each team member is a unique person who deserves interactions handled in a unique manner. Understanding each member can help with group dynamics.

Be sure to analyze the frequency and quality of the use of LMX. This will foster productivity, innovation, and growth of your people. Make LMX a part of your organization's telework plan.

Asynchronous Approach

The asynchronous approach allows responses to coworkers to be at the discretion of the receiving member's discretion and removes or greatly reduces restrictions on the hours of the day an individual chooses to work. Some would say that this represents an unreasonable relaxation of standards, but there is something else that is much more important. The change in standards is a symbol of trust and empowerment and, as we have discussed at several points in this book, it is an opportunity for people to be more productive. Trust and empowerment can lead to increased levels of loyalty and commitment and organizations will find their people will tend to work longer hours, take less sick leave, and exhibit more ownership of goals and objectives (Brown, 2011).

Figure 2. Asynchronous Approach

The asynchronous approach also deemphasizes meetings. Instead, companies are turning to cross-organizational platforms where current and new initiatives are developed, and feedback is collected using a collaborative tool. Read-ahead documents and videos are used to expose everyone to the material and start forming their opinions without being burdened by time-zone differences and unwieldy calendar matching exercises.

For instance, students at the University of Applied Sciences in Upper Austria demonstrated an asynchronous remote support system that addressed four goals, listed in Figure 3 (Reisner-Kollmann & Aschauer, p. 1). The system allows participants to interact with the technology, and with others, whenever it is most convenient. There is no need to have everyone participate simultaneously because the system collects and stores all the data regardless of the input location or time. Many companies are taking this approach.

Figure 3. Asynchronous Collaboration
(Reisner-Kollmann & Aschauer, p. 1)

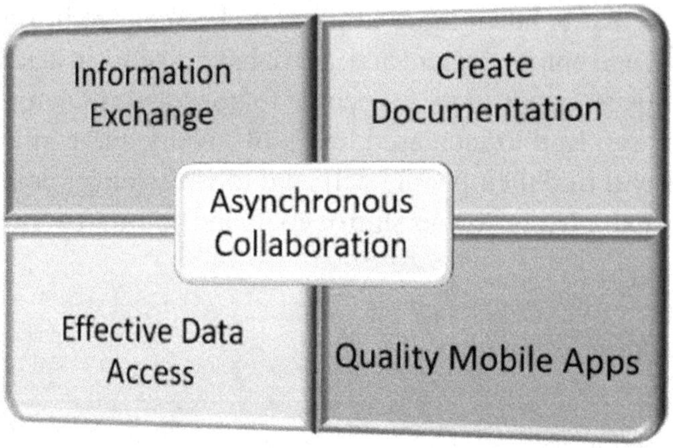

Asynchronous collaboration features the exchange of information between local and remote locations and the creation of documentation necessary to effectively exchange information over time. Equally important is the use of existing data from all sources and ensuring it can be easily accessed both remotely and on-site. Asynchronous operations are improved with mobile apps, which should be simplified by moving complex tasks to a desktop app that is easily accessible.

The bottom-line benefit to asynchronous approaches may be found in the sharing and analysis of information. Reports and their feedback are compiled and incorporated into summaries that can be used for decision making. Asynchronous and/or online collaborations allow flexibility and convenience in reviewing and may provide broader discussions and more comprehensive outcomes.

The organization can now benefit from constant feedback from deep-thinking workers. Workers are now free to manage necessary contacts with managers and other employees while taking care of their work-life balance in the process. Minimizing meetings turns focus to ensuring the quality of those fewer meetings that are held because they are scheduled in response to employee-determined issues.

Focus on Key Plan Features

Every telework plan needs some key features that will make it more valuable to everyone involved. Start with finding ways to replace or enhance face-to-face contact opportunities between leaders and members. This keeps the leader informed and ensures that the member's belonging needs are being met. They feel a part of the team, they feel that their inputs are valued, and they know the desire to keep them involved is a two-way street.

Figure 4. Key Plan Features

The telework plan should anticipate the future need for mass teleworking in a crisis to address health, safety, and/or security considerations. Regular updates are important to keep current. Benchmarking of other organizations' successes and lessons learned can only serve to improve your organization's plan.

Success is highly dependent on trustworthiness as well as flexibility, which includes preparing the workspace to accept and embrace mobile workers any time necessary. As we learned in the age of COVID-19, people may need to move in and out of the organization's headquarters as telework requirements or practices evolve.

In fact, many companies are embracing work-from-home solutions that will likely last long beyond the end of the COVID-19 pandemic. According to a June 25, 2020, CNN Business article, "*These companies plan to make working from home the new normal. As in forever* (McLean, 2020)." The companies mentioned are Facebook, Twitter, Square, Shopify, Groupe PSA, Box, and Slack. Facebook is planning have as many as 50% of their employees working remotely within the next five to 10 years. Twitter has announced that it will allow some of its workforce to "continue working from home 'forever,' if they choose (McLean, 2020)." Square plans to continue work from home once the pandemic ends, allowing employees to work from their desired location. This is intended to keep workers happy and healthy by allowing them to find and/or build a work environment that suits them.

Shopify's CEO has announced that due to COVID-19 there is no longer any office centricity, making his company digital by default. The company will be reworking its physical spaces to allow permanent remote work. Groupe PSA is seeking agility in this new environment by allowing all non-production staff to work remotely. The company cited positive remote work experiences as it redesigns its offices for in-person collaboration and a reduced real estate footprint. The company is now seeking improved work-life balance and easier commutes.

Box went from about 15 percent of its workforce being remote before the pandemic to allowing all 2,000 of its employees to work remotely through the end of 2020. The company says it intends to remain fully virtual in the future and would aid people wishing to set up home offices. Slack's CEO announced in a panel discussion that employees would be allowed to work from home indefinitely.

...it's going to be very, very hard to walk back," CEO Stewart Butterfield told Bloomberg's Emily Chang. "If you go down this path and 20% of your employees are remote and 50% of them adjusted the way they work and where they live to work in an environment where they're in the office a day or two a week and then at home the rest, unwinding that is a little bit hard to imagine (McLean, 2020).

Full Telework Commitment

Figure 5. Telework Commitment

Organizations and leaders must show full commitment to the teleworking program regardless of how many people are teleworking. Of course, if no one in the organization is teleworking and the organization sees no scenario where it would be possible or necessary to telework, then there is no reason to commit to the practice. However, as COVID-19 taught us, anything can happen. The bottom line is that even if only one or two people in the organization are teleworking, a plan is necessary.

Do not let the teleworker be the forgotten person. Maintain regular communications and find ways to include them in the operational rhythm each day even when they are at home. This ensures that they are connected regardless of where they sit. The organization gets the two-way benefit that the leader is informed and aware and the member is connected to all operations.

Showing commitment to telework means involving everyone in the process and making sure everyone understands the fundamentals: What is the organization's telework policy? How do I find out if I qualify? What are the rules for teleworking? How do I remain connected with my supervisor and my team when I'm teleworking? These are the critical questions, but there will be many more.

Using the LMX theory is a good way to demonstrate full leadership commitment. Be sure to stress the education program so you can ensure there is shared understanding of the rules and so that you can foster the member behaviors you need to make teleworking an organizational and personal success. Finally, determine some metrics based on the goals and objectives you set to get you to full capability. Then measure and refine your program on a recurring timetable.

Manage Leadership Controversies

Leaders should strive to manage the issues that stand in the way of gaining the full benefits of telework. We previously discussed motivation and leadership historical perspectives. During that discussion, we highlighted Latham's four leadership controversies. Some form of each of them may present obstacles to the full commitment to telework suggested above.

Leaders should:

- Understand the limitations of money as a motivator
- Manage the differences in intrinsic and extrinsic motivators and use this approach to your best advantage
- Understand the causal relationship between job satisfaction and job performance
- Recognize the importance of participation in decision making as a motivational technique for employees

Figure 6. Leadership Controversies

There are several ways to address these issues, and they all involve exhibiting strong leadership. Leaders should be transparent professionals who maintain regular communications with their team. Those communications must be both one-on-one and group conversations to get the best results. Regular meetings should be scheduled to encourage collaboration and reduce feelings of isolation. Leaders must ensure that there is a purpose for each meeting and must pay attention to good time management.

Perform regular maintenance checks. This is not micromanagement. This is checking with your team members to find out if they need something from you and to set expectations. This is also the way to foster accountability because the regular checks give members regular opportunities to share information and even get guidance on course corrections.

In short, there are five ways to support your team and provide the ideal environment for telework. First, effective communication that is regular and ensures feedback is essential. Second, provide emotional and social support to help your team members find the right work-life balance. Third, ensure that you have a process to assess productivity and promote engagement to take advantage of the improved performance we have shown telework can deliver. Fourth, leaders should provide the necessary technology for telework programs but should also monitor the industry to keep the technology at the cutting edge. Fifth, keep in mind that telework is recommended to improve health, safety, security, and employee happiness. Work to achieve those goals.

Remember that telework programs consider those who are working remotely AND those who are in the office. Making this work for all involved should be reflected in your strategic priorities. Your pre-COVID-19 strategic priorities may not have included telework, so make sure there is room for them now. There are remote learning success stories that may fit your organization's needs, buy you may need to do additional research to find the answers that fit your organization's situation.

Improve Communication

No discussion that covers ways to improve the work environment through trustworthiness, performance, and productivity can be considered complete without considering communication. Communication has been discussed throughout the book, but it deserves a special focus in this section dedicated to recommended approaches.

Figure 7. Communication Improvements

Focus communication on trust to build relationships that drive messages from sender to receiver promoting feedback at every opportunity. Expectation, Value, and Return (EVR) can be used to ensure your communications are totally focused. EVR uses three keys to demonstrate shared value (Brown Sr, 2016, p. 186). EVR was developed to explain social media participation and get buy-in, but it has evolved to mean the way in which multiple actors exchange information or something else of value, coming away with a shared value proposition. In this way, the receiver is shown the WIIFM – what's in it for me. They can then be motivated to continue the interaction because of an EXPECTATION of VALUE in RETURN. They get dynamic two-way or multi-way (teams) interaction, they get valued information exchange, and their contributions or ideas get recognition that matters to others. In this way EVR gives you the tools to effectively connect with others.

Once teams are communicating, leader commitment builds trust and avoids uncertainty. This is done by ensuring that you tailor the message to the receiver, that you tell the truth, that you seek shared value with the receiver, and that you stayed engaged until you get feedback to ensure the message is received in the way it was intended. Commitment allows the sender to collaborate and get involved in a meaningful way and builds confidence in the receiver. People respond favorably to this kind of interaction.

Vision is an end state for communication that assists in understanding the necessary current and future interaction needs and courses of actions. The leader's vision considers what is necessary for the team to continue efficient operations and translates that information into concrete, consistent messages to the team. Relationships developed by the leader in this way will endure in the short and long term and should assist with team building. Marshall Loeb and Stephen Kindel say vision comes from three places: experience, knowledge, and imagination (1999).

Experience lets you visualize from the way you live. Knowledge lets you visualize from what you've learned. Imagination springs from the randomness of life because it synthesizes knowledge and experience, but it's also connected to desire. By taking your life experience and factoring in all the possibilities and all the ways that you can see yourself and the world, your imagination allows you to grasp the possibility that waits just over the horizon. Luck and possibilities are intertwined because a change in luck can determine your possibilities. And possibility is the stuff of visions.

Teams must remember that good communication requires awareness. Everyone on the team shares a responsibility to connect, analyze the others in the interaction, and share information that matters. Everyone is also responsible to listen and find ways to determine if the information was received and seek feedback. Then the parties in the interaction assess the shared value and decide if the communication should continue. This is not always done, but it is good to keep this level of detail in mind to ensure you are sending something of value and getting value in return.

Communicating well requires engagement that makes sense of the way people connect. This approach finds ways to help communicators discover like-minded people and share valuable information with them. Senders are in search of unfettered trust where we put our lives and our communication needs in the hands of people we might not trust otherwise. We create social capital and exchange valuable content. This communication is valuable to people getting together, creating community, listening to each other, understanding the message, and providing feedback.

Engagement enhances communication by addressing the topics and challenges we face every day (Leinonen, Järvelä, & Häkkinen, 2005; Nardi & Whittaker, 2002). Senders must ensure that they do not overwhelm the receiver and cause communication meltdown that ends the conversation. The message and the environment must be managed to achieve the communication success. Verifying shared value in the ways described delivers dependable communication channels, coordinated messages, and valuable feedback.

FUTURE RESEARCH DIRECTIONS

A longitudinal research effort examining an asynchronous approach to teleworking and team cohesion would be a valuable next step to my research and the recommendations offered here. This study could address trust, empowerment, loyalty, commitment, and ownership to analyze their impacts on organizational operations. This kind of research could also evaluate the use of collaborative tools such as mobile apps, focusing on, for instance, desktop applications that are easily accessible regardless of the worker's location.

Future research could also examine factors that influence telework. These include the limitations of money as a motivator, intrinsic and extrinsic motivators, causal relationships between job satisfaction and job performance, and participative decision making. All these factors are at play, intentionally or unintentionally, when organizations are dealing with their work force in determining whether they work onsite or remotely.

CONCLUSION

Many communication theories make similar recommendations for communicators as shown below. These abilities are important to communicating effectively.

- Alleviate uncertainty
- Provide needed assistance throughout the communication activity
- Deal with interpersonal deception
- Adjust to communication partners who seek or avoid the issue at hand
- Protect privacy and control information
- Create and nurture long-term relationships

People build trust by sharing emotions to work on eliminating uncertainty through collaborative activities. Building trust is aided by shared value, common understanding, and deliberative conversations where there is ample give and take between the participants.

REFERENCES

Brown, M., Sr. (2011). *Social networking and individual performance: Examining predictors of participation* (Ph.D.). Old Dominion University, United States. Retrieved from http://proquest.umi.com/pqdweb?did=2355291551&Fmt=7&clientId=3505&RQT=309&VName=PQD

Brown, M. A. Sr. (2016). *Solutions for High-touch Communications in a High-tech World.* IGI Global.

Denzin, N. K. (2012). Triangulation 2.0. *Journal of Mixed Methods Research*, *6*(2), 80–88. doi:10.1177/1558689812437186

Leinonen, P., Järvelä, S., & Häkkinen, P. (2005). Conceptualizing the Awareness of Collaboration: A Qualitative Study of a Global Virtual Team. *Comput Supported Coop Work Computer Supported Cooperative Work*, *14*(4), 301–322. doi:10.100710606-005-9002-z

Loeb, M., & Kindel, S. (1999). *Leadership for Dummies.* IDG Books Worldwide, Inc.

McLean, R. (2020). *These companies plan to make working from home the new normal. As in forever*. CNN Business.

Nardi, B. A., & Whittaker, S. (2002). The place of face-to-face communication in distributed work. Distributed. *Work (Reading, Mass.)*, ▪▪▪, 83–110.

Reisner-Kollmann, I., & Aschauer, A. (n.d.). *Design and Implementation of Asynchronous Remote Support. Academic Press.*

Chapter 13
The Future

ABSTRACT

This book addresses understanding of and solutions to teleworking, trustworthiness, and performance issues. Overall, it suggests using a strategic approach that encourages participation and that is required to achieve, understand, and build buy-in for teleworking. The organizationally sanctioned program must exist. The use of LMX is beneficial in exploring the factors that contribute to motivating the target audience: employees. A culture of self-motivation is necessary to empower employees, but there must also be a culture of enforcement when needed. Finally, buy-in at all levels of the organizations is crucial to the success of a telework program. The parts of the strategic approach mentioned here will be enhanced with the resources provided in this book: how to develop leaders, motivating employees, increasing productivity, using EI, managing radical change, and learning from the research provided. Viewed through the lens of a management context, these components make the recommended strategic approach possible and can deliver an effective framework for results.

BACKGROUND

My great friend Leslie Krohn, who honored me by writing the preface to the book, exactly captures the challenge I faced with this project at the outset. "There are many issues to consider, many perspectives to address." Whether organizations and leaders want to deal with telework or not, it is on the minds of a large portion of their workforce. Interestingly, there are varying beliefs

DOI: 10.4018/978-1-7998-8950-2.ch013

about wanting a relief from working from home and getting back in touch with people, and about wanting to stay home and reduce costs and have more say in where they work. These are compelling issues that exist every day in part because of COVID but in part because of advances in technology and the discovery of how to eliminate or reduce brick and mortar costs.

Let us look at the issue of telework in a very basic way. Imagine you are the owner of a company that employs 10 people. You conducted a survey and 3 of your staff reported their productivity increased when they teleworked. Half of your staff reported that they favored telework. Half of your staff reported that they were job hunting and the top "want" on their list was work-life balance. Four members of your staff reported that they would change jobs if they could choose their work location at least part of the time. Would these telework numbers change your position on telework?

In much of my research, both quantitative and qualitative, I found that this type of information is not collected when telework decision are made. Of course, organizations must make financial and manpower decisions and there are considerations about whether the work can be done remotely. There is even the valid argument that in-person work situations allow a higher degree of feedback, visual cues, and spontaneity. However, would any of that be possible if your workforce goes elsewhere so they can telework? Also, can you be completely comfortable making decisions about telework without knowing the level at which people are committed to find a telework solution that improves their work-life balance.

One of the simplest ways to look at the issue is in terms of commute, but you must view it from the worker's perspective, not the leader's. I have endured the Washington, D.C., rush hour commute and the Hampton Roads Tunnel, Norfolk, Va., commute. Amid yet another 1-hour, 1-way drive to or from work, telework looks so attractive.

As we have discussed throughout, COVID forced the world into telework and people found old, new, and innovative ways to get the job done. Yes, businesses folded but many survived and some prospered. The world found a way to work from home and be efficient. Now, even if it was not peak efficiency, some hesitate or refuse to go back to the old way. There is a lot of talk about hybrid solutions that can work but using LMX Theory makes it simple. Do you know what work-life situation your current employees want? Do you want to keep them in your organization? You must know the answers to both, so that you can take the proper action. The action you take may be about telework, or promotions, or work assignments, but you must act.

Figure 1 is an overview of how we can take a long look at the data collected. Imagine that 3 in 10 or 4 in 10 or 5 in 10 of your workforce was in favor of doing something. Would you be in favor of it too? We will take an exact look at the numbers later in this chapter.

Figure 1. Overview of Surveys on Telework

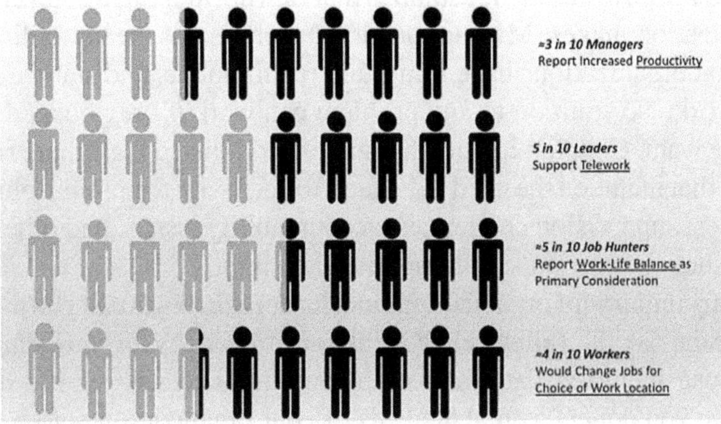

The chart above is an indication of the importance of leaders engaging with members – LMX. This engagement is important because I believe that finding innovative ways to use telework and let people work where they want to can improve the work environment and earn loyalty. This engagement must be a dialogue with feedback and continued interaction until the parties reach a shared understanding. You must revisit that shared understanding whenever there is uncertainty about its status.

The necessary relationships are created through regular communication that allows the leader to understand who their members are on and off the job. I remember I had a great supervisor who started each day with "What brings you to work today?" This really demonstrated that he was interested in what mattered to me. This kind of communication creates shared understanding that is so valuable in effective organizations. It's important to find out what workers want, what they like, what makes them tick, and incorporate that into the way you lead them. Sometimes you can't find a fit, but that too is a growth opportunity.

I have a running joke with someone who worked for me before. I always say, "I get you," to let that person know that I'm listening and I'm trying to maintain our shared understanding.

Engaging your team members and working to include their desires as part of your organizational goal, where possible, can bring success. This focus can provide great benefits in terms of enriched employees who are loyal and who want to stay with the organization.

Before we move on, let me establish that I am not judging whatever decision an organization makes. My support of telework is not meant to diminish or ignore that organizations have important requirements and standards for in-person work. No solution to any problem can work if only one side can get what they want. Chapter 2, Our Changing World, listed legitimate risks with telework that included the need to be face-to-face with the public, onboarding difficulties, supervision challenges, accountability issues, and other factors. These issues cannot and should not be taken lightly.

Now my inquiry for organizations and leaders becomes can you mitigate or eliminate the risks and allow telework at some frequency for some employees? Do you use memory, data, and employee input to answer the question? Also, have you done a formal analysis of your organization before and after COVID, and does that analysis include employee input? I have talked with a few organizations that analyzed the before and after with two things that I consider to be limitations. Either the analysis did not consider employee input, or employee input was not a significant part of the factors on which the decision was made.

My approach allows organizations to look at all factors and make informed decisions. It is beneficial whether organizations work though it on their own or contract out for expert evaluation, assistance, and implementation. I am sure that people's desire to telework and technological advances to make it easier and more productive will continue to grow. Organizations would do well to take advantage of those issues and create employee-friendly situations that do not harm the bottom line.

This inquiry began with a thirst for an understanding of the ways in which COVID-19 affected the world's workforce. As it forced us to quarantine and use telework to move the economy forward, our world of work was changed; maybe forever. So, what did we learn?

The questions were easy.

- What are the social and technical factors that are important for leaders when teleworking or other remote work situations are created or increased in response to a crisis?
- What tradeoffs are caused in telework in terms of trustworthiness, performance, and other factors?
- How can you change the minds of leaders and managers who are against teleworking?
- How can you improve teleworking so everyone can create trust and improve performance?
- Can there be an overarching strategy for addressing telework issues on a national or international scale?

This educational journey pursues many of those answers, but this is only a start. It is part of the world's new beginning in understanding the world of work. Using the data and analysis in this work demonstrates ways to achieve the necessary shared understanding that will allow leaders and members to openly discuss the challenges presented by teleworking. This journey has addressed impediments or obstacles that organizations could remove or reduce to enable members to accomplish the same amount of work they are currently doing in the office, but in a shorter duration of time while teleworking.

Figure 2. LinkedIn Telework Poll

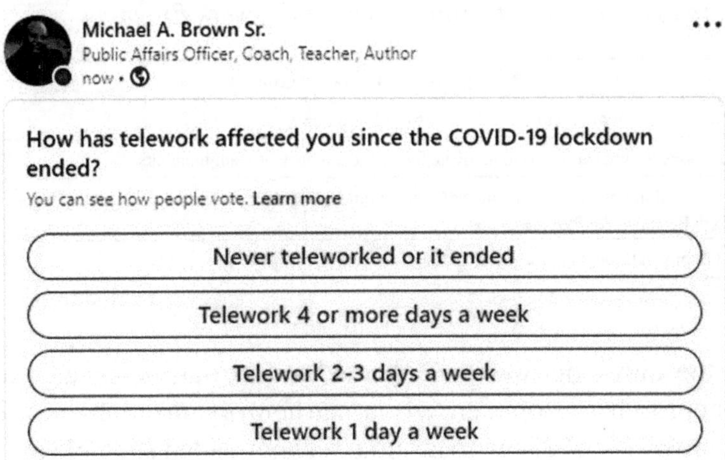

Focusing on continuing use of telework is relevant in our changing world. A three-day, informal LinkedIn poll (Table 1) demonstrated that 20% never teleworked, 59% teleworked 4 or more days a week, 12% teleworked 2-3 days a week, and 9% teleworked 1 day a week or less.

The goal of this work is to provide the most thorough evaluation to date of telework. The numbers above, and all the research cited in this work, demonstrate the widespread use of telework. Table 1 illustrates the formula for telework success.

The evaluation seeks to understand how to build strengths and mitigate weaknesses in trustworthiness and performance as they are applied in organizational development. The knowledge in this work is intended to address the teleworking perceptions of leaders and members in terms of promoting increased trustworthiness and improved performance. The action plan suggested below is the result of this book's learning journey.

Before reading the plan, we should keep in mind that three data points were used to help us identify what is required to set employees up for success. These three points also aid us to determine how leaders and managers can be persuaded that telework can be a viable solution leading to continued and increased productivity. We used these data points to focus our effort and attention on telework, trustworthiness, and performance. They are the Telework Act of 2010, a March 2021 Telework, Trustworthiness, and Telework Survey, and personal interviews.

Table 1. Strategic Approach to Build Effective Telework Programs

Effective Telework Programs
Improve or create a formal or organizationally sanctioned program
LMX that addresses the pros and cons to motivate the target audience of team members
Continuation of a culture of self-motivation and/or enforcement to ensure success (it is hoped that this culture already exists in the organization)
Development of buy in throughout the organization

Given the knowledge we have collected and the data points we reference, a strategic approach is recommended that can help organizations build effective telework programs. We now focus on a recommended strategic approach to improve teleworking. This is a plan that combines the analysis and conclusions from the previous chapters to arrive at a solution.

The strategic approach makes four assumptions. The first assumption is that organizations are in favor of telework at some level. The second assumption is that organizations will create formal telework programs to avoid the ad hoc ways that COVID-19 forced them to employ telework. The third assumption is that organizations will accept the use of LMX theory to guide the supervisor-employee interaction leading to efficient telework. The fourth assumption is that organizations will continue to use telework once the world has defeated COVID-19.

In Fiscal Year 2013, the General Services Administration (GSA) instituted open space configurations. In this approach, GSA increased the number of people sharing workstations in renewed teleworking and hoteling arrangements. This provided more locations where employees could "…to informally meet, gather, and exchange ideas; plug in and collaborate; or unplug and concentrate (Denison et al., 2014).

The suggested strategic approach encourages participation and identifies what is required to achieve, understand, and build buy-in for teleworking. The organizationally sanctioned program must exist. The use of LMX is beneficial in addressing the factors that contribute to motivating the target audience of team members. A culture of self-motivation is necessary to empower members, but there must also be a culture of enforcement when needed. Finally, buy-in at all levels of the organizations is crucial to the success of the telework program.

The parts of the strategic approach mentioned here will be enhanced with the resources provided in this book. We have covered the influence of COVID-19 that drove the world to maximum telework. We examined how to telework, the changes in our world, building trustworthiness, and improving performance. We reinforced all that knowledge with information about historical, theoretical, and best-practice information. We reviewed current research and recommended approaches for conducting effective telework programs. These things make the recommended strategic approach possible and can deliver outstanding results.

Improve or Create a Formal or Organizationally Sanctioned Program

A reasonable approach to teleworking should focus on schedule, communications, and goals to achieve effectiveness. Work with employees to set up a schedule that provides structure and adheres to core business hours when everyone can stay in contact. Stress regular breaks to achieve work-life balance and carefully manage the schedule of group meetings and consistent one-on-one talks between leaders and members. Keep pop-up meetings to a minimum in terms of frequency and length of time. Do this to reduce intrusions on the regular tempo of operations and afford people the maximum time to do assigned work.

Organizations can build good programs by leveraging good leadership and management practices, such as paying attention to personal and professional issues and adjusting as necessary, using e-leadership, and modeling best practices. E-leadership is the use of information technology to produce a desired change in attitudes, feelings, behavior, performance, or thinking.

The plan must be structured to deal with common issues like balancing family and work, LMX issues that involve trustworthiness, performance, and accountability, accepting changes and/or improvements in the way we work, and managing the ever-changing ways people communicate. If organizations and leaders do not pay attention to these issues, they will find reluctance or resistance to returning to the old way of doing things. For instance, as America recovers from COVID-19, we are seeing people who do not want to go back to working in an office or who just choose not to go back to work at all.

The plan must account for reasons that some leaders cite when resisting teleworking. Those reasons include, but are not limited to, the organization handles and/or produces classified materials, the organization must be interpersonally collaborative and interactive, workers need structure and supervision to be productive, and communication is more effective in person. We have discussed the counter argument to these obstacles to teleworking, but there must be open and honest discussions to address reluctance or resistance.

If organizations are invested in employee happiness and work-life balance, they should pay attention to the influence telework can have on employee retention, for instance. Research in 2007 revealed that 37% of employees would change jobs if they could find a new job that delivered an opportunity to work where they wanted to work even if their current job offered more incentives (Gallup, p. 149)." More than half of employees said they would seek a new job to get greater work-life balance.

According to a 2021 Gallup Panel report, 23% of workers would stay remote if given the option and 44% of workers prefer to continue working remotely (Saad & Hickman). The Gallup Panel is a research entity that examines, with quick turnaround of results, U.S. adults' opinions on a wide range of emerging and relevant issues. According to the panel website, Gallup "maintains demographic profiles of all Panel members, using this information to draw stratified samples or samples of low-incidence populations that are otherwise difficult to reach." Gallup is a multimode panel with about 100,000 members that offers a representative sample of all American households.

To increase the reality of this effort, I interviewed 13 people to get their views on teleworking. The recurring issues from those interviews can be helpful when creating or assessing a telework program. The issues are distractions, fatigue, accountability, communication, productivity, technology, coping, work hours, resources, and plan approaches. They can be used to improve employee engagement. Let me give you an overview of the things that workers talked about in those interviews.

Workers discussed how teleworking reduced distractions allowing them to pursue small goals and finish projects in one day. They also commented about how tiring or stressful it can be at the computer all day. This was balanced by comments about workers back in the office now having to take work home without overtime pay. There were discussions about personal accountability in addressing transportation issues of staying at home versus being in the office. There were discussions about leadership accountability in making sure the workplace is safe in our current situation of vaccinated and unvaccinated workers as we saw the COVID numbers spike back up in July and August 2021.

Communication is always important and there are indications from the interviews that there is work to be done whether employees are in the office or remote. Workers are concerned with isolation or inability to compete for promotions and awards, but there are also indications that organizations must have good methods to bring employees back to work to alleviate these issues. We can see in everyday news or social media about the strained conversations or negotiations between workers who have proved they can work from home and organizations that want them back in the office.

Workers feel they can be productive teleworking and they are, in many cases, not willing to come back to the office because "that's how it has always been." Many are willing to give up the job for an opportunity to work from home. This work has quoted several sources that show leaders who see increased productivity, but that does not seem to be creating exceptionally large movements to full or partial telework. But workers want to know they are trusted by their leadership to produce at acceptable levels so they can govern themselves, have flexible work arrangements, and manage their work-life balance. Some workers want to know that the technological improvements in meetings, office product generation software, and even time and attendance checks can lead to greater opportunities for telework.

Three quotes are important to understand the factor called "coping."

- *There are many good things about telework, including the ability to focus on certain aspects of work without many distractions. I also do not end up having to drive home from work late at night on dark, cold nights from the office.*
- *I do not have to deal with the daily 2- or 2.5-hour commute to and from work. I like the flexibility. I can sleep in for an extra hour every morning. I can focus better.*
- *What is good is that it is a time saver, in the fact that you do not have to worry about the commute. So, you get that time back.*

Some workers expressed concerns that when teleworking the workday starts too early and never ends, which is not the case when working in the office. Some reported that there is an implicit telework expectation that you should be always available. They stress the importance of setting boundaries that everyone must follow in the telework situation. Finally, people surveyed had an overall wish to have leadership consistency, telework training, and a telework agreement or plan at the outset to address some of the issues discussed here. One said, "I am excited about the future of teleworking; it is a win-win for both the organization and its employees. Organizational objectives can be realized while at the same time meeting the needs of employees." We will talk more about the needs of employees and the wishes of employers.

Now we move to another study, done by Upwork, which provides good rationale for moving beyond resistance and incorporating a sound telework plan (Ozimek, 2020, p. 5). The Upwork study shows optimism that productivity has increased and will continue to do so despite many responses about why remote work worked poorly. The survey reported that 32.2% of hiring managers reported an increase in productivity as opposed to only 22.5% who reported a decrease.

We should also keep in mind some of the data collected in the survey from Chapter 11. The results showed a great deal of support for teleworking in the survey population.

- Organizational support for teleworking ranged from "moderate" to "a great deal" for most survey participants

- Seventy-four percent of participants said their supervisor or boss believe they are putting in a full day while teleworking
- Participants were highly positive about supervisor or boss understanding of the challenge of working from home, with 78% reporting that their leadership was supportive
- Some participants point out the need for bosses to understand the issues of finishing work on time, time management, length of the workday, lack of connection to other members of the team, and people having to pay for their own work expenses while at home
- Participants also reported the importance of employee-centered concerns like work life balance, space constraints, lack of a quiet space to work, distractions, self-motivation, childcare issues, lack of belonging, lack of an end time for the workday, and difficult communications
- Still, most survey participants felt that their supervisor or boss cares about the challenge of working from home

The details are relevant for our examination because there was more than a fair amount of leadership participants in the survey. In fact, 77 of the 132 respondents were in some type of leadership position: president/CEO/etc., upper management, mid-level management, and supervisor. While the results of this survey cannot be generalized to an entire population, a convenience sample allowed gathering data from an exceptionally large population. This method is helpful when the researcher's time, workforce, or resources are limited. The method was useful in this case to generate and analyze results that can be later used to create entire population generalizations. This was a first attempt by the researchers in an area of inquiry, and it is hoped that there will be more studies like it in the future. This effort is an example of how other research projects can explore and test existing theories as they apply to teleworking, trustworthiness, and performance.

LMX That Addresses the Pros and Cons to Motivate the Target Audience of Team Members

LMX theory explains how leadership affects members, teams, and organizations by creating and nurturing leader-member relationships. The leader should treat each member in a unique way and build teams based on the knowledge gained in this manner. There are some criticisms of this approach because the work-related attitudes and behaviors tend to depend so strongly on how people are treated by their leader. On the positive side, the relationships that leaders create can contribute to good EI. This is because LMX theory's central concept focuses on the processes that occur when leaders and members benefit from mature relationships or partnerships. LMX also allows a special focus on determining the members' primary abilities and skills.

Another important consideration is to pay attention to what is really happening when engaging with members. For instance, one of the surveys quoted earlier in this book stated that more than 60 percent of the employees surveyed said they preferred immediate feedback, but less than 25 percent said they received it (Stillman, 2012). This reference showed us the differing viewpoints of leaders and members in terms of how information is shared. This kind of difficulty must be resolved to avoid communication or engagement disconnects that hinder work relationships and business operations.

To avoid this kind of disconnect, leaders need to perform maintenance, which requires applying a balanced management approach, allowing creativity, making regular level checks, and evaluating effectively. It is important to step back from the action and observe the group at work. Getting a wider view can reveal some considerations that would not otherwise come to light.

Team members have as much responsibility for success as leaders. They should support the organization by committing to goals and objectives. Their great contributions include understanding the stated agenda and working within their roles. They should support the team by accomplishing tasks and by pitching in to help coworkers when their own work is done, leading to great personal and team performance. This is personal accountability, and it is invaluable to effective teams.

Team members own their work, which is a way of describing acceptance of responsibility. They must also own the benefits of success and the penalties of failure. Great team members are accountable and demand to be personally responsible for the outcome.

All of this means leaders can prosper by being calm when there is chaos, deliberate when there is doubt, and caring when there is trouble. Make sure your team pursues opportunities and accepts challenges.

Continuation of a Culture of Self-Motivation and/or Enforcement to Ensure Success

Let us hope that this culture already exists in the organization. Even if it does, building or improving trust in teleworking by understanding personal versus organizational views is a constant necessity. By getting everyone involved in the discussion we can make sure that people are willing to admit mistakes, acknowledge weaknesses, applaud strengths, and lean on each other for help. Trustworthiness now has a chance to increase. Trusting can be hard because everyone might have to give up a little bit of themselves to allow trust to grow. People might have to trust someone early and without any guarantee that things will work out.

A quality environment relies on being good in five areas: people, purpose, support, contributions, and appreciation. Leaders should manage the makeup of their team and nurture relationships. The organization must promote a one team, one purpose approach where everyone is on a singular mission to perform at a high level. Trustworthiness and accountability are needed to provide and ensure proper support throughout the organization. This allows goal achievement. When the team works together to build social capital the organization profits. The sum of the parts is important. Appreciation is about recognition and reward. Whether it is on-the-spot or an annual award, people are motivated by "thank you."

Motivation can be situational, requiring that leaders make sound judgements based on a good understanding of human interaction. We have discussed many types of interactions in this examination. It is important to weigh the interests of the participants and make collaborative decisions whenever possible.

Everyone's survival and wellbeing and dictate the way motivation processes operate. This is about fulfilling people's needs. People must understand their environment and leadership can help in that regard. Leaders must understand how people's needs interrelate and make sense of the motivational effort. The ever-evolving interest in individual differences must go together with continuing examination of and attention to individual and organizational needs.

Development of Buy in Throughout the Organization

Telework can deliver many organizational benefits. The literature reviewed in this text, combined with surveys, tells us that telework can increase the level of member commitment. Increasing the flexibility and convenience of telework can also have positive effects on member commitment. Also, if members are happy with the ability to telework and balance family situations and work with innovations like work from home, work at regional satellite facilities, or flexible commuting strategies, they may exhibit increased loyalty to the organization (Alamillo, 2020; Beauregard et al., 2019; Marx et al., 2021; Ravalet & Rérat, 2019).

Determining what matters to members in terms of work-life balance and using that information to enrich their job through telework enhances the value of the position. Job enrichment improves the fit between the worker and the organization, showing the worker the level at which the organization cares about them. Job enrichment through telework can lead to happy employees who can control their own actions and work situation.

Leaders can achieve job enrichment through telework success by focusing on four themes:

1. Frequent teleworkers have a high degree of feelings of isolation
2. Some teleworkers feel they are forgotten or dismissed in terms of operations
3. Teleworkers may have belonging issues related to the isolation of the practice
4. E-leaders must provide active, mutual, continuous communication through socializing activities to enhance cohesion and feelings of togetherness (Even, 2020, pp. 11-12; Lilian, 2014)

Leaders should foster shared roles and identities and use training that focuses on best practices and collaboration with members to achieve the best results. Through the personal interviews in Chapter 2, we learned about the commonalities of thought related to telework brought on by COVID-19: distractions, fatigue, accountability, communication, productivity, technology, coping, work hours, resources, and plan approaches.

We should also keep in mind some of the data collected in the survey from Chapter 11. The results showed a great deal of support for teleworking in the survey population.

- Organizational support for teleworking ranged from "moderate" to "a great deal" for most survey participants
- Seventy-four percent of participants said their supervisor or boss believe they are putting in a full day while teleworking
- Participants were highly positive about supervisor or boss understanding of the challenge of working from home, with 78% reporting that their leadership was supportive
- Some participants point out the need for bosses to understand the issues of finishing work on time, time management, length of the workday,

lack of connection to other members of the team, and people having to pay for their own work expenses while at home

- Participants also reported the importance of employee-centered concerns like work life balance, space constraints, lack of a quiet space to work, distractions, self-motivation, childcare issues, lack of belonging, lack of an end time for the workday, and difficult communications
- Still, most survey participants felt that their supervisor or boss cares about the challenge of working from home

The details are relevant for our examination because there was good involvement of leadership in the survey. In fact, 58% were in some type of leadership position: president/CEO/etc., upper management, mid-level management, and supervisor.

FUTURE RESEARCH DIRECTIONS

A new version of the qualitative survey featuring interviews should be expanded. The population should include the views of workers, leaders/supervisors, and CEOs or top-level executives to address the disconnect that is indicated in this work in terms of how each group feels about other groups' interest in and management of work life balance and employee satisfaction. At every step of the current analysis, a lack of shared understanding was indicated at some level.

Also, a longitudinal study of trustworthiness and performance comparing onsite and remote workers would add great value to this area of inquiry. Employer-employee expectations and outcomes are critical issues for discovery.

CONCLUSION

The information gained from the interviews can help us reinforce what we know, discover what we do not know, and identify what we should ask questions about. We will call this approach, "Ideas and Actions" (Table 2) to focus attention on the ways in which people think about teleworking, both positively and negatively.

- **Reinforce:** Treat telework as a team activity and let all the members participate in developing or improving the organization's policy.

Foster confidence and set a path to success by ensuring that everyone understands how the telework policy will affect their situation.

Table 2. Ideas and Actions

Idea	Action
Reinforce	Get in touch with what we know about our current experience.
Discover	Understand the issues that leaders and members face and start the conversation.
Identify	Find new and better ways to be productive.

As organizations move to telework, their members demonstrate higher engagement levels. Some employers report that they are experiencing positive impacts on job satisfaction and loyalty. Research also shows that teleworkers are less likely to leave their current organization than non-teleworkers.

- **Discover:** Find best ways to adjust to the organization's new team dynamics. Some organizations designate office spaces where people can take any available desk space, allowing flexibility based on who is working on-site on any given day. Establishing core hours to get the maximum numbers of your staff together at every opportunity will help. This would be an ideal time for meetings.

Find the best way to communicate with your team. If organizations deemphasize how long it takes for a member to answer an email, it reduces stress for both sides. Leaders can send email when members might be sleeping, and members can determine the best time to answer the email. Regular check-ins throughout the week can be used to report status and ask questions.

- **Identify:** One good example of improvements in teleworking is a two-sentence policy announced in Summer 2020 by Siemens, one of the largest companies in the world headquartered in Germany with more than 380,000 employees (https://www.inc.com/justin-bariso/this-companys-new-2-sentence-remote-work-policy-is-best-ive-ever-heard.html). The company announced that it was working a new normal corporate culture by allowing all employees to work from wherever they want for two or three days a week.

Roland Busch, the deputy CEO and labor director of Siemens, wrote on Twitter "...The coronavirus crisis has triggered a surge in digitalization. We have always had mobile working at Siemens, but now we are taking it a step further. The basis for this forward-looking working model is further development of our corporate culture. These changes will also be associated with a different leadership style, one that focuses on outcomes rather than on time spent at the office." See the press release for the company policy: https://press.siemens.com/global/en/pressrelease/siemens-establish-mobile-working-core-component-new-normal.

REFERENCES

Alamillo, J. (2020). *Teleworking Benefits for Los Angeles County Employees*. California State University.

Alderfer, C. P. (1969). An empirical test of a new theory of human needs. *Organizational Behavior and Human Performance*, *4*(2), 142–175. doi:10.1016/0030-5073(69)90004-X

Analytics, G. W. (2013). *The Bottom Line on Telework*. Academic Press.

Atkinson, J. W. (1964). *An Introduction to Motivation*. Van Nostrand.

Avolio, B. J., Kahai, S., & Dodge, G. E. (2000). E-leadership: Implications for theory, research, and practice. *The Leadership Quarterly*, *11*(4), 615–668. doi:10.1016/S1048-9843(00)00062-X

Bachmann, R. (2001). Trust, power and control in trans-organizational relations. *Organization Studies*, *22*(2), 337–365. doi:10.1177/0170840601222007

Bachmann, R., Knights, D., & Sydow, J. (2001). Special Issue: Trust and control in organizational relations. *Organization Studies*, *22*(2). Advance online publication. doi:10.1177/0170840601222007

Bandura, A. (1969). *Principles of behavior modification*. Holt, Rinehart and Winston.

Bandura, A. (1977a). *Social Learning Theory*. Prentice-Hall.

Bandura, A. (1986). Social foundations of thought and action. Academic Press.

Bates, C. (2016). A methodology study of Hersey and Blanchard situational leadership theory. *Int J Adv Eng Technol Manage Appl Sci*, *3*(11), 42–48.

Beauregard, T. A., Basile, K. A., & Canonico, E. (2019). *Telework: Outcomes and facilitators for employees*. Academic Press.

Becerra, M., & Gupta, A. K. (2003). Perceived trustworthiness within the organization: The moderating impact of communication frequency on trustor and trustee effects. *Organization Science*, *14*(1), 32–44. doi:10.1287/orsc.14.1.32.12815

Belzunegui-Eraso, A., & Erro-Garcés, A. (2020). Teleworking in the Context of the Covid-19 Crisis. *Sustainability*, *12*(9), 3662. doi:10.3390u12093662

Berman, E. M., & West, J. P. (2008). Managing Emotional Intelligence in U.S. Cities: A Study of Social Skills among Public Managers. *Public Administration Review*, *68*(4), 742–758. doi:10.1111/j.1540-6210.2008.00912.x

Blenko, M. W., Mankins, M. C., & Rogers, P. (2010). *Decide & deliver: 5 steps to breakthrough performance in your organization*. Harvard Business Press.

Brayfield, A. H., & Crockett, W. H. (1955). Employee attitudes and employee performance. *Psychological Bulletin*, *52*(5), 396–424. doi:10.1037/h0045899 PMID:13266929

Brown, C., Smith, P. R., Arduengo, N., & Taylor, M. (2016). Trusting telework in the federal government. *Qualitative Report*, *21*, 87.

Brown, M., Sr. (2011). *Social networking and individual performance: Examining predictors of participation* (Ph.D.). Old Dominion University. Retrieved from http://proquest.umi.com/pqdweb?did=2355291551&Fmt=7&clientId=3505&RQT=309&VName=PQD

Brown, M. A. Sr. (2016). *Solutions for High-touch Communications in a High-tech World*. IGI Global.

Brown, M. A. Sr. (2017a). *Solutions for High-Touch Communications in a High-Tech World*. IGI Global. doi:10.4018/978-1-5225-1897-6

Brown, M. A. Sr. (2017b). *Motivationally Intelligent Leadership: Emerging Research and Opportunities: Emerging Research and Opportunities*. IGI Global.

Bughin, J. R., & Cincera, M. (2020). *FOG and teleworking: Some labor economics of covid-19*. Academic Press.

Caillier, J. G. (2012). The Impact of Teleworking on Work Motivation in a U.S. Federal Government Agency. *American Review of Public Administration, 42*(4), 461–480. doi:10.1177/0275074011409394

Campbell, J. P., Dunnette, M. D., Lawler, E. E. III, & Weick, K. E. Jr. (1970). *Managerial Behavior, Performance and Effectiveness*. McGraw-Hill.

Cascio, W. F. (2000). Managing a virtual workplace. *The Academy of Management Perspectives, 14*(3), 81–90. doi:10.5465/ame.2000.4468068

Caudron, S. (1999). The Hard Case for Soft Skills. *Workforce, 78*(7), 60–66.

Chen, C. C., Peng, M. W., & Saparito, P. A. (2002). Individualism, Collectivism, and Opportunism: A Cultural Perspective on Transaction Cost Economics. *Journal of Management, 28*(4), 567–583. doi:10.1177/014920630202800405

Cherniss, C., & Goleman, D. (2001). *The Emotionally Intelligence Workplace: How to Select for, Measure, and Improve Emotional Intelligence in Individuals, Groups, and Organizations*. San Francisco: Jossey-Bass.

Choudhury, P., Foroughi, C., & Larson, B. Z. (2020). Work-from-Anywhere: The Productivity Effects of Geographic Flexibility. *Academy of Management Proceedings, 2020*(1), 21199. doi:10.5465/AMBPP.2020.225

Coch, L., & French, J. R. P. Jr. (1948). Overcoming resistance to change. *Human Relations, 1*(4), 512–532. doi:10.1177/001872674800100408

Collins, J. C. (2009). *Good to great: why some companies make the leap ... and others don't*. Collins.

Contreras, F., Baykal, E., & Abid, G. (2020). E-Leadership and Teleworking in Times of COVID-19 and Beyond: What We Know and Where Do We Go. *Frontiers in Psychology, 11*(3484), 590271. Advance online publication. doi:10.3389/fpsyg.2020.590271 PMID:33362656

Cook, J., DeMarco, J., Doherty, W., & Jones, Y. (2013). OPM's 2012 Telework Report Shows Vast Opportunities for Improvement. *Public Management, 42*(4), 13.

Cooper, R. K. (1997). Applying Emotional Intelligence in the Workplace. *Training & Development, 51*(12), 31–38.

Corman, R. (1999). *Glory: photographs of athletes*. Morrow.

Dansereau, F. Jr, Graen, G., & Haga, W. J. (1975). A vertical dyad linkage approach to leadership within formal organizations: A longitudinal investigation of the role making process. *Organizational Behavior and Human Performance*, *13*(1), 46–78. doi:10.1016/0030-5073(75)90005-7

Day, F. C., & Burbach, M. E. (2015). Does organization sector matter in leading teleworker teams? A comparative case study. *International Journal of Business Research and Development*, *3*(4). Advance online publication. doi:10.24102/ijbrd.v3i4.547

de Vries, H., Tummers, L., & Bekkers, V. (2019). The Benefits of Teleworking in the Public Sector: Reality or Rhetoric? *Review of Public Personnel Administration*, *39*(4), 570–593. doi:10.1177/0734371X18760124

Dearborn, K. (2002). Studies in Emotional Intelligence Redefine Our Approach to Leadership Development. *Public Personnel Management*, *31*(4), 523–530. doi:10.1177/009102600203100408

Denison, M. B., Banks, D., Bosley, E., Hyduke, B., James, K., Lefkowitz, E., ... Prochaska, G. (2014). Effective engagement strategies for an increasingly dispersed workforce. *Public Management*, *43*(3), 62.

Denzin, N. K. (2012). Triangulation 2.0. *Journal of Mixed Methods Research*, *6*(2), 80–88. doi:10.1177/1558689812437186

Dirks, K. T., & Ferrin, D. L. (2001). The role of trust in organizational settings. *Organization Science*, *12*(4), 450–467. doi:10.1287/orsc.12.4.450.10640

Driver, J., & Aalst, M. v. (2010). *You say more than you think: the 7-day plan for using the new body language to get what you want*. Crown Publishers.

Druskat, U., & Wolff, S. (2001). Building the Emotional Intelligence of Groups. *Harvard Business Review*, *79*(3), 81–90. PMID:11246926

Erdogan, B., & Bauer, T. N. (2015). Leader–Member Exchange Theory. In J. D. Wright (Ed.), *International Encyclopedia of the Social & Behavioral Sciences* (2nd ed., pp. 641–647). Elsevier. doi:10.1016/B978-0-08-097086-8.22010-2

Evan, M., & Berman, J. P. W. (2008). Managing Emotional Intelligence in U.S. Cities: A Study of Social Skills among Public Managers. *Public Administration Review*, *68*(4), 742–758. doi:10.1111/j.1540-6210.2008.00912.x

EvenA. (2020). The Evolution of Work: Best Practices for Avoiding Social and Organizational Isolation in Telework Employees. *Available at* SSRN 3543122. doi:10.2139/ssrn.3543122

Ferrin, D. L., & Dirks, K. T. (2003). The use of rewards to increase and decrease trust: Mediating processes and differential effects. *Organization Science*, *14*(1), 18–31. doi:10.1287/orsc.14.1.18.12809

Ferrin, D. L., Dirks, K. T., & Shah, P. P. (2006). Direct and indirect effects of third-party relationships on interpersonal trust. *The Journal of Applied Psychology*, *91*(4), 870–883. doi:10.1037/0021-9010.91.4.870 PMID:16834511

Frank Messina, E. D. (2011). *Two-And-A-Half Minutes To "Effective"*. Daily Thoughts for Improving Your Effectiveness in the Areas of Communications, Coaching, and Delegation.

Frayne, C. A., & Latham, G. P. (1987). Application of social learning theory to employee self-management of attendance. *The Journal of Applied Psychology*, *72*(3), 387–392. doi:10.1037/0021-9010.72.3.387

Galford, R. M., & Drapeau, A. S. (2003). The Enemies of Trust. *Harvard Business Review*. Retrieved from https://hbr.org/2003/02/the-enemies-of-trust

Gambetta, D. (1988a). *Trust: making and breaking cooperative relations*. B. Blackwell.

Gambetta, D. (1988b). *Trust: Making and breaking cooperative relations*. Academic Press.

Ghiselli, E. E., & Brown, C. W. (1948). *Personnel and industrial psychology*. Academic Press.

Gilbreth, F. B., & Gilbreth, L. M. (1917). *Applied motion study: A collection of papers on the efficient method to industrial preparedness*. Sturgis & Walton Company.

Goldsmith, S., & Eggers, W. D. (2004). *Governing by Network: The New Shape of the Public Sector*. Washington, DC: Brookings Institute Press.

Goldstein, A. P., & Sorcher, M. (1974). *Changing Supervisory Behavior*. Pergammon.

Goleman, D. (1995). *Emotional Intelligence*. Bantam.

Goleman, D. (Ed.). (2001). *The Emotionally Intelligent Workplace* (Vol. 27-44). Jossey-Bass.

Goleman, D. (2006). *Social Intelligence*. Bantam.

Gowing, M. K. (Ed.). (2001). *The Emotionally Intelligent Workplace*. Jossey-Bass.

Graen, G. B., & Uhl-Bien, M. (1995). Relationship-based approach to leadership: Development of leader-member exchange (LMX) theory of leadership over 25 years: Applying a multi-level multi-domain perspective. *The Leadership Quarterly*, *6*(2), 219–247. doi:10.1016/1048-9843(95)90036-5

Greer, T. W., & Payne, S. C. (2014). Overcoming telework challenges: Outcomes of successful telework strategies. *The Psychologist Manager Journal*, *17*(2), 87–111. doi:10.1037/mgr0000014

Gursakal, N., Oguzlar, A., Aydin, Z. B., & Tuzunturk, S. (2009). Measuring trust in an intra-organisational context using Social Network Analysis. *International Journal of Management and Enterprise Development*, *6*(4), 494–512. doi:10.1504/IJMED.2009.024238

Hatala, J. P., & Fleming, P. R. (2007). Making Transfer Climate Visible: Utilizing Social Network Analysis to Facilitate the Transfer of Training. *Human Resource Development Review*, *6*(1), 33–63. doi:10.1177/1534484306297116

Henderson, D., Wayne, S., Shore, L., Bommer, W., & Tetrick, L. (2008). Leader-Member Exchange, Differentiation, and Psychological Contract Fulfillment: A Multilevel Examination. *The Journal of Applied Psychology*, *93*(6), 1208–1219. doi:10.1037/a0012678 PMID:19025243

Herzberg, F. (1966). *Work and the nature of man*. World Pub. Co.

Hogan, R., & Hogan, J. (2001). Assessing leadership: A view from the dark side. *International Journal of Selection and Assessment*, *9*(1-2), 40–51. doi:10.1111/1468-2389.00162

Hood, C., & Lodge, M. (2004). Competency, Bureaucracy, and Public Management Reform: A Competency Analysis. *Governance: An International Journal of Policy, Administration and Institutions*, *17*(3), 313–333. doi:10.1111/j.0952-1895.2004.00248.x

Hu, J., & Liden, R. (2013). Relative Leader–Member Exchange Within Team Contexts: How and when Social Comparison Impacts Individual Effectiveness. *Personnel Psychology*, *66*(1), 127–172. Advance online publication. doi:10.1111/peps.12008

Huse, E. F., & Bowditch, J. L. (1977). *Behavior in Organizations: A Systems Approach to Managing*. Addison-Wesley.

Huy, Q. N. (1999). Emotional Capability, Emotional Intelligence, and Radical Change. *Academy of Management Review*, *24*(2), 325–345. doi:10.5465/amr.1999.1893939

Jackson, K. S., Wilson, D., & Borden, D. (2020). Telework: Achievements and Blunders. *Journal of Government Financial Management*, *69*(1), 58–59.

Jacobs, R. L. (Ed.). (2001). *The Emotionally Intelligent Workplace*. Jossey-Bass.

James, W. (1892). *Psychology. Academic Press.*

James, W. (2007). *The principles of psychology* (Vol. 1). Cosimo, Inc.

Janse, B. (2019). Leader-Member Exchange Theory (LMX). *Toolshero*. Retrieved from Retrieved May 11,2021: https://www.toolshero.com/management/leader-member-exchange-theory-lmx/

Kaplan, A. M., & Haenlein, M. (2010). Users of the world, unite! The challenges and opportunities of Social Media. *Business Horizons*, *53*(1), 59–68. doi:10.1016/j.bushor.2009.09.003

Kast, E. F., & Rosenzweig, J. E. (1979). *Organization and Management: A Systems Approach*. McGraw-Hill.

Kim, D. H. (1993). The link between individual learning and organizational learning. *Sloan Management Review*, *35*(Fall), 379–500.

Koestenbaum, P. (1991). *Leadership: the inner side of greatness: a philosophy for leaders*. Jossey-Bass.

Korman, A. K. (1974). *The Psychology of Motivation*. Prentice-Hall.

Kramer, R. M. (1996). *Trust in organizations: Frontiers of theory and research*. Sage Publications.

Kramer, R. M. (1999). Trust and distrust in organizations: Emerging perspectives, enduring questions. *Annual Review of Psychology*, *50*(1), 569–598. doi:10.1146/annurev.psych.50.1.569 PMID:15012464

Lane, C., & Bachmann, R. (1998). *Trust within and between organizations: Conceptual issues and empirical applications*. Oxford University Press.

Latham, G. P. (2012). Work motivation: History, theory, research, and practice. *Sage (Atlanta, Ga.)*. Advance online publication. doi:10.4135/9781506335520

Lawler, E. J., Thye, S. R., & Yoon, J. (2000). Emotion and Group Cohesion in Productive Exchange 1. *American Journal of Sociology*, *106*(3), 616–657. doi:10.1086/318965

Leinonen, P., Järvelä, S., & Häkkinen, P. (2005). Conceptualizing the Awareness of Collaboration: A Qualitative Study of a Global Virtual Team. *Comput Supported Coop Work Computer Supported Cooperative Work*, *14*(4), 301–322. doi:10.100710606-005-9002-z

Lewicki, R. J., & Bunker, B. B. (1995). Trust in relationships. *Administrative Science Quarterly*, *5*(1), 583–601.

Lewin, K. (1942). *Field theory and learning*. Academic Press.

Lewin, K. (1951). *Field Theory in Social Science*. Harper and Row.

Light, P. C. (2005). *The Four Pillars of High Performance: How Robust Organizations Achieve Extraordinary Results*. McGraw-Hill.

Likert, R. (1961). *New patterns of management*. Academic Press.

Lilian, S. C. (2014). Virtual teams: Opportunities and challenges for e-leaders. *Procedia: Social and Behavioral Sciences*, *110*, 1251–1261. doi:10.1016/j.sbspro.2013.12.972

Locke, E. A. (1965a). Interaction of ability and motivation in performance. *Perceptual and Motor Skills*, *21*(3), 719–725. doi:10.2466/pms.1965.21.3.719 PMID:5855908

Locke, E. A. (1965b). The relationship of task success to task liking and satisfaction. *The Journal of Applied Psychology*, *49*(5), 379–385. doi:10.1037/h0022520 PMID:5828990

Locke, E. A. (1968). Toward a theory of task motivation and incentives. *Organizational Behavior and Human Performance*, *3*(2), 157–189. doi:10.1016/0030-5073(68)90004-4

Locke, E. A. (1991). The motivation sequence, the motivation hub, and the motivation core. *Organizational Behavior and Human Decision Processes*, *50*(2), 288–299. doi:10.1016/0749-5978(91)90023-M

Loeb, M., & Kindel, S. (1999). *Leadership for Dummies*. IDG Books Worldwide, Inc.

Luhmann, N. (1988). Familiarity, confidence, trust: Problems and alternatives. In D. Gambetta (Ed.), *Trust: Making and breaking cooperative relations*. Basil Blackwell.

Luthans, F. (1977). *Organizational Behavior*. McGraw-Hill.

Macaleer, W. D., & Shannon, J. B. (2002). Emotional Intelligence: How Does it Affect Leadership? *Employment Relations Today*, *29*(3), 9–19. doi:10.1002/ert.10047

Mace, C. A. (1935). *Incentives. Some Experimental Studies*. Academic Press.

Maier, N. R. F. (1949). *Frustration: The study of behavior without a goal*. McGraw-Hill New York.

Manz, C. C., & Sims, H. P. Jr. (1981). Vicarious Learning: The Influence of Modeling on Organizational Behavior. *Academy of Management Review*, *6*(1), 105–113. doi:10.5465/amr.1981.4288021

Marx, C. K., Reimann, M., & Diewald, M. (2021). Do Work–Life Measures Really Matter? The Impact of Flexible Working Hours and Home-Based Teleworking in Preventing Voluntary Employee Exits. *Social Sciences*, *10*(1), 9. doi:10.3390ocsci10010009

Maslow, A. H. (1943). A theory of human motivation. *Psychological Review*, *50*(4), 370–396. doi:10.1037/h0054346

Maslow, A. H. (1970). *Motivation and personality*. Harper & Row.

Mayo, E., Follett, M. P., & McGregor, D. (1949). *Organization theory*. Penguine Education.

McAllister, D. J., Lewicki, R. J., & Chaturvedi, S. (2006). Trust in developing relationships: from theory to measurement. *Academy of Management Proceedings*. 10.5465/ambpp.2006.22897235

McClelland, D. C. (1961). *The Achieving Society*. Van Nostrand. doi:10.1037/14359-000

McEvily, B., Perrone, V., & Zaheer, A. (2003). Introduction to the special issue on trust in an organizational context. *Organization Science*, *14*(1), 1–4. doi:10.1287/orsc.14.1.1.12812

McEvily, B., Perrone, V., & Zaheer, A. (2003). Trust as an organizing principle. *Organization Science*, *14*(1), 91–103. doi:10.1287/orsc.14.1.91.12814

McGregor, D. (1960). Theory X and theory Y. *Organization Theory*, *358*(1), 374.

McLean, R. (2020). *These companies plan to make working from home the new normal. As in forever.* CNN Business.

Miao, C., Humphrey, R. H., & Qian, S. (2016). Leader emotional intelligence and subordinate job satisfaction: A meta-analysis of main, mediator, and moderator effects. *Personality and Individual Differences*, *102*, 13–24. doi:10.1016/j.paid.2016.06.056

Miner, J. (2005). Essential theories of motivation and leadership. *Organizational Behavior*, 1-25.

Miner, J. B. (1984). The validity and usefulness of theories in an emerging organizational science. *Academy of Management Review*, *9*(2), 296–306. doi:10.5465/amr.1984.4277659

Miner, J. B. (2005). *Organizational Behavior 1: Essential Theories of Motivation and Leadership*. M.E. Sharpe.

Miner, J. B. (2015). *Organizational behavior 3*. Routledge.

Mitchell, T. R. (1982). Motivation: New Directions for Theory, Research, and Practice. *Academy of Management Review*, *7*(1), 80–88. doi:10.5465/amr.1982.4285467

Muchinsky, P. M. (1977). A Comparison of within- and Across-Subjects Analyses of the Expectancy-Valence Model for Predicting Effort. *Academy of Management Journal*, *20*(1), 154–158.

Münsterberg, H. (1915). Psychology, general and applied. D. Appleton. doi:10.1037/11627-000

Nakrošienė, A., Bučiūnienė, I., & Goštautaitė, B. (2019). Working from home: Characteristics and outcomes of telework. *International Journal of Manpower*, *40*(1), 87–101. doi:10.1108/IJM-07-2017-0172

Nardi, B. A., & Whittaker, S. (2002). The place of face-to-face communication in distributed work. *Distributed Work*, 83-110.

NCHS. (2001). First marriage dissolution, divorce, and remarriage. Academic Press.

Newell, S., & Swan, J. (2000). Trust and inter-organizational networking. *Human Relations*, *53*(10), 1287–1328. doi:10.1177/a014106

O'Keeffe, S. W. (2008). Shifting federal telework into drive. *Public Management*, *37*(1), 47.

O'Reilly, C. A. III. (1991). Organizational behavior: Where we've been, where we're going. *Annual Review of Psychology*, *42*(1), 427–458. doi:10.1146/annurev.ps.42.020191.002235 PMID:19090761

Oldham, G. R., Hackman, J. R., & Pearce, J. L. (1976). Conditions under which employees respond positively to enriched work. *The Journal of Applied Psychology*, *61*(4), 395–403. doi:10.1037/0021-9010.61.4.395

OzimekA. (2020). The future of remote work. *Available at* SSRN 3638597.

Park, S., & Cho, Y. (2020). Does telework status affect the behavior and perception of supervisors? Examining task behavior and perception in the telework context. *International Journal of Human Resource Management*, 1–26. doi:10.1080/09585192.2020.1777183

Pinder, C. C. (1984). *Work motivation: Theory, issues, and applications*. Scott Foresman & Company.

Porter, L. W. (1961). A study of perceived need satisfactions in bottom and middle management jobs. *The Journal of Applied Psychology*, *45*(1), 1–10. doi:10.1037/h0043121

Preno, G. (2020). *Long-term effects of teleworking during Covid-19 quarantine*. California State University.

Rainisch, G., Undurraga, E. A., & Chowell, G. (2020). A dynamic modeling tool for estimating healthcare demand from the COVID19 epidemic and evaluating population-wide interventions. *International Journal of Infectious Diseases*, *96*, 376–383. doi:10.1016/j.ijid.2020.05.043 PMID:32425631

Ravalet, E., & Rérat, P. (2019). Teleworking: Decreasing mobility or increasing tolerance of commuting distances? *Built Environment*, *45*(4), 582–602. doi:10.2148/benv.45.4.582

Rawlins, C. (1992). *Introduction to management*. HarperCollins Publishers.

Rezvani, A., Chang, A., Wiewiora, A., Ashkanasy, N. M., Jordan, P. J., & Zolin, R. (2016). Manager emotional intelligence and project success: The mediating role of job satisfaction and trust. *International Journal of Project Management*, *34*(7), 1112–1122. doi:10.1016/j.ijproman.2016.05.012

Rice, R. E. (1992). Task Analyzability, Use of New Media, and Effectiveness: A Multi-Site Exploration of Media Richness. *Organization Science*, *3*(4), 475–500. doi:10.1287/orsc.3.4.475

Roberts, K. H., & O'Reilly, C. A. III. (1973). *Some problems in measuring organizational communication*. Retrieved from Rosenbaum, B. L. (1978). New uses for behavioral modeling. *The Personnel Administrator*, 27–28.

Rousseau, D. M., Sitkin, S. B., Burt, R. S., & Camerer, C. (1998). Not so different after all: A cross-discipline view of trust. *Academy of Management Review*, *23*(3), 393–404. doi:10.5465/amr.1998.926617

Rousseau, D. M., Sitkin, S. B., Burt, R. S., & Camerer, C. (1998). Not so different after all: A cross-discipline view of trust. *Academy of Management Review*, *23*(3), 393–404. doi:10.5465/amr.1998.926617

Ryan, T. A., & Smith, P. C. (1954). *Principles of industrial psychology*. Academic Press.

Saad, L., & Hickman, A. (2021). Majority of U.S. Workers Continue to Punch. In *Virtually*. Gallup Panel.

Sako, M. (1992). *Prices, quality, and trust: inter-firm relations in Britain and Japan*. Cambridge University Press. doi:10.1017/CBO9780511520723

Shapiro, D. L., Sheppard, B. H., & Cheraskin, L. (1992). Business on a handshake. *Negotiation Journal*, *8*(4), 365–377. doi:10.1111/j.1571-9979.1992.tb00679.x

Singh, H. K., & Verma, S. (2020). *Understanding the Challenges of Mandatory Telework Adoption and Its Effect on Employee Engagement.* Paper presented at the International Working Conference on Transfer and Diffusion of IT.

Skinner, B. F. (1950). Are theories of learning necessary? *Psychological Review*, *57*(4), 193–216. doi:10.1037/h0054367 PMID:15440996

Skinner, B. F. (1966). What is the experimental analysis of behavior? *Journal of the Experimental Analysis of Behavior*, *9*(3), 213–218. doi:10.1901/jeab.1966.9-213 PMID:16811287

Smigla, J. E., & Pastoria, G. (2000). Emotional Intelligence: Some Have It, Others Can Learn. *The CPA Journal*, *70*(6), 60–61.

Smith, S. A., Patmos, A., & Pitts, M. J. (2018). Communication and teleworking: A study of communication channel satisfaction, personality, and job satisfaction for teleworking employees. *International Journal of Business Communication*, *55*(1), 44–68. doi:10.1177/2329488415589101

Snyder, K. (2012). Enhancing telework: A guide to virtual leadership. *Public Management*, *41*(1), 11–14.

Sosik, J. J., & Megerian, L. E. (1999). Understanding Leader Emotional Intelligence and Performance. *Group & Organization Management*, *24*(3), 367–390. doi:10.1177/1059601199243006

Stagner, R. (1956). *Psychology of industrial conflict.* Academic Press.

Stillman, J. (2012). Do Bosses and Employees See Eye to Eye on Anything? *Inc.com.* Retrieved from https://www.inc.com/jessica-stillman/do-bosses-and-employee-see-eye-to-eye-on-anything.html

Tavares, A. I. (2017). Telework and health effects review. *International Journal of Healthcare*, *3*(2), 30. doi:10.5430/ijh.v3n2p30

Taylor, F. W. (2004). *Scientific management.* Routledge. doi:10.4324/9780203498569

Thorndike, E. L. (1917). The curve of work and the curve of satisfyingness. *The Journal of Applied Psychology*, *1*(3), 265–267. doi:10.1037/h0074929

Thurstone, L. L. (1927). Three psychophysical laws. *Psychological Review*, *34*(6), 424–432. doi:10.1037/h0073028

Thurstone, L. L. (1931). The measurement of social attitudes. *Journal of Abnormal and Social Psychology, 26*(3), 249–269. doi:10.1037/h0070363

Tiffin, J. (1948). Industrial noise and hearing. *The Journal of Applied Psychology, 32*(5), 476–489. doi:10.1037/h0061762 PMID:18889449

Vasel, K. (2021). *'I don't have to choose between lifestyle and career.' How remote work changed these people's lives.* Retrieved from https://www.cnn.com/2021/03/15/success/remote-work-changed-lives-pandemic/index.html

Vibert, C. (2004). *Theories of macro organizational behavior: A handbook of ideas and explanations.* ME Sharpe.

Vidyarthi, P. R., Liden, R. C., Anand, S., Erdogan, B., & Ghosh, S. (2010). Where do I stand? Examining the effects of leader–member exchange social comparison on employee work behaviors. *The Journal of Applied Psychology, 95*(5), 849–861. doi:10.1037/a0020033 PMID:20718513

Viteles, M. S. (1953). *Motivation and morale in industry.* Academic Press.

Viteles, M. S., & Brief, A. (1932). *Industrial psychology.* WW Norton.

Vroom, V. H. (1964). *Work and motivation.* Academic Press.

Vroom, V. H. (1964). *Work and Motivation.* Wiley.

Watson, J. B. (2017). *Behaviorism.* Routledge. doi:10.4324/9781351314329

Weisberg, A., & Porell, M. (2011). Moving telework from compliance to competitiveness. *Public Management, 40*(1), 12.

Weiss, H. M. (1978). Social learning of work values in organizations. *The Journal of Applied Psychology, 63*(6), 711–718. doi:10.1037/0021-9010.63.6.711

Wicker, F. W., Brown, G., Wiehe, J. A., Hagen, A. S., & Reed, J. L. (1993). On reconsidering Maslow: An examination of the deprivation/domination proposition. *Journal of Research in Personality, 27*(2), 118–133. doi:10.1006/jrpe.1993.1008

Woolcock, M., & Narayan, D. (2000). Social Capital: Implications for Development Theory, Research, and Policy. *The World Bank Research Observer, 15*(2), 225–249. doi:10.1093/wbro/15.2.225

Wyatt, S., Fraser, J., & Stock, F. (1929). *The effects of monotony in work.* Industrial Fatigue Research Board.

Wyatt, S., Frost, L., & Stock, F. (1934). Incentives in repetitive work. Industrial Health Research Board (Great Britain) Report (69).

Zucker, L. G. (1986). Production of trust: Institutional sources of economic structure. In B. M. Staw & L. L. Cummings (Eds.), *Research in organisational behaviour* (Vol. 8). JAI.

APPENDIX 1: SURVEY

Telework, Trust, and Performance Survey

Informed Consent

You are invited to partipate in a short online survey designed to gauge the level of trust demonstrated towards employees while they are performing job duties through telework.

Study Title: Telework and Trust

Purpose of the Study: This study is designed to gauge the level of trust demonstrated towards employees while they are performing their job duties through telework.

Procedures: Participants are requested to complete a short online survey. This survey should take no more than fifteen minutes to complete.

Potential Risks of Participating: This survey carries little to no risk to participants, other than possible discomfort in answering some of the questions that could be more sensitive in nature.

Potential Benefits of Particpating: Participation in the survey research will help to raise awareness regarding trust in telework and is designed to help organizations to better manage employees while they are working from home.

Compensation: There is no compensation for completing the survey.

Confidentiality: Survey responses will be gathered through SurveyMonkey.com using a web collector and your responses will remain anonymous. Your names will not be used in any report.

Voluntary participation: Your participation in this study is completely voluntary. There is no penalty for not participating. You may also refuse to answer any of the questions we ask you and you are free to stop answering the survey questions at any point.

Right to withdraw from the study: You have the right to withdraw from the study at any time without consequence.

Whom to contact if you have questions about the study: The two researchers, Dr. Denise Siegfeldt at dsiegfeldt@fit.edu or Dr. Michael A. Brown, Sr. at mbrown@fit.edu

Whom to contact about your rights as a research participant in the study:

Dr. Jignya Patel
IRB Chairperson
150 West University Blvd.
Melbourne, FL 32901
Email: jpatel@fit.edu Phone: 321.674.8104

1. **Agreement:** I have read the survey procedure described above. I voluntarily agree to participate in the survey and I have received a copy of this description. Please feel free to print a copy of the consent form for your records.

Electronic Consent: Please choose your response below by either clicking on the "Agree" button or the "Disagree" button.

Agree
Disagree

2. Are you required to account for daily activities while teleworking and/or commuting?
    a. Online Presence While Teleworking? Yes No
    b. Performance/Productivity While Commuting? Yes No
3. Does your organization use an automated system for daily online accountability and work performance?
    a. Yes
    b. No

If yes, please identify the system (or systems) that is used by your employer.

____

____

4. Do you believe your employees are working:
    a. Less than 8 hours per day
    b. 8 hours per day

   c. More than 8 hours
   d. Some other time frame
   e. N/A – I do not manage or supervise others
5. How strongly do you believe in your organization's support for teleworking?
   a. A great deal
   b. A lot
   c. A moderate amount
   d. A little
   e. None at all
   f. Don't know
6. Do you think your supervisor/boss believes that you are working a full day?
   a. Yes
   b. No
   c. Don't know
7. Do you believe your supervisor/boss understands the challenge of working from home?
   a. Yes
   b. No
   c. Don't know
8. What are some challenges the supervisor/boss should understand?
9. Do you believe your supervisor/boss cares about the challenge of working from home?
   a. Yes
   b. No
   c. Don't know
10. What is your position?
   a. President/CEO/etc.
   b. Supervisor
   c. Upper Management
   d. Employee/Worker
   e. Mid-Level Management
   f. Other (please specify)

APPENDIX 2: INFORMED CONSENT FORM

Informed Consent

You are invited to participate in an online survey designed to gauge the level of trust demonstrated towards employees while they are performing job duties through telework.

Study Title: Telework and Trust

Purpose of the Study: <This study is designed to gauge the level of trust demonstrated towards employees while they are performing their job duties through telework.>

Procedures: <Participants are requested to complete a short survey online survey. The survey should take no more than fifteen minutes to complete.>

Potential Risks of Participating: <This survey carries little to no risk to participants, other than possible discomfort in answering some of the questions that could be more sensitive in nature>

Potential Benefits of Participating: <Participation in the survey research will help to raise awareness regarding trust in telework and is designed to help organizations to better manage employees while they are working from home.>

Compensation: < There is no compensation for completing the survey>

Confidentiality: < Survey responses will be gathered through SurveyMonkey.com using a web collector and your responses will remain anonymous. Your name will not be used in any report.)

Voluntary participation: Your participation in this study is completely voluntary. There is no penalty for not participating. You may also refuse to answer any of the questions we ask you and you are free to stop answering the survey questions at any point.

Right to withdraw from the study: You have the right to withdraw from the study at any time without consequence.

Whom to contact if you have questions about the study: <The two researchers, Dr. Michael A. Brown, Sr. at mbrown@fit.edu and Dr. Denise Siegfeldt at dsiegfeldt@fit.edu or

Whom to contact about your rights as a research participant in the study:

Dr. Jignya Patel
IRB Chairperson
150 West University Blvd.

Melbourne, FL 32901

Email: jpatel@fit.edu [REMOVED HYPERLINK FIELD] Phone: 321.674.8104

Agreement: I have read the survey procedure described above. I voluntarily agree to participate in the survey, and I have received a copy of this description. Please feel free to print a copy of the consent form for your records.

Electronic Consent: Please choose your response below by either clicking on the "Agree" button or the "Disagree" button.

Agree

Disagree

APPENDIX 3: FLORIDA INSTITUTE OF TECHNOLOGY EXEMPT APPLICATION

Figure 3.

Florida Institute of Technology

RESEARCH INVOLVING HUMAN PARTICIPANTS
EXEMPT APPLICATION

This form shall be used if there is **minimal risk** to human subjects; one of the categories on the next page applies to the research. If there is more than minimal risk associated with the research (none of the conditions apply) or if the research utilizes a special population (children, prisoners, institutionalized individuals, etc.), please use the expedited/full application form found on the IRB website.

You should consult the university's document "Principles, Policy, and Applicability for Research Involving Human Subjects" and instructions on the IRB Committee website prior to completion of this form.
https://www.fit.edu/research/compliance--regulations/institutional-review-board

Submit via email to FIT_IRB@fit.edu.

IRB Contact Information:
Dr. Jignya Patel
IRB Chairperson
FIT_IRB@fit.edu
321-674-7347

INVESTIGATOR INFORMATION

Title of Project Telework and Trust

Date of Submission Feb. 8, 2021

Expected Project Start Date February 22, 2021 Expected Project Duration March 15, 2021

Principal Investigator Dr. Denise Siegfeldt

Title Associate Professor, Business and Director, Hampton Roads Education Center

Academic Unit Nathan M. Bisk College of Business

Phone (757) 887-2488 Email dsiegfeldt@fit.edu

List all co-investigator(s). Please include name, title, academic unit/affiliation and email.

Dr. Michael A. Brown, Sr., Ph.D.
Adjunct Instructor, Education Centers
mbrown@fit.edu
dr.michael.brown76@gmail.com
(757) 876-6589

Florida Institute of Technology · Institutional Review Board
150 West University Boulevard, Melbourne, FL 32901-6975 • 321-674-7347 • FIT_IRB@fit.edu

FY-064-118
Page 1 of 7

Figure 4.

Florida Institute of Technology

RESEARCH INVOLVING HUMAN PARTICIPANTS
EXEMPT APPLICATION

CATEGORIES OF EXEMPT RESEARCH

Research must choose one:

- [ ] Research conducted in established or commonly accepted educational settings, involving **normal educational practices**, such as:
  a. research on regular and special education instruction strategies, or
  b. research on the effectiveness of or the comparison among instruction techniques, curricula or classroom management methods.

- [ ] Research involving the use of **educational tests (cognitive, diagnostic, aptitude, achievement), survey procedures, interview procedures or observation of public behavior** unless:
  a. the subjects can be identified, directly or through identifiers linked to the subjects and
  b. any disclosure of subjects' responses outside the research could reasonably place the subjects at risk of criminal or civil liability or be damaging to the subjects' financial standing, employability or reputation.
  Note: This exemption does not apply to survey procedures or interviews involving minors.

- [x] Research involving the use of educational tests, survey or interview procedures, or observation of **public behavior** if:
  a. the subjects are elected or appointed public officials or candidates for public office, or
  b. the confidentiality of the personally identifiable information will be maintained throughout the research and thereafter.

- [ ] Research involving the **collection or study of existing data, documents, records or specimens** if these sources are publicly available or if the information is recorded by the investigator in such a manner that subjects cannot be identified, indirectly or through identifiers linked to the subjects.

- [ ] Research and demonstration projects that are conducted by or subject to the approval of department or agency heads and that are designed to study, evaluate or otherwise examine:
  a. **public benefit or service programs**,
  b. procedures for obtaining benefits or services under those programs,
  c. possible changes in or alternatives to those programs or procedures, or
  d. possible changes in methods or levels of payment for benefits or services under those programs.

- [ ] **Taste and food quality evaluation** and consumer acceptance studies if:
  a. wholesome foods without additives are consumed, or
  b. food is consumed that contains food ingredients found to be safe by the Food and Drug Administration or approved by the Environmental Protection Agency or the Food Safety and Inspection Service of the U.S. Department of Agriculture.

RESEARCH FUNDING

If any part of this study will be funded by an external funding source, you must note the funding source and award/solicitation number below:

No external funding source

Florida Institute of Technology • Institutional Review Board
150 West University Boulevard, Melbourne, FL 32901-6975 • 321-674-7347 • FIT_IRB@fit.edu

PY-064-11B
Page 2 of 7

Figure 5.

Florida Institute of Technology — **RESEARCH INVOLVING HUMAN PARTICIPANTS EXEMPT APPLICATION**

ANSWER THE FOLLOWING QUESTIONS AS THOROUGHLY AS POSSIBLE.

1. List the objectives of the proposed project.

To contribute to the body of knowledge that currently exists on telework and trust.

To identify problems that exist with telecommuting and what can be done to remedy them to enable employees to be productive.

To develop an academic paper that includes results of the survey.

ABSTRACT: We focus on rules for teleworking generated by the COVID-19 that exist without a national strategy. The project will address telework and trust issues: performance, accountability, effectiveness, and efficiency. It will address the need for and existence of a shared understanding where leaders and employees openly discuss the challenges telework presents. The project also asks whether there are impediments or obstacles that organizations could remove or reduce to enable employees to accomplish the same amount of work they are currently doing in the office, but in a shorter duration of time while telecommuting.

E-MAIL INTRODUCTION
The attached survey on telework and trust is intended to identify problems that exist with telecommuting and to identify what can be done to remedy these issues and allow employees to be productive. The study also contributes to the teleworking body of knowledge. Your responses are completely anonymous with absolutely no way of identifying any participants. Once you have started the survey, you may end participation at any time. To get to the survey, simply click on this link (https://www.surveymonkey.com/r/QSR8673), or paste it into your browser.
If you have any questions or comments about the survey, please contact Dr. Denise Siegfeldt, dsiegfeldt@fit.edu, or Dr. Michael Brown, mbrown@fit.edu.
Any feedback you provide is greatly appreciated. Again, thank you for your time and willingness to participate.

2. Describe the research project design/methodology. Discuss how you will conduct your study, and what measurement instruments you are using. Attach all research materials to this application. Please describe your study in enough detail so the IRB can identify what you are doing and why.

This research project will utilize survey research as the methodology for the study. The survey instrument is attached.
People will take the survey using Survey Monkey and the data will remain anonymous. Confidentiality will be maintained. The Survey Monkey-produced analysis will be used for the purposes of the project.

Florida Institute of Technology • Institutional Review Board
150 West University Boulevard, Melbourne, FL 32901-6975 • 321-674-7347 • FIT_IRB@fit.edu

FY-064-118
Page 5 of 7

Figure 6.

Florida Institute of Technology

RESEARCH INVOLVING HUMAN PARTICIPANTS
EXEMPT APPLICATION

3. Describe the characteristics of the participant population, including number, age, sex and recruitment strategy (attach actual recruitment email text, recruitment fliers, etc).

The participant population will be working adults. The recruitment strategy that will be used is to send an email out to a minimum of 100 people, inviting them to take the survey using Survey Monkey. We have also requested that the Virginia Peninsula Chamber of Commerce send the Survey Monkey link to their members. That request is pending.

4. Describe any potential risks to the participants (physical, psychological, social, legal, etc.) and assess their likelihood and seriousness. Describe steps that will be taken to mitigate each risk.

There is no risk that is expected for the participants.

Florida Institute of Technology • Institutional Review Board
150 West University Boulevard, Melbourne, FL 32901-6975 • 321-674-7347 • FIT_IRB@fit.edu

FY-064-118
Page 4 of 7

Figure 7.

Florida Institute of Technology **RESEARCH INVOLVING HUMAN PARTICIPANTS EXEMPT APPLICATION**

5. Describe the procedures you will use to maintain the confidentiality and privacy of your research participants and project data. If video or audio recordings will be made, you must review the video/audio recording policy found on the IRB website and address precautions you will take in this section.

The identify of the participants will remain anonymous when they complete the survey using Survey Monkey. Data will be compiled and any identifying information will be kept confidential and not included in the data used for the article.

6. Describe your plan for informed consent (attach proposed form).

The Informed Consent will be part of the actual survey. There will be an Electronic Consent Button. See Informed Consent:

You are invited to participate in an online survey designed to gauge the level of trust demonstrated towards employees while they are performing job duties through telework.

Study Title: Telework and Trust

Purpose of the Study: <This study is designed to gauge the level of trust demonstrated towards employees while they are performing their job duties through telework.>

Procedures: <Participants are requested to complete a short survey online survey. The survey should take no more than fifteen minutes to complete.>

Potential Risks of Participating: <This survey carries little to no risk to participants, other than possible discomfort in answering some of the questions that could be more sensitive in nature>

Potential Benefits of Participating: <Participation in the survey research will help to raise awareness regarding trust in telework and is designed to help organizations to better manage employees while there are working from home.>

Compensation: < There is no compensation for completing the survey>

Confidentiality: < Survey responses will be gathered through SurveyMonkey.com using a web collector and your responses will remain anonymous. Your name will not be used in any report.)

Voluntary participation:
Your participation in this study is completely voluntary. There is no penalty for not participating. You may also refuse to answer any of the questions we ask you and you are free to stop answering the survey questions at any point.

Florida Institute of Technology · Institutional Review Board
150 West University Boulevard, Melbourne, FL 32901-6975 • 321-674-7347 • FIT_IRB@fit.edu

FY-064-118
Page 5 of 7

Figure 8.

Florida Institute of Technology **RESEARCH INVOLVING HUMAN PARTICIPANTS**
EXEMPT APPLICATION

7. Discuss the importance of the knowledge that will result from your study (benefits to the field and to society) and what benefits will accrue to your participants (if any). Include information about participant compensation if appropriate.

The study results will help to raise awareness regarding trust in those who are teleworking and the results will help organizations to better manage employees while they are working from home.

The survey will be voluntary and there will be no compensation for the participants.

8. Explain how your proposed study meets criteria for exemption from Institutional Review Board review (as outlined on page 2 of this form).

This proposed study meets the criteria of the third category for exemption from the Institutional Review Board, on page 2 of this form. The research will involve a survey and the confidentiality of personally identifiable information will be maintained throughout the study and thereafter. Personally identifiable information is not expected but should a respondent provide it, the information will be held confidential and will not be used.

Florida Institute of Technology • Institutional Review Board
150 West University Boulevard, Melbourne, FL 32901-6975 • 321-674-7347 • FIT_IRB@fit.edu

FY-064-118
Page 6 of 7

Figure 9.

Florida Institute of Technology **RESEARCH INVOLVING HUMAN PARTICIPANTS EXEMPT APPLICATION**

SIGNATURE ASSURANCES

I understand Florida Institute of Technology's policy concerning research involving human participants and I agree:

1. to accept responsibility for the scientific and ethical conduct of this research study.
2. to obtain prior approval from the Institutional Review Board before amending or altering the research protocol or implementing changes in the approved consent form.
3. to immediately report to the IRB any serious adverse reactions and/or unanticipated effects on subjects which may occur as a result of this study.
4. to complete, on request by the IRB, a Continuation Review Form if the study exceeds its estimated duration.

PI Signature ______________________________ Date ____________

PI Signature (print) ______________________________

ADVISOR ASSURANCE: IF PRIMARY INVESTIGATOR IS A STUDENT

This is to certify that I have reviewed this research protocol and that I attest to the scientific merit of the study, the necessity for the use of human subjects in the study to the student's academic program, and the competency of the student to conduct the project.

Major Advisor Signature ______________________________ Date ____________

Major Advisor (print) ______________________________

ACADEMIC UNIT HEAD: IT IS THE PI'S RESPONSIBILITY TO OBTAIN THIS SIGNATURE

This is to certify that I have reviewed this research protocol and that I attest to the scientific merit of this study and the competency of the investigator(s) to conduct the study.

Academic Unit Head Signature ______________________________ Date ____________

Academic Unit Head (print) ______________________________

FOR IRB USE ONLY

IRB Approval ______________________________ Date ____________

IRB # ______________________________

Florida Institute of Technology • Institutional Review Board
150 West University Boulevard, Melbourne, FL 32901-6975 • 321-674-7347 • FIT_IRB@fit.edu

PY-064-118
Page 7 of 7

Conclusion

Think about your position or belief on telework. Which matches you?

- Do not support telework.
- Support some level of telework.
- Use telework to the fullest extent possible.

This book has covered the pros and cons of each of these positions. What organizations and their leaders do now should be based on a recurring theme in leadership and management supported by LMX Theory.

Telework is an investment in your people to give them flexibility in the interest of improving their work-life balance.

Accepting the use of telework is investing in your people. If organizations start with addressing member desires as their goal, instead of the bottom line or verification of whether and how people are working, telework can provide great benefits in terms of enriched employees who are loyal and who want to stay with the organization.

Leaders can develop and nurture telework success by starting with understanding the desires of their members. Whether the focus is on the in-group or the out-group, the leader develops trustworthiness, improves performance, and exhibits and commands accountability to create strong relationships throughout the team.

The focus of the book is rules for teleworking generated by the coronavirus pandemic (COVID-19) that exist without a national strategy. The intent at the outset was to address implications for everyday situations, take a new look at teleworking in all situations regardless of the reasons that make it necessary or prudent, address telework factors beginning with trustworthiness and performance, and discuss the need for shared understanding where leaders and members openly discuss the challenges presented by teleworking.

What we have achieved is a deeper evaluation of telework than is currently available in relevant literature. Our intent is to build strengths and mitigate weaknesses in telework as it relates to organizational development. Ultimately, we examine whether organizations have made decisions to mandate or encourage teleworking formally and informally, making the possibility of participation available to the whole organization.

This text began by stating the author's goal to make clear to readers the important relationship between telework, trustworthiness, and performance. To achieve that goal, we looked well beyond trustworthiness and performance and analyzed a range of factors critical to teleworking success: leadership development, motivation, productivity, emotional intelligence, and radical change.

Overall, we have examined the ways in which COVID-19 changed our lives and forced the use of telework and other social distancing solutions to protect our health. Even today we are learning more about balancing family and work, about the changes in how and why the world goes to work, and about new and dynamic ways in which people communicate.

This book represents a deep dive into telework to see its strengths and weaknesses as we work to determine the best ways forward with and without COVID-19. We paid close attention to the things that may cause organizations and their leaders to avoid the use of telework, and we have tried to alleviate or explain those reasons for resistance. We have used qualitative and quantitative research to understand the thoughts and feelings of leaders and members in the hopes that it will create a shared understanding that makes telework attractive in many situations. We also used research to demonstrate that organizations are experiencing increased loyalty, performance, and productivity from their members.

Of course, we have not found all the definitive answers. Certainly, this examination is fully in favor of teleworking as both an answer and a solution to organizational development now and in the future. But we urge organizations to at least consider using telework before we are faced with the next crisis that will make this kind of work situation necessary. The world has found such goodness in allowing its workforce to telework, and it would be a shame to revert to "the way we have always done it" because it is easy or because we can. There have been some extraordinary discoveries in the ways telework can be used. There have been some amazing people who have taken the negativity of COVID-19 and the despair of loss of life and closing of businesses and turned it into positive, productive business streams. It is important to capture the full range of positivity for our future.

COVID-19 has helped us understand that the combination of increased trustworthiness and improved performance can make telework the right choice in both steady-state, day-to-day work, and during times of crisis. If we capture all that we have learned, telework can help us all prosper in the workplace and in life.

As I close the book on this examination, the world is in flux where COVID is concerned. In the U.S., the nation rushed to vaccinate everyone but as of August 2021 only half of the country was fully vaccinated according to media reports. At the same time, the Delta variant is growing and having a devastating effect on the unvaccinated. A Centers for Disease Control (CDC) report (https://www.cdc.gov/coronavirus/2019-ncov/variants/delta-variant.html), updated on Aug. 6, 2021, listed that "The Delta variant causes more infections and spreads faster that early forms of SARS-CoV-2." The findings at that site show that the Delta variant is nearly twice as contagious than what we experienced before. According to new data, the Delta variant might cause more severe illness in unvaccinated people than previous strains. The greatest concern is unvaccinated people, however, there are cases of breakthrough infections in fully vaccinated people. Fully vaccinated people, according to CDC, can transmit the virus to other people, but they appear to be infectious for a shorter period.

There has also been talk about booster vaccines for certain individuals. I share this information because we could face another pandemic or world crisis at any time. Telework is a way to keep people safe and working while taking care of organizational issues. Capturing what we have learn from the way the world changed because of COVID is important. Just as important is finding a way to use the lessons learned to posture for what tomorrow may bring.

I hope that other researchers will look favorably on my work and continue to analyze telework, trustworthiness, and performance at the organizational level. I suggest that future inquiries keep a focus on the interplay between leaders and members and how their engagement is crucial to success. This interplay is always present, so it is important to accept it and work to make it beneficial throughout the organization. More importantly, I hope that my continuing research is helpful to organizations and individuals.

Finally, I hope to continue to meet great people in this discovery so that I can continue discussion of this exciting area of discovery!

About the Author

Michael A. "Doc" Brown, Sr., Ph.D. has authored several books and is an accomplished public speaker. He has coached different sports at the recreation league, middle school, junior varsity, high school, and adult levels. He earned his Public Administration and Urban Policy degree, International Business, from Old Dominion University (ODU) in May 2011. He is teaching online social media, public relations, and communication courses for Florida Institute of Technology. He is a Navy civil servant working as a public affairs officer in Norfolk, Virginia. This PR professional has 40-plus years of military and civilian experience combined. He is an Air Force retiree who served 24 years in uniform.

Index

S

T

V

W

Z

www.ingramcontent.com/pod-product-compliance
Lightning Source LLC
LaVergne TN
LVHW081326300926
849161LV00008B/1893